AF697728

GREAT JUDGMENTS OF THE EUROPEAN COURT OF JUSTICE

Great Judgments of the European Court of Justice presents a new approach to understanding the landmark decisions of the European Court of Justice in the 1960s and 1970s. By comparing the Court's doctrines to the enforcement and escape mechanisms employed by more common forms of trade treaty, it demonstrates how the individual rights created by the doctrine of direct effect were connected to the practical challenges of trade politics among the European states and, in particular, to the suppression of unilateral safeguard mechanisms and inter-state retaliation. Drawing on the writings and speeches of French judge and President of the Court, Robert Lecourt, it demonstrates that one of the Court's most influential judges shared this understanding of the logic of direct effect. This book offers a distinctive interpretation of the Court of Justice's early years, as well as of the purpose of the fundamental principles of European law.

WILLIAM PHELAN is Associate Professor and Jean Monnet Chair of EU Politics and Law at Trinity College Dublin. His previous book on the European Court of Justice, entitled *In Place of Inter-state Retaliation* (2015), was awarded the Brian Farrell Book Prize of the Political Studies Association of Ireland.

GREAT JUDGMENTS OF THE EUROPEAN COURT OF JUSTICE

Rethinking the Landmark Decisions of the Foundational Period

WILLIAM PHELAN
Trinity College, Dublin

CAMBRIDGE
UNIVERSITY PRESS

CAMBRIDGE
UNIVERSITY PRESS

University Printing House, Cambridge CB2 8BS, United Kingdom

One Liberty Plaza, 20th Floor, New York, NY 10006, USA

477 Williamstown Road, Port Melbourne, VIC 3207, Australia

314–321, 3rd Floor, Plot 3, Splendor Forum, Jasola District Centre, New Delhi – 110025, India

79 Anson Road, #06–04/06, Singapore 079906

Cambridge University Press is part of the University of Cambridge.

It furthers the University's mission by disseminating knowledge in the pursuit of education, learning, and research at the highest international levels of excellence.

www.cambridge.org
Information on this title: www.cambridge.org/9781108499088
DOI: 10.1017/9781108615020

© William Phelan 2019

This publication is in copyright. Subject to statutory exception and to the provisions of relevant collective licensing agreements, no reproduction of any part may take place without the written permission of Cambridge University Press.

First published 2019

Printed and bound in Great Britain by Clays Ltd, Elcograf S.p.A.

A catalogue record for this publication is available from the British Library.

Library of Congress Cataloging-in-Publication Data
Names: Phelan, William (College teacher)
Title: Great judgments of the European Court of Justice : rethinking the landmark decisions of the foundational period / William Phelan, Trinity College, Dublin.
Description: Cambridge, United Kingdom ; New York, NY, USA : Cambridge University Press, 2019. | Includes bibliographical references and index.
Identifiers: LCCN 2018061705 | ISBN 9781108499088 (hardback : alk. paper) | ISBN 9781108713122 (pbk. : alk. paper)
Subjects: LCSH: Law–European Union countries–Cases. | Court of Justice of the European Union.
Classification: LCC KJE947 .P486 2019 | DDC 341.242/2284–dc23
LC record available at https://lccn.loc.gov/2018061705

ISBN 978-1-108-49908-8 Hardback

Cambridge University Press has no responsibility for the persistence or accuracy of URLs for external or third-party internet websites referred to in this publication and does not guarantee that any content on such websites is, or will remain, accurate or appropriate.

We never see the true state of our condition, till it is illustrated to us by its contraries; nor know how to value what we enjoy, but by the want of it.

Daniel Defoe, *Robinson Crusoe* (1719)

Déjà des organismes internationaux ont été créés pour limiter et si possible empêcher les conflits violents entre les peuples et pour substituer le droit à la violence. C'est ce principe qui arrêta autrefois les guerres privées qu'on emploie aujourd'hui pour empêcher les guerres mondiales. C'est l'interdiction pour quiconque, individus ou nations, de recourir à la violence et l'obligation pour tous de s'adresser au juge au lieu de se faire justice à soi-même. Ainsi ce principe s'est-il toujours développé parallèlement avec le Droit. Dès que le Droit s'étend à un domaine nouveau, ce principe apparaît à la base. Son extension est si considérable et si visible que limité autrefois aux conflits d'intérêts privés il tend sans cesse à s'appliquer aux litiges entre les peuples. C'est ainsi qu'en droit international il s'est traduit surtout pendant les dix dernières années, par la création d'organismes internationaux : Société des Nations, conférences internationales (conférences du désarmement), tribunaux internationaux qui jouent un rôle si important dans les rapports des États. Ces organismes sont appelés à empêcher les violences entre les peuples, et à interdire aux nations comme il est depuis longtemps défendu aux particuliers, de se faire justice à soi-même . . .

Robert Lecourt, *Nature juridique de l'action en réintégrande : étude de la jurisprudence française* (A.-D., Paris, 1931)

CONTENTS

TABLES

ACKNOWLEDGEMENTS

The inspiration for this book began during my time as visiting fellow at the European University Institute (EUI) in Fiesole, just outside Florence, in 2014. There is nowhere better to think deeply about European law than in the EUI's sunny gardens and shaded cloisters with the company of brilliant students and distinguished scholars. Over many coffees and lunches during those six months, I was repeatedly struck by the divergence between the celebrated works of legal scholarship which placed great emphasis on the European Court of Justice's (ECJ) rejection of inter-state retaliation in the 1964 *Dairy Products* case,[1] and the many experts on European law who seemed completely unaware of that judgment. This unfamiliarity was no doubt due to the fact that *Dairy Products* has been entirely omitted from many accounts of the early years of European law and from prominent collections of the Court of Justice's classic cases.

It seemed obvious to me, however, that the prohibition on inter-state retaliation announced by the Court in *Dairy Products* in 1964 was the partner of – perhaps even the inspiration for – the individual rights and role for national courts so famously announced by the Court in *Van Gend en Loos* in 1963. That view in turn seemed to bewilder most of the European lawyers I met in Fiesole, even though the EUI was simultaneously hosting a well-attended seminar series on the World Trade Organization where the possibility of using direct effect as an alternative to retaliatory enforcement was debated nearly every week. The purpose of this book is to make clear the connection between direct effect and the abolition of inter-state retaliation in the early years of the European legal order, and to embed this connection in our understanding of the Court's most important judgments. I also well remember my conversation with an eminent professor who pointed out that even if we can now recognize

[1] Those celebrated works of scholarship include the best-known article by the then President of the European University Institute, Joseph Weiler (Weiler 1991: 2422).

a strong relationship between direct effect and European law's rejection of inter-state retaliation, there was still the separate question of whether the relevant judges on the Court of Justice understood that relationship back when the foundations, of European law were first being built. That observation led me to intensify my research into the remarkable ECJ judge Robert Lecourt and, despite the challenges of closed archives and lost private papers, I hope that this book offers convincing evidence that judge Lecourt was fully aware of that connection.

A project of this sort is only possible with the support of many friends and collaborators. A number of generous colleagues were kind enough to read part or all of the book in draft form, or commented on draft chapters at conferences or workshops. I am grateful for comments and criticism from Gerald Butler, Gareth Davies, Peter Lindseth, Mario Mendez, Fernanda Nicola, and Fabien Terpan. Those who offered helpful feedback over coffee or otherwise from the very beginning include Loïc Azoulai, Marise Cremona, Bruno de Witte, Oran Doyle, Nial Fennelly, Dimitry Kochenov, Brigid Laffan, Petros Mavroidis, Ernst-Ulrich Petersmann, Diarmuid Rossa Phelan, and Michel Waelbroeck, as well as patient colleagues at both the Department of Political Science and the School of Law here at Trinity College Dublin. I have also benefited from the writings and encouragement of many of the "new historians" of European law, particularly Bill Davies, Morten Rasmussen, Antoine Vauchez, and again Peter Lindseth, without whose prior historical researches this book could never have been written. Two Trinity College PhD students – Brady Gordon and Dáire McCormack-George – offered outstanding research assistance.

For the invitation to visit at the EUI, and for many conversations on France, Germany, and Europe over the years, I am especially indebted to Ulrich Krotz. For an unexpected welcome in Fiesole, I thank Duncan McDonnell and Elena Messina. I would like to thank Paolo Gori for our conversations about his early years at the Court of Justice, and for a wonderful tour of Prato. I am particularly grateful to Joseph Weiler who understood the project immediately, encouraged it warmly, and advised me to keep the book short. I have done my best, but for any failings on that account, or any other, I must remain solely responsible.

This project has been generously supported by the Jean Monnet Chair in EU Politics and Law at Trinity College Dublin and by Trinity College's Arts and Social Sciences Benefactions Fund. Draft papers or chapters were presented at meetings of the Irish Association of Law Teachers in Maynooth and the European Union Studies Association in Miami, and at seminars held at the Irish Jurisprudence Society at Trinity College Dublin, the Sutherland Law of School at University College Dublin, and the European University Institute in Fiesole. This book draws on material that has appeared in *European Law Journal*, *European Journal of International Law*, *International Journal of Constitutional Law*, and *Irish Journal of European Law*. I thank both editors and reviewers for their feedback and criticism. Finally, it has been a pleasure to work with Finola O'Sullivan and her team at Cambridge University Press.

Of course it is family that helps us through the challenges of long and demanding projects, and one of the pleasures of sabbatical leave near Florence is that your family members are keen to come and visit, including my parents, Cel and Bill, who have supported first my own opportunities and now our growing family in so many ways. I cannot begin to properly express my gratitude for all their sacrifices. Above all my love to Haiyan and to our wonderful boys – Hubert who enjoyed our daily visits to Pasticceria Alcedo on the Via Gramsci and Bill who still has that delight to look forward to.

ABBREVIATIONS

ECHR	European Convention on Human Rights
ECJ	European Court of Justice
ECSC	European Coal and Steel Community
EEC	European Economic Community
EU	European Union
GATT	General Agreement on Tariffs and Trade
NAFTA	North American Free Trade Agreement
WTO	World Trade Organization

EUROPEAN COURT OF JUSTICE CASES

PREAMBLE AND SELECTED PROVISIONS OF THE TREATY OF ROME

In the discussions of the decisions of the European Court that follow, we will refer repeatedly to certain provisions of the Treaty of Rome, above all Articles 5, 164, 169, 170, 171, 177, 189, 219, and 226, as well as the Treaty's Preamble. These texts are set out here for ease of reference, and following there is a table setting out how these provisions of the Treaty of Rome relate to provisions of the current European Treaties as of 2018.

Preamble

DETERMINED to lay the foundations of an ever-closer union among the peoples of Europe,

RESOLVED to ensure the economic and social progress of their countries by common action to eliminate the barriers which divide Europe,

AFFIRMING as the essential objective of their efforts the constant improvement of the living and working conditions of their peoples,

RECOGNISING that the removal of existing obstacles calls for concerted action in order to guarantee steady expansion, balanced trade and fair competition,

ANXIOUS to strengthen the unity of their economies and to ensure their harmonious development by reducing the differences existing between the various regions and the backwardness of the less favoured regions,

DESIRING to contribute, by means of a common commercial policy, to the progressive abolition of restrictions on international trade,

INTENDING to confirm the solidarity which binds Europe and the overseas countries and desiring to ensure the development of their prosperity, in accordance with the principles of the Charter of the United Nations,

RESOLVED by thus pooling their resources to preserve and strengthen peace and liberty, and calling upon the other peoples of Europe who share their ideal to join in their efforts,

HAVE DECIDED to create a European Economic Community . . .

Article 5

Member States shall take all appropriate measures, whether general or particular, to ensure fulfilment of the obligations arising out of this Treaty or resulting from action taken by the institutions of the Community. They shall facilitate the achievement of the Community's tasks.They shall abstain from any measure which could jeopardise the attainment of the objections of this Treaty.

Article 164

The Court of Justice shall ensure that in the interpretation and application of this Treaty the law is observed.

Article 169

If the Commission considers that a Member State has failed to fulfil an obligation under this Treaty, it shall deliver a reasoned opinion on the matter after giving the State concerned the opportunity to submit its observations. If the State concerned does not comply with the opinion within the period laid down by the Commission, the latter may bring the matter before the Court of Justice.

Article 170

A Member State which considers that another Member State has failed to fulfil an obligation under this Treaty may bring the matter before the Court of Justice.

Before a Member State brings an action against another Member State for an alleged infringement of an obligation under this Treaty, it shall bring the matter before the Commission. The Commission shall deliver a reasoned opinion after each of the States concerned has been given the opportunity to submit its own case and its observations on the other party's case both orally and in writing.

If the Commission has not delivered an opinion within three months of the date on which the matter was brought before it, the absence of such opinion shall not prevent the matter from being brought before the Court of Justice.

Article 171

If the Court of Justice finds that a Member State has failed to fulfil an obligation under this Treaty, the State shall be required to take the necessary measures to comply with the judgment of the Court of Justice.

Article 177

The Court of Justice shall have jurisdiction to give preliminary rulings concerning:

(a) the interpretation of this Treaty;
(b) the validity and interpretation of acts of the institutions of the Community;
(c) the interpretation of the statutes of bodies established by an act of the Council,

where those statutes so provide. Where such a question is raised before any court or tribunal of a Member State, that court or tribunal may, if it considers that a decision on the question is necessary to enable it to give judgment, request the Court of Justice to give a ruling thereon. Where any such question is raised in a case pending before a court or tribunal of a Member State, against whose decisions there is no judicial remedy under national law, that court or tribunal shall bring the matter before the Court of Justice.

Article 189

In order to carry out their task the Council and the Commission shall, in accordance with the provisions of this Treaty, make regulations, issue directives, take decisions, make recommendations or deliver opinions.

A regulation shall have general application. It shall be binding in its entirety and directly applicable in all Member States.

A directive shall be binding, as to the result to be achieved, upon each Member State to which it is addressed, but shall leave to the national authorities the choice of form and methods.

A decision shall be binding in its entirety upon those to whom it is addressed. Recommendations and opinions shall have no binding force.

Article 219

Member States undertake not to submit a dispute concerning the interpretation or application of this Treaty to any method of settlement other than those provided for therein.

Article 226

1. If, during the transitional period, difficulties arise which are serious and liable to persist in any sector of the economy or which could bring about serious deterioration in the economic situation of a given area, a Member State may apply for authorisation to take protective measures in order to rectify the situation and adjust the sector concerned to the economy of the common market.
2. On application by the State concerned, the Commission shall, by emergency procedure, determine without delay the protective measures which it considers necessary, specifying the circumstances and the manner in which they are to be put into effect.
3. The measures authorised under paragraph 2 may involve derogations from the rules of this Treaty, to such an extent and for such periods as are strictly necessary in order to attain the objectives referred to in paragraph 1. Priority shall be given to such measures as will least disturb the functioning of the common market.

EQUIVALENCE TABLE OF TREATY ARTICLES

Treaty of Rome (1957) – Treaty on European Union (TEU) and Treaty on the Functioning of the European Union (TFEU), the consolidated foundational treaties of the European Union, as constituted and amended by the Single European Act, the Maastricht Treaty, the Amsterdam Treaty, the Nice Treaty and the Lisbon Treaty.

Treaty of Rome	Current Status
Article 5	Replaced in substance by art 5 TEU.
Article 164	Repealed and replaced in substance by art 19 TEU.
Article 169	Amended by art 2(7) Lisbon Treaty; now art 258 TFEU.
Article 170	Amended by art 2(7) Lisbon Treaty; now art 259 TFEU.
Article 171	Amended by art 2(7) Lisbon Treaty; now art 260 TFEU.
Article 177	Amended by art 2(7) Lisbon Treaty; now art 267 TFEU.
Article 189	Amended by art 2(234) Lisbon Treaty; now art 288 TFEU.
Article 219	Art 344 TFEU.
Article 226	Repealed by art 6(75) Amsterdam Treaty.

Introduction

The study of the early judgments of the European Court of Justice has long been recognized as the best way to understand the most important principles of European law. After all, the doctrines on which the European legal order has come to rely over time were only very partially set out in the Treaty of Rome. It is therefore the celebrated judgments of the Court of Justice itself in the 1960s and 1970s – *Van Gend en Loos*, *Costa* v. *ENEL*, *Van Duyn*, *Simmenthal*, and so on – that first developed the most important doctrines of European law. The publication of *Grands Arrêts de la Cour de Justice des Communautés européennes* by Boulouis and Chevallier in 1974 was perhaps the first of what have been many attempts to elaborate the essential principles of the European legal order through a compilation and analysis of the "great judgments" of its Court. This book's approach to these famous cases will nevertheless be new to many readers for two reasons.

First, this book is inspired by the premise that one can only understand the profound impact of the Court's early judgments through detailed comparisons with dispute settlement and enforcement arrangements in other treaty systems. "A person who knows only one country basically knows no country well" has long been the motto of comparativist scholars, and our knowledge of treaty-based dispute settlement can benefit from a similar insight.[1] Much has been written on the *sui generis* nature of the European Treaties, including subtle discussions of competing visions of "federalism", "supranationalism", and "constitutionalism", but the analyses that I personally have found most compelling are those that identify the European legal order's special distinctions based on concrete divergences from the fundamental organizing principles of more common forms of international trade treaty.[2] The Treaty

[1] Lipset 1993: 121.

[2] Phelan 2012, Phelan 2015b, Phelan 2018. For an alternative approach to examining the Court's judgments "in context", see the fascinating "EU Law Stories" volume recently edited by Nicola and Davies (Nicola and Davies 2017).

of Rome, of course, was more than an ordinary trade treaty and contained from the start many ambitious non-trade obligations. But the "Common Market" was always at the heart of the European Economic Community and trade-related disputes – including *Van Gend en Loos* itself – often provided the basis for the Court's most important judgments. By looking at how other trade treaties have addressed similar problems we will better understand what was new and different about the European legal order.

Such a comparative approach benefits from the fact that the European legal order, as the Court of Justice developed it, came to demonstrate very specific and important distinctions from other prominent trade treaty systems. Trade treaties, for example, frequently provide participating states with the possibility of imposing retaliatory trade sanctions against their trading partners for failing to fulfil their obligations. The availability of this self-help form of enforcement is widely acknowledged as an essential component of the dispute settlement and enforcement system of today's global trade regime, the World Trade Organization (WTO). The possibility of self-help methods of enforcement – countermeasures, reprisals, retaliation – is also often understood to provide an irreplaceable enforcement function in general international law. Despite the apparently vital importance of such mechanisms in other contexts, however, the European legal order established by the Treaty of Rome has consistently rejected any possible resort to such behaviours by the European member states since 1964.

Trade treaties also frequently provide participating states with extensive opportunities unilaterally to reimpose trade barriers if industries are facing particular difficulties, or unilaterally to derogate from treaty obligations for various public policy reasons, subject at best only to *ex post* controls by treaty institutions, or prudence in light of potentially unwelcome responses-in-kind by their trading partners. Known variously as "escape" or "safety valve" mechanisms, the availability of such unilateral safeguards is also often understood to be an indispensable element in any demanding trade treaty system, and is indeed again widely acknowledged as essential to the political viability of today's WTO. Despite the apparently vital importance of such instruments in many other treaty contexts, however, the European legal order has again remarkably and consistently rejected the unilateral use of such safeguard and derogation mechanisms by the European member states since the early 1960s. The European legal order therefore takes a very unusual approach to managing the challenges both of enforcement and escape in international treaty politics.

The identification of the European legal order's special distinctions as its rejection of inter-state retaliation and unilateral safeguard mechanisms offers a satisfyingly specific vision of the ambitions and achievements of European legal integration in comparative context. This raises the question, however, of how European law's distinctive approach to enforcement and escape came about. These features of the European legal order are rarely mentioned – let alone the central focus of inquiry – in commentaries on the landmark decisions of the Court of Justice or accounts of the early development of Community law. Where then did these principles come from? Were they explicitly provided for in the Treaty of Rome itself? Or was there perhaps a separate line of judgments by the Court of Justice, supplementary to those so prominently emphasized in leading accounts, where European law's approach to enforcement and escape was founded and nurtured to full growth? Such noteworthy features of treaty law and politics are hardly likely to have developed by accident, and are more likely to have been the final results of much deliberation and planning by both drafters of the Treaty and members of the Court.

As it turns out, a concentration on these particular distinctions of the European legal order does indeed, at times, turn our focus towards lesser-known provisions of the Treaty of Rome, as well as towards some of the less prominent judgments of its Court of Justice. Perhaps surprisingly, however, the story of the European legal order's rejection of inter-state retaliation and unilateral safeguard mechanisms also turns out to be closely intertwined with the principles announced in the already famous early judgments of the Court of Justice, such as *Van Gend en Loos* and *Costa* v. *ENEL*. Indeed, as this book will show, the greatest innovations of the European legal order, including the new role for individual rights and national courts provided for by the doctrines of direct effect and supremacy, are directly linked to addressing the practical problem of how to effectively enforce trade obligations between states in an international treaty system without making use of such mechanisms. This book will demonstrate the logical connection between self-help, safeguards, and individual rights in the early years of European law, and thus put forward a new understanding of the purpose and impact of the great judgments of the Court of Justice in its most important and creative period.

To be sure, there is already a strand of European law scholarship that concentrates on the Court of Justice's rejection of inter-state retaliation and the 1964 *Dairy Products* judgment in which this principle was first announced. However, most such discussions concentrate on the question of whether, and if so under what circumstances, the European member states might revert to the self-help, retaliatory, enforcement mechanisms provided for in general international law.[3] That debate has certainly been very stimulating, and its influence can be found throughout this book. We will not share, however, the insistent focus of this scholarship on such hypothetical "fall back" scenarios. We are more interested in how the European legal order managed to "leap forward", and develop effectively in the first place without the availability of such otherwise pervasive mechanisms of treaty enforcement.

Second, this approach to understanding the Court's early judgments will be reinforced by examining the ways in which the challenges of self-help and safeguards were discussed by some of the lawyers then most closely involved in the work of the Court of Justice. We will give special attention to a contemporary commentary on *Costa* v. *ENEL* written by the then recently retired ECJ judge Nicola Catalano, as well as to a remarkable 1967 book on safeguards by the influential judge's assistant Paolo Gori.[4] Our primary focus, however, will be on the discussions of direct effect and self-help in the writings of Robert Lecourt, French judge from 1962, and President of the Court of Justice from 1967 to 1976.

Lecourt had already led a long and varied career before he joined the Court. Like many aspiring French politicians before the war, he was trained in the law and practised as a lawyer first in Rouen and then in Paris.[5] Politically, Lecourt was a left-leaning Catholic activist and became a prominent member of the Catholic and Gaullist Resistance under the German occupation. Lecourt "furnished part of the arms which enabled the Paris Police to take part in the insurrectional fighting at the time of the liberation", noted a brief biography provided by the British Foreign Office in 1950.[6] After the war he was elected to the National Assembly as a representative of the French Christian Democratic party *Mouvement Républicain Populaire*, and served several times as both parliamentary party leader and as Minister of Justice. A longstanding campaigner for European unity, Lecourt was prominent in the postwar transnational networks that brought together French, German, and other Christian

[3] Above all, Simma 1985, Gradoni 2008.

[4] Catalano 1964, Gori 1967. Gori held a position as "legal *attaché*" – what would now be called a *référendaire* – to a judge of the ECJ, working first for judge Catalano, then from 1962 for his replacement, judge Trabucchi.

[5] Le Beguec 1989.

[6] British Documents on Foreign Affairs, Volume 23, Germany, France and Western Europe (General), January 1950–December 1950, p. 143.

Democratic politicians to debate the future of Europe.[7] Finally, before his appointment to the Court of Justice in 1962, Lecourt served as Minister of State in the Fifth Republic that General de Gaulle had founded in 1958.[8]

At the Court of Justice, Lecourt appears to have been extremely influential. The Court's *Van Gend en Loos* judgment declaring the direct effect of European law in early 1963 has been attributed to Lecourt's arrival as a judge in May of the previous year.[9] By the early 1970s, the Court has been described as "dominated" by the "formidable French President, Robert Lecourt".[10] His role in the early years of European law has been compared by both the Court's admirers and its critics to that of Chief Justice John Marshall in the early years of the United States Supreme Court.[11] If European law was in effect created by the Court of Justice, Lecourt was "present at the creation" and indeed one of the leading "creators". No other single judge has had such a profound influence on the development of European law.

Despite this, however, discussions of the early landmark judgments of European law rarely attempt to investigate Lecourt's own understanding of their purpose or importance. There are many reasons for this, of course. Above all, the Court of Justice (unlike, in this respect, the United States Supreme Court) produces only a single judgment presented by the Court as a whole, with no separately signed dissenting or concurring opinions. The individuality of particular judges' participation in the Court's decisions is thus officially obscured. The judges themselves are sworn to secrecy about their internal deliberations, and both judges and their assistants typically remain discreet about the internal functioning of the Court. The Court as an institution refuses to allow access to any materials that might reveal how its judges reached their decisions, even

[7] Pappini 1996.

[8] See obituaries of Robert Lecourt in *Le Figaro*, 14 August 2004, p. 12 and *Le Monde*, 15 August 2004, p. 12. Neither these obituaries nor the outline of Lecourt's life in Vera Fritz's valuable recent biographical survey of judges and advocates-general of the early ECJ does justice to the many and varied features of Lecourt's long career, which has yet to be adequately studied (Fritz 2018: 241–248). See also Bernier's account of the reception of European law in France, in which Lecourt plays a prominent role (Bernier 2018). A continuing research project on Robert Lecourt is being pursued by the present author with the assistance of the Jean Monnet Chair in EU Politics and Law at Trinity College Dublin.

[9] Rasmussen 2008: 98, Vauchez 2010, Fritz 2018: 144–148.

[10] Edward 2001: 180.

[11] E.g. Rasmussen 1983: 160, Cassuto 2015: 76.

these many decades later.[12] Detailed direct evidence for Lecourt's contributions to the Court's internal deliberations is therefore unavailable. Lecourt himself published no memoirs of his time on the Court.[13] His best-known book on European law – the 1976 *L'Europe des juges* – is often considered bland and atheoretical, aimed squarely at popularizing European law with "legal practitioners".[14] Perhaps most unfortunately of all, Lecourt appears to have had his private papers destroyed prior to his death.[15] So neither Lecourt nor the Court of Justice have made it easy for us to trace Lecourt's personal impact on the birth of the European legal order.

Despite these challenges and obstacles, the importance of Lecourt's role in the Court's early years suggests that our understanding of the Court's judgments will be enhanced by looking carefully at Lecourt's own discussions of Community law. That will be our approach throughout this book. We will draw attention to interesting passages from *L'Europe des juges*, but some of Lecourt's other discussions of the direct-effect doctrine – whether in public speeches, law journals, or Christian Democratic publications – are even more illuminating. To be sure, we only have access to a small portion of Lecourt's writings over his years on the Court, and the apparent destruction of his private papers is a great loss for history. Such material as is available, however, repeatedly indicates that Lecourt held a very specific and likely unexpected outlook on the purpose and effects of the Court's greatest judgments.

One surviving piece of indirect evidence for Lecourt's contribution to the development of European law can be found in his early legal scholarship. Long before he joined the Court of Justice, Lecourt completed a doctoral dissertation on litigation in French property disputes, addressing in particular an action before the French courts known as the *réintégrande*, which provided for the restitution of property to a person who had been arbitrarily dispossessed, often by a country neighbour, sometimes by the state. To be sure, this topic might seem far from the international challenges that would later face the European Court of Justice. Compared to previous scholarship, however, Lecourt's approach to the *réintégrande* emphasized that its central purpose was to counteract

12 ECLR Editorial Comments 2014.

13 Lecourt did write a book chapter entitled "The Court of Justice seen from the interior" but it was far from a "tell-all" memoir (Lecourt 1981).

14 Lecourt 1976a, cf. Schermers 1977.

15 Rasmussen 2010: 654 ft 58.

arbitrary self-help in property disputes.[16] For Lecourt, *réintégrande* was based on the principle that "no one can take the law into their own hands" – "*la réintégrande est fondée sur le principe qu'il est interdit de se faire justice à soi-même*".[17] He stressed the *réintégrande*'s role in suppressing arbitrary self-help much more than its importance in, for example, the protection of property ownership.[18] Contrary to French legal tradition, Lecourt also celebrated the development of this legal instrument by the French courts themselves in response to economic and social needs when legislative texts were "silent or ambiguous".[19] If, as has been suggested, the development of European law from the 1960s onwards was in many ways the product of the "personal judicial philosophies" of a small coterie of judges acting under the leadership of Robert Lecourt, then it is important to note that the personal judicial philosophy that Lecourt himself brought to the Court of Justice encompassed both a profound rejection of any form of self-help in law enforcement as well as an openness to ambitious developments of the law by courts themselves.[20]

A passage from the final pages of Lecourt's dissertation extended his discussion of the suppression of self-help in French property disputes to the more ambitious project of suppressing self-help in international law:[21]

16 Lecourt 1931. The first discussion by this author of Lecourt's doctoral dissertation appeared in the *European Journal of International Law*, on which this section draws, and to which the reader is referred for a more extensive treatment (Phelan 2017).

17 Michelet, writing decades later, summarised Lecourt's contribution as the claim that "*la réintégrande est fondée sur le principe qu'il est interdit de se faire justice à soi-même*" (Michelet 1973: 180).

18 Lecourt 1931: 11, similarly 241–242, 279–280.

19 Lecourt 1931: 236, 282.

20 Rasmussen 2009: 11. On the active role of the Court of Justice in interpreting the Treaties, see e.g. Lecourt's 1973 speech where he explains that the Community judge has less occasion, compared to judges within the national legal order, to limit their role to the "simple exegesis of texts": "More than in legal systems that have matured over the length of centuries, the Court of Justice, charged with the interpretation of a recent law, must more often supplement its appreciation either by investigation into the useful effect [*effet utile*] of the provisions under litigation, or, in certain circumstances, by a concern for the object to be obtained in the general logic of the treaties" (Lecourt 1973a: 15).

21 Lecourt 1931: 284–285. Note that Lecourt's focus on the suppression of self-help in law enforcement was not limited to this passage, rather it was the single-minded and relentless focus of his doctoral dissertation as a whole. Furthermore, Lecourt's discussion of the *réintégrande* demonstrated that his objection was not limited to the possibility of violence but to the possibility of self-help as such in legal disputes (Lecourt 1931: 212).

> International law is virtually in its origins, starting at the point where domestic law began.
>
> States have agreed to outlaw violence now and put the "war outside the law." And these ideas are progressing every day. Already international organizations have been created to limit and if possible prevent violent conflicts between peoples and the right to substitute violence with law. The very principle that once stopped private wars we use today to prevent world wars. This is the prohibition for anyone, individuals or nations, to resort to violence and the obligation of all to present themselves before a judge instead of taking the law into their own hands. This principle has always developed in parallel with the Law. Where the Law extends to a new area, this principle appears as a foundation. Its extension is so great and so visible that although once limited to conflicts between private interests it now constantly tends to apply to disputes between peoples. This has been reflected in international law especially during the last decade through the creation of international organizations: the League of Nations, international conferences (disarmament conferences), international tribunals that play an important role in the relations between States. These organizations are called upon to prevent violence between peoples and prohibit nations, just as it has long been forbidden to individuals, from taking the law into their own hands [*à interdire aux nations, comme il est depuis longtemps défendu aux particuliers, de se faire justice à soi-même*].

As we will see, Lecourt maintained his interest in the suppression of self-help as a means of enforcing treaty obligations throughout his time as a judge at the Court of Justice.

In short, therefore, during the early years of the European Economic Community, influential lawyers working at the Court of Justice performed a sort of X-ray analysis of the Treaty to draw out the hidden meanings and significances of its provisions and institutions.[22] Here we in turn will perform a similar X-ray analysis of some of the writings of those very lawyers, drawing out as best we can the concerns and priorities that informed their approaches to enforcement and escape in the Treaty of Rome.

Building on comparisons with other treaty systems as well as on the writings of Lecourt and others, this book will put forward the argument that the great doctrines of European law must be understood to have a much closer relationship to the practical problems of international trade politics than is often understood. On current accounts, the special

[22] The expression is Lecourt's (Lecourt 1965: 21).

distinction of the European legal order is often to be found in the role of the private individual, empowered by the doctrine of direct effect to vindicate rights derived from the Treaties before their own national courts. This new enforcement role for private individuals is matched by a new enforcement role for national courts, whose obligation to vindicate the rights of individuals was confirmed and strengthened by the doctrine of the supremacy of Community law over conflicting national law. So the litigating private individual, above all, is both the Community legal order's "new actor" and the main beneficiary of doctrines set out in these great judgments of the Court of Justice. It is in that sense that *Van Gend en Loos* founded a new European "citizenship", albeit primarily a "market citizenship", and placed "the individual" at the centre of the European legal order.[23] It is no wonder that much analysis of the "interests" underlying the creation and development of the Community legal order stress above all the way that this new legal system was profoundly in the interests of both those litigating individuals and the newly empowered national courts.[24]

Such accounts of the creation of the European legal order can be wonderful, even inspiring. They are also unsatisfying. Treaties organize a relationship between states. Dominant approaches to the founding doctrines of Community law, and the great judgments in which they were first set out, however, often almost entirely ignore the relationship between states, and focus instead on how these doctrines structured the relationship between the treaty system itself, on the one hand, and private individuals and national courts on the other. The Treaty of Rome, as the Court of Justice interpreted it, did of course set out a distinctive enforcement role for private individuals and national courts. But a treaty system that provides a distinctive enforcement role for private individuals and national courts remains a treaty system that organizes a relationship between its participating states. European law's new role for individuals and national courts therefore must be understood as part of a solution to *international collective action problems* common to international trade treaties, where individual states have powerful incentives to behave in ways that produce collectively suboptimal outcomes. As it is, many prominent accounts of the creation of the Community legal order, and many paeans to the role of the individual within European law, offer little or no attempt to describe how these new doctrines contributed

[23] Robert 1963, Everson 1995, Weiler 2014: 103.

[24] Most influentially, Weiler 1991.

to addressing such international collective action problems. Well, that cannot be right. Here instead we will make that connection our central focus, and demonstrate that direct effect was intimately and specifically connected with the Community legal order's rejection of both self-help and unilateral safeguards by the European states, and thus to a much wider group of beneficiaries than those litigating individuals or "empowered" national courts.

In order to keep the contribution of this book carefully focused, it will discuss only a select group of the Court's most foundational judgments on the structure and organization of the Community legal order. Some of these are very well-known and would be included in any account of the development of the European legal order – *Van Gend en Loos*, *Costa* v. *ENEL*, *Internationale Handelsgesellschaft*, *Van Duyn*, *Simmenthal*, and perhaps *Sheep Meat*. We will discuss another judgment that is certainly well-known, but rarely used to understand the development of the European legal order as it relates to the legal obligations between the European states – the *International Fruit* judgment on the relationship of the Community to the General Agreement on Tariffs and Trade (GATT) global trade regime, founded in 1948 and the forerunner of today's WTO. Finally, the book will also discuss two judgments which, while their importance has not always been well recognized, should, I argue, be understood to have played a similarly vital role in the construction of the European legal order – the *Pork Products* and *Dairy Products* judgments of 1961 and 1964 respectively.

These great decisions of the Court of Justice have given birth to reams of commentary, illuminating diverse facets of these judgments and their influence on later decisions of courts both European and national. Previous scholarship on these cases will therefore be discussed selectively and with no futile attempt at comprehensiveness. Many of these judgments, and the subsequent decisions that confirmed and extended their ambits, have by themselves been the subject of distinguished and often lengthy monographs, whose thoroughness we cannot aim to match.[25] For the same reason, we do not aim to produce a complete history of the early years of the European Court of Justice, an assessment of all the

[25] Among monographs that I have found most useful on these leading cases, and the most important associated judgments, are Gori on *Pork Products*, Claes on *Costa* and *Simmenthal*, Gradoni on *Dairy Products*, Mendez on *International Fruit*, and Prechal on *Van Duyn* (Gori 1967, Prechal 2005, Claes 2006, Gradoni 2008, Mendez 2013).

lawyers of distinction who influenced its development,[26] or even a comprehensive account of all of judge Lecourt's contributions to European legal integration.[27] We aim instead at setting out a largely overlooked perspective on the purposes and effects of the most important of the Court's early judgments and at justifying this perspective as an essential one in any attempt to understand the beginnings of European law.

Throughout the text we refer to the provisions of the Treaty as they were set out in the Treaty of Rome, rather than as they have been renumbered in various subsequent revisions. Such an approach is required by our focus on the Court's early decisions, in the context of the challenges facing the Court at the time. For the convenience of the reader, the texts of the most relevant provisions of the Treaty of Rome, as well as its Preamble, and an equivalence table matching the provisions of the Treaty of Rome with the relevant provisions of the current European Treaties, are set out at the front of this book.

"Community law" and "European law" are used interchangeably throughout. All translations of non-English language scholarship, and of the writings of Robert Lecourt, are my own.

We should perhaps say a brief word about the format in which the book presents its argument. The European legal order was built by the Court of Justice judgment by judgment, and a judgment-by-judgment analysis of the Court's progress is therefore the appropriate way in which to explain its principles and development. Make no mistake, however,

[26] Other influential early ECJ judges include Alberto Trabucchi and Pierre Pescatore, and outside the Court itself scholarship has increasingly emphasized the key role played by Michel Gaudet and Walter Much as directors of the Legal Service of the European Commission (Bailleux 2013, Boerger and Rasmussen 2017, Fritz 2018). Indeed, as Somek has emphasized, there is a continuing debate about the relative contributions of Lecourt and Gaudet to the creation of the direct-effect doctrine (Somek 2017: 66 ft 57). No doubt both had a vital role to play. This book advances these debates by bringing to light previously neglected evidence of Lecourt's thinking about the new doctrines of European law.

[27] A comprehensive account of the impact of Robert Lecourt on European integration and European law would require an engagement with a much fuller range of Lecourt's activities and published writings over many decades as well as his involvement with a variety of political movements and Catholic organizations during his long career. One focus would have to be Lecourt's long experience as a journalist and propagandist, which may have contributed to the Court's many activities to generate public and legal attention for its new role. Even a full consideration of all of Lecourt's writings directly on the subject of European law is beyond the scope of this monograph, which concentrates on demonstrating the relationship between direct effect, self-help, and safeguards in the early years of European legal order.

this is neither casebook nor coursebook, but a monograph setting forward a focused argument about the development of European law by following a line of reasoning through the texts of, and debates about, the Court's landmark early judgments. For each ruling, the chapter first summarizes the facts of the case, the mundane and principled issues at trial, the contending parties and so on, as well as the essential parts of the Advocate General's opinion and the judgment of the Court. Indeed, a focus on Court's own words is often helpful for our task, as summaries of the Court's judgments not infrequently "trim" important aspects of the Court's reasoning or insert references to Treaty provisions that the Court's own judgment did not contain. It next briefly discusses some of the related cases, prior or subsequent, where the Court addressed or modified the points of principle advanced in the foundational case under discussion. The discussion then concentrates on demonstrating new perspectives on the Court's decisions in the light of the texts of the judgments, contemporary scholarship, relevant writings by judge Lecourt and other influential lawyers closely connected to the Court, and, above all, the European legal order's distinctive approach to enforcement and escape in comparison with the alternatives commonly employed by other trade treaties.

The chapters that follow discuss the European Court of Justice's decisions largely chronologically, starting with *Pork Products*, before proceeding to *Van Gend en Loos*, *Costa* v. *ENEL*, *Dairy Products*, *International Fruit*, *Van Duyn*, *Simmenthal*, and *Sheep Meat*. A further chapter then discusses the 1970 case *Internationale Handelsgesellschaft*, whose focus on possible conflicts between European law and national constitutional rights requires a somewhat separate treatment.[28] No attempt has been made press the individual chapters into approximately equal size, and our discussions of *Van Gend en Loos*, *Costa* v. *ENEL*, *Dairy Products*, and *International Fruit* are the most extensive.

The book concludes with an essay entitled "States and Individuals in the Great Judgments of the European Court of Justice, 1961–1979".

[28] These nine cases are not, of course, the only landmark judgments of the Court of Justice during the 1960s and 1970s, and perhaps not even the only landmark judgments during this period relevant to the argument being advanced by this book. They are however the most important ones for our argument about the development of the European legal order's distinctive approach to enforcement and escape in intra-European trade.

1

Pork Products, 1961

No Unilateral Safeguards

The Case before the Court

This case came to the Court of Justice as a consequence of the Article 169 procedure, which provided that if the Commission considered that a member state had failed to fulfil an obligation under the Treaty, then the Commission could deliver a reasoned opinion on the matter after allowing the state concerned the opportunity to submit its observations.[1] If the state did not comply with the opinion within the period laid down, the Commission could bring the matter before the Court. Article 171 provided that, if the Court found that a state had failed to fulfil its Treaty obligations, then the state "shall be required to take the necessary measures to comply with the judgment of the Court of Justice". *Pork Products* was the first dispute heard by the Court concerning the Treaty of Rome.

One of the provisions establishing a customs union between the member states – Article 31 – required that the "Member States refrain from introducing between themselves any new quantitative restrictions or measures having equivalent effect", adding provisions by which the member states were to supply the Commission with lists of products liberalized within the framework of the Organization for European Economic Cooperation (OEEC), as the standstill requirement related only to those products so liberalized. In December 1958, the Italian government supplied the Commission with a list of products liberalized by it in pursuance of the decisions of the OEEC, which included "swine, other than those for slaughter", "pig fat", and "meat" broadly defined. However, in June 1960, an Italian inter-ministerial order provided for the suspension until the end of August 1960 of all imports (including those from the other member states) of various products including "live swine", "pigmeat", and "unrendered pig fat". As Advocate General

[1] Case 7/61 *Commission* v. *Italy (Pork Products)* [1961] ECR 317.

Lagrange pointed out, it was clear that the products described in this inter-ministerial order were the same products specified in the list of liberalized products earlier provided by the Italian Government to the Commission, products therefore for which an import prohibition could not subsequently be enacted. The Italian government had justified the inter-ministerial order to the Commission by declaring that it was of an "absolutely provisional nature", in response to a "crisis" in the pigmeat market. Subsequent orders of the Italian government continued the suspension of imports until the end of December 1960, and indeed, even after the Commission had issued its reasoned opinion, as required by Article 169, specifying the Commission's opinion that the Italian government was failing to fulfil its obligation under the Treaty, the ban on imports of these products was further extended until March 1961.

The Italian government, responding to the Commission's reasoned opinion, stated that it hoped "that the Commission will be able to agree, pursuant to the power conferred on it by Article 226 of the Treaty of Rome, to the measures taken to deal with the exceptional situation on the Italian market". Article 226 allowed any member state suffering from "difficulties . . . which are serious and liable to persist in any sector of the economy" to "apply for authorization to take protective measures in order to rectify the situation and adjust the sector concerned to the economy of the Common Market". It further specified that the Commission should "by emergency procedure" determine "without delay" the protective measures it considers necessary, including derogations from the rules of the treaty, but only to the extent and for such periods as were strictly necessary.

The Commission decided that it would interpret the Italian government's communication as an application for authorization of the suspension of imports as a protective measure under Article 226. It added that such an application would not bring about the suspension of the Article 169 proceedings. Furthermore, before the dispute was heard by the Court, the Commission decided to decline the application made under Article 226, and instead suggested that the Italian government introduce a system of minimum prices as referred to in Article 44 of the Treaty, which the Italian government went on to introduce from July 1961, several months before the Court of Justice's judgment.

The Advocate General, Maurice Lagrange, rejected the view that use of the Article 169 procedure to bring the Italian government before the Court no longer served any purpose if the Italian government had finally come to fulfil its obligations. Lagrange argued that only where a member state had complied with the demands of the Commission's reasoned opinion within the prescribed period was the Commission unable to bring the matter before the Court, whereas if the member state did not comply with the opinion within the prescribed period, it loses this "potential benefit" and the Article 169 procedure may then continue to assess, not whether the reasoned opinion of the Commission has been observed, but whether or not there had been a failure in relation to the Treaty.

Moving to the substance of the case, Advocate General Lagrange explained that the first question arising is whether the re-establishment by a state, even temporarily, of measures restricting imports of products consolidated between the member states under Article 31 is contrary to the provisions of that Article. Here, Lagrange stated, "there can be no doubt that the answer is in the affirmative". Lagrange therefore rejected the claims of the Italian government that Article 226 applied to this case and that the Commission should have come to a decision about applying it, even though the Commission had not been requested by the Italian government to do so until January 1961. Lagrange emphasized that the protective clauses provided by Article 226 could "only be used within the framework of the special procedure provided for in that article, that is to say, on application by the government concerned". Such measures were "completely exceptional" and "the least that one is entitled to demand" for a procedure with such serious consequences is "an unequivocal, formal application by the government concerned".

Second, the Italian government had argued that "the need for quick action" led it to take for itself the provisional measures required by the circumstances. As Lagrange explained, the Italian government "calls upon the general principles of public law whereby every state is entitled to make such provisional measures as are necessary in the case of serious occurrences". Lagrange replied that, whether or not such principles may be relied upon in the context of the Treaty of Rome was a very difficult question, but "what is certain is that the argument may not be relied on in this instance, as it so happens that there is a formal provision, Article 226, which itself lays down an emergency procedure". Lagrange therefore dismissed the argument based on urgency. The Advocate General likewise found unconvincing a late attempt by the Italian government to appeal to the exceptions to the free movement of goods set out in Article 36 of the Treaty, relating to "public policy" or "protection of life and health" of Italian swine. The Advocate General concluded by stating his opinion that the Italian Republic should be found by the Court to have failed to fulfil an obligation under the Treaty of Rome.

On 19 December 1961, the Court of Justice's judgment largely confirmed the views of the Advocate General. The Court stated that, if a member state failed to comply with the Commission's reasoned opinion within the prescribed period, "there is no question that the Commission has the right to obtain the Court's judgment on that member state's failure to fulfil the obligations following from the treaty". Only if the member state had complied with the reasoned opinion within the prescribed period would the Commission lose that right. Turning to the substantive issue, the Court rejected the contention of the Italian government that the measures were provisional and that Italy intended to re-establish freedom for imports of the products concerned as quickly as possible. Rather, the Court declared, "The 'standstill' obligation laid down by Article 31 is absolute. It comprises no exceptions, not even partial or temporary ones. The interpretation pleaded by the defendant would open the way to unilateral actions by member states going directly against the aim pursued by the Treaty in relation to the free movement of goods."

The Court then went on to find that protective measures under Article 226 of the Treaty "could only be authorized within the framework of the special procedure prescribed by that article, that is to say, on unequivocal, formal application by the government concerned". The Court also rejected arguments based on "necessity and urgency", stating that "the very fact that an emergency procedure has been provided excludes any unilateral action by member states, which may not therefore rely on either the urgency or seriousness of the situation to evade the procedure of Article 226".

Finally, the Court considered and rejected the Italian government's contention that the Commission should have "inquired spontaneously whether Article 36 was applicable in this case". "Article 36", the Court explained, "as distinct from Article 226, is directed to eventualities of a non-economic kind ... In particular, it does not establish a generic protective clause additional to that provided by Article 226 and allowing member states to derogate by unilateral action from the procedure and guarantees laid down by that Article." The Court therefore found that the Italian government, by provisionally suspending imports of products from other member states, had failed to fulfil the obligations of Article 31 of the Treaty of Rome.

Related Cases

As the Court of Justice's first judgment concerning the European Economic Community treaty, there are no prior cases vis-à-vis provisions of the Treaty of Rome that are related to the *Pork Products* case. As for later cases, various decisions of the Court of Justice in the 1960s demonstrate the Court's continued insistence that the strict nature of the safeguard regime within the Common Market. These include the February 1964 case *Handelsvereniging Rotterdam* v. *Minister van Landbouw*, where the Court insisted that the Commission in making use of the Article 226 safeguard mechanism, "must use the means which are least likely to have an adverse effect on the state, a sector of whose economic activity is affected by the measures authorized"; the June 1965 case *Italy* v. *Commission*, where the Court rejected Italy's claim that the Commission (following an application in line with the Article 226 procedure) had not authorized sufficient protection for Italian silk; and the July 1965 case *Toepfer and Getreide-Import Gesellschaft* v. *Commission*, where the Court annulled the decision of the Commission authorizing Germany to retain protectionist measures against maize imports, finding that the Commission had likely exaggerated the impact of such imports on the German markets.[2]

On a broader note, as the following chapters will set out, the principle defended in *Pork Products* – that the adoption of safeguard measures or derogations by individual member states within the European Community could only be permitted on the basis of prior authorization by the European institutions as provided for by the Treaties – can be connected to many, perhaps all, of the great decisions of the Court of Justice over the 1960s and 1970s. Indeed, this principle formed part of the Court's reasoning in such important decisions as *Costa* v. *ENEL*, *Dairy Products*, *Van Duyn*, *Sheep Meat*, and, by way of contrast, *International Fruit*.

Analysis and Context

The *Pork Products* judgment is rarely included in prominent texts and surveys of the development of European law, or in collections of the

[2] Cases 73 & 74/63 *Handelsvereniging Rotterdam* v. *Minister van Landbouw* [1964] ECR 1, Case 32/64 *Italy* v. *Commission* [1965] ECR 365, and Case 106 & 107/63 *Toepfer and Getreide-Import Gesellschaft* v. *Commission* [1965] ECR 405.

Court's famous judgments.[3] At most, *Pork Products* may be referred to when explaining, for example, that the Commission's reasoned opinions cannot be subject to an action for annulment, or that the Court can make a finding that a state has acted illegally even if the state has by that point remedied its conduct.[4] Approaches such as these leave the central aspect of *Pork Products* – that the unilateral adoption of safeguard measures by the member states was prohibited by the Treaty – largely disconnected from the great judgments of the Court of Justice in the years that followed.

Like other early decisions of the European Court, however, the significance of *Pork Products* may best be understood in the context of treaty provisions and state practices in other trade-related treaty regimes, above all those related to the enforcement of, and escape from, demanding treaty obligations. The treaty provisions and state practices most relevant to *Pork Products* are provisions for, and state use of, emergency or safeguard measures within international trade regimes.

One of the most striking aspects of many trade treaties is their generous provision of "escape" or "safety valve" mechanisms by which policy-makers in the participating states can impose trade restrictions to protect domestic industries facing difficulties as a result of imports from their treaty partners.[5] Thus many a treaty regime both requires its member states to reduce trade barriers vis-à-vis their treaty partners and, at the same time, provides a *smorgasbord* of instruments by which the same member states can reintroduce such trade barriers where their domestic industries are facing actual or possible injury from this treaty-agreed reduction in trade barriers. Such safeguards, sometimes called "trade remedies", are pervasive and include anti-dumping measures, countervailing duties, "industry safeguards" strictly defined, procedures for states to withdraw from previously agreed obligations, and

[3] It is omitted entirely in e.g. Craig and de Búrca 2011, Weatherill 2014, Schütze 2016, and only included in Arnull 2006: 161 ft 10 as the Court's first judgment in an EEC Case. *Pork Products* is not included as a "basic community case" or a "classic of EU law" in either Rudden and Rossa Phelan 1997 or Maduro and Azoulai 2010. The *Pork Products* decision was delivered before judge Lecourt joined the Court in 1962, but is however mentioned in *L'Europe des juges*, where Lecourt emphasizes that Article 36 did not provide a generic safeguard additional to that provided in Article 226, and that *Pork Products* provided an unusual example of progress in the control of quantitative restrictions through use of the Article 169 procedure, rather than actions by private individuals (Lecourt 1976a: 39, 43, 46, 47).

[4] Chalmers et al. 2014: 363, Craig and de Búrca 2015: 440, 444.

[5] Rosendorff and Milner 2001.

derogations justified by various public policy purposes. As Pelc writes in his recent study of escape clauses in global and regional trade treaties, "as long as there have been formal rules binding sovereign states, there have been additional rules put in place allowing states temporary breaches of their commitments".[6] Indeed, the role of such mechanisms were prominently debated in postwar trade politics, with United States President Truman issuing an Executive Order in 1947 requiring that all future US trade agreements contain a clause providing that, where imports threatened domestic producers with serious injury, "the United States shall be free to withdraw the [trade] concession, in whole or in part, or to modify it, to the extent or for such time as may be necessary to prevent such injury".[7]

As Truman's order shows, these mechanisms are most commonly available at the unilateral option of policy-makers in the participating states, both as specified in relevant treaty provisions and even more so in actual state practice. Certainly there was, for example, no prior international control on the use of such mechanisms by the members of the postwar multilateral trade regime, the General Agreement on Tariffs and Trade (GATT), set up in 1948 and replaced in 1994 by its successor, the World Trade Organization (WTO).[8] This combination of demanding obligations and readily available escape mechanisms within the same treaty is, so the argument goes, justified because state policy-makers are more likely to accept challenging trade obligations where they are also provided with "insurance" mechanisms that allow them subsequently actively to vary the degree of trade openness or policy convergence as domestic circumstances require.[9] Indeed, the Italian government's argument in *Pork Products*, that its restrictions on trade were of an "absolutely provisional nature", in response to a "crisis" in the pigmeat market,

[6] Pelc 2016: 6.

[7] Executive Order 9832 (February 25 1947), Part 1, Article 1, Kim 2010: 42.

[8] E.g. Trebilcock et al. 2013: 412. Such escape and derogation mechanisms are also available in, for example, other prominent trade treaty systems such as the NAFTA (North American Free Trade Area), the Mercosur (The Common Market of the South), and the Andean Community (The Andean Community of Nations), albeit sometimes subject to more demanding regulations than those of the GATT/WTO – see Teh et al. 2007, Voon 2010. On the Andean Community in particular see Phelan 2015a, noting for example that an intra-Andean safeguard could be levied by Andean states for four months on a provisional basis, even in cases where the measure was eventually considered to be unwarranted by the Andean Secretariat.

[9] E.g. Rosendorff and Milner 2001, Fischer and Prusa 2003.

corresponds exactly to the situation that such emergency safeguard mechanisms are designed to address.

Now it is true that the provision of such mechanisms may help otherwise reluctant policy-makers to allow the lowering of trade barriers within a treaty system, and similarly may reduce pressures on states to completely exit from treaty systems when demanding obligations become politically difficult.[10] Those important considerations aside, however, such mechanisms have little to recommend them. By allowing the domestic economic and political difficulties of trade openness to be managed through the temporary, and sometimes "temporary", restriction or effective closure of international trade in particular products, such mechanisms invite the continual disruption of international economic exchange as internal conditions – above all, interest group politics – within individual treaty states so require.[11] Furthermore, the unilateral use of such mechanisms by state policy-makers naturally tends to prompt policy-makers in other states within the same treaty regime to respond by imposing similar trade restrictions of their own, whether because (as is sometimes the case) the safeguard mechanisms explicitly entitle them to do so on the basis of reciprocity or because they are prompted to make their own use of unilaterally available safeguards. Such an international market can therefore easily become cluttered by the proliferation of such "provisional" and "temporary" measures. Both in themselves, therefore, and in their potential for such "chain reactions", such safeguard mechanisms, allowing states to effectively unilaterally restrict access to their home market for the goods and services produced in their trade partners' jurisdictions, damage the reliability of international economic exchange for trading businesses and individuals. Even the latent availability of such safeguards brings its own form of uncertainty to international trade.

In short, the question of how and under what circumstances safeguard measures may be adopted by states is one of the central international collective action problems facing any international trade treaty system. State policy-makers often demand that suitable safeguards be available in the case of difficult circumstances within their own jurisdictions but are simultaneously critical of the damage to reliable trading conditions arising from safeguards unilaterally employed by policy-makers in other states.

[10] Rosendorff and Milner 2001, and, with particular relevance to European legal integration, Phelan 2016b.

[11] Rosendorff and Milner 2001.

Individual incentives for states to unilaterally adopt such safeguards produce international tensions and a collectively suboptimal outcome.

The creation of a reliable Common Market in postwar western Europe therefore required not only the provision of a set of rules reducing barriers to trade and facilitating all forms of economic exchange between the participating European states. It also required the provision of a set of arrangements to manage claims by state policy-makers that they faced unforeseen and difficult situations, to allow for temporary deviations from such rules, to permit – frankly put – protectionist measures contrary to prior treaty commitments be allowed to continue when circumstances so required it, particularly in the European Economic Community's early and transitional years. This important practical aspect of trade politics needed to be addressed, however, in a manner compatible with developing a highly reliable market between the participating states, first by effectively restricting the availability of common forms of safeguard and then by transitioning to a system where even such restricted forms of safeguard would no longer be available.

The Treaty of Rome did indeed provide for such mechanisms. Seen in comparative context, however, the provisions for such safeguard mechanisms included in the Treaty of Rome have a striking quality. The most prominent such mechanism was that set out in Article 226 of the Treaty, which provided that "derogations from the rules of this Treaty" might be allowed to individual member states during the EEC Treaty's long transitional period until the end of 1969, where "difficulties arise which are serious and liable to persist in any sector of the economy or which could bring about serious deterioration in the economic situation of a given area". In those aspects, this relatively all-purpose escape mechanism had many similarities from those of many other trade-related treaty systems.

However – and this is the essential point – the Article 226 procedure was not available at the unilateral option of the individual member states. Rather, it provided that if such difficulties arise, "a Member State may apply for authorisation to take protective measures" and "the Commission shall, by emergency procedure, determine without delay the protective measures which it considers necessary, specifying the circumstances and the manner in which they are to be put into effect". The safeguard mechanism provided by Article 226 of the Treaty therefore, and this is true *mutatis mutandis* of various other trade-related safeguard mechanisms provided for in the Treaty of Rome, was a safeguard mechanism whereby the member states were required to *ask* the European institutions in advance for permission to adopt such measures.

The requirement that no such safeguards could be employed except as provided for by the Treaties, and in those cases were subject to prior control by common institutions, is remarkable, and as explained above one of the clear distinctions of the European Common Market in contrast to many other international trade regimes.[12]

The Treaty of Rome's provisions requiring safeguards and derogations to be authorized by the European institutions were a critical aspect of the Treaty's design. The design of such institutional controls was, for example, prominently discussed in the 1956 Spaak Report, where the administration of derogations and safeguard clauses was one listed as one of the essential activities for the functioning of the then proposed Common Market. The administration of safeguards could not be submitted to a vote of the governments, it explained, which could lead to vetoes, haggling between governments, or coalitions of interests rather than an objective assessment of what the law required. The creation of an institution – what would become the European Commission – with its own authority and a common responsibility therefore appeared indispensable.[13] That institution would then authorize the use of derogations and safeguards as necessary and as provided for by the Treaty.[14]

[12] Scholarship on safeguards, trade remedies, and other escape mechanisms in international trade regimes repeatedly confirms that these commonly tend to be readily available to policy-makers within the participating states, other than within the European Treaty system. Voon, for example, explains that of her collection of well over one hundred regional trade agreements, "only one" – the EU Treaty – has abolished all three of the most prominent forms of trade remedies (anti-dumping, countervailing, and safeguard measures) among its members (Voon 2010: 647, see also Roitinger 2004: 207, Teh et al. 2007: 26). Pelc in his recent discussion of escape clauses in nearly 600 trade agreements argues that "deeper" agreements tend to provide participating states with more trade flexibility mechanisms, but that the European Union is "the most notable outlier to the depth–flexibility relationship" – "a deep agreement by any measure, it is also one where designers have abolished all forms of trade remedies" (Pelc 2016: 186). Note that the European Community's abolition of these trade remedies is connected to the Community's ambitious competition policy, as the imposition of such "safeguard" trade barriers may be justified by state policy-makers on the basis of alleged anti-competitive behaviour by firms, or subsidies provided to firms by public authorities, in other trading states.

[13] *Rapport des chefs de délégation aux ministres des affaires étrangères* [Spaak Report], Brussels, 21 Apr. 1956, p. 24.

[14] The Spaak Report repeatedly returns to the design and role of safeguards and derogations necessary for the proposed Common Market, explaining, for example, that safeguards and derogations must be temporary with a fixed term (p. 19), that derogations during and even after the transitional period would be within agreed limits and would require the agreement of common [i.e. European] institutions (p. 20), that safeguards related to the

That is the principle that the Court defended in *Pork Products*. Neither the Advocate General nor the Court denied that some sort of safeguard mechanism might have been justified by the impact of intra-Community trade on the Italian pigmeat market. Both firmly rejected, however, that it was for the Italian government unilaterally to adopt any such safeguard mechanisms, emphasizing instead the requirement for the Italian government to submit an application, as required by the Treaty, to the European Commission to request the possible use of such measures. The Italian government was behaving as many governments do in many trade regimes – indeed as today's EU, and the European Communities before it, does in its external trade with non-European states within the global trade regime organized by the postwar GATT or today's WTO – by adopting provisional measures contrary to prior treaty obligations in response to economic difficulties affecting a sensitive industry. The Court of Justice insisted, however, that such normal behaviour could not continue *within* the European Economic Community. It is not too much to say that the specificity of the Treaty of Rome's approach to organizing the market between its participating states was at stake in the *Pork Products* case, and that the Court's decision here had profound consequences for many years to come.

The Court's judgment appeared stronger on point of principle than in its demonstration of an effective mechanism to reliably prevent such behaviours, however. After all, Italy had unilaterally introduced these trade barriers without the authorization of the European institutions, and had persisted with these policies even after the Commission had issued a reasoned opinion explaining why they were contrary to Italy's obligations under the Treaty. While Italy had indeed eventually changed its policies, there was little to prevent Italy or other member states from doing the same again in the future, and enjoying the benefits of such trade barriers as safeguards until the Court condemned their actions, or indeed beyond, instead of applying for such permission in advance. Thus the

common external tariff would require the agreement of the Commission and a limited duration (p. 33), that liberalization of trade between the member states already agreed under the scope of the OECE could not be withdrawn except where the proposed treaty itself authorized the possibility of safeguards (p. 36), that the Commission be granted the right to allow safeguards to industries disadvantaged by distortions of competition (p. 63), and that the treaty should provide for the possibility of safeguards authorized by the Commission to manage the movement of workers (p. 90). See *Rapport des chefs de délégation aux ministres des affaires étrangères* [Spaak Report], Brussels, 21 Apr. 1956.

Pork Products case contains both a clear statement of the Court's commitment to one of the distinctive principles of the Common Market as set out in the Treaty of Rome and at the same time reveals the inadequacy of the instruments that the Treaty had provided – most prominently, the Article 169 procedure, initiated by the Commission and leading to a declaratory judgment of the Court – to ensure that these principles were reliably adhered to.

This disjunction did not go unnoticed. Among analyses of European law's approach to safeguards prior to the Court's *Van Gend en Loos* judgment in 1963, perhaps the most interesting is Wenner's assessment of *Pork Products* in the 1962 *Aussenwirtschaftsdienst des Betreibs-Beraters*.[15] In a careful consideration of the case in light of the developing legal aspects of the Treaty of Rome regime as a whole, Wenner convincingly identified two related limitations of the system. The first was that the length of time associated with the use of the Article 169 procedure by the Commission to bring member states before the Court for allegations that they had failed to fulfil an obligation under the Treaty. A state could therefore continue to protect its industry for a long time despite being its behaviour being complained about before the Court of Justice. The second was that the implementation of an Article 171 finding by the Court that a member state had failed to fulfil an obligation under the Treaty remained in the hands of the member state. The Treaty did not, so Wenner made clear, provide the Court or Commission with the ability to authorize sanctions against the member states.[16] Thus protectionism of this sort by the member states could continue even after an authoritative finding by the Court. Wenner's analysis of the real availability of unilateral safeguards within the structure of the Treaty of Rome is unanswerable, and indeed matches similar analyses of "escape mechanisms" in other trade-related treaties, where the nature of safeguards on offer is sometimes characterized not so much by the rules establishing the scenarios for properly exercising them but by the time periods provided for before any concrete sanction can be authorized for their improper use.[17]

[15] Wenner 1962.

[16] Wenner 1962: 111, including ft 6 noting that the Treaty of Rome did not provide for sanctions against the member states similar to those provided for in Article 88 of the Treaty of Paris establishing the European Coal and Steel Community treaty.

[17] E.g. Brewster 2011.

The conclusion of this analysis for Wenner was that effectiveness of the Treaty appeared to rely on the "goodwill" of the member states.[18] Finding this unsatisfactory, Wenner then turned to argue that the weaknesses of the Treaty system would be reduced to the extent that provisions of the Treaty received direct effect in the national legal orders.[19] In that case, individuals could call on the judges of their own country to enforce the Treaty's requirements. Wenner did note that the direct effect of Regulations, one of the Treaty's main rule-making instruments, had been explicitly provided for in Article 189 of the Treaty, and that the Treaty provided a monopoly of its interpretation to the Court of Justice through the Article 177 procedure, but the argument for direct effect is driven primarily by the limited effectiveness of the legal control of the member states through the Article 169 procedure as revealed by the *Pork Products* safeguards case.[20] Wenner concluded by inviting the Court of Justice to address these issues in the near future.[21]

Wenner's 1962 assessment of *Pork Products*, it can be noted, is entirely compatible with the logic of the Court of Justice's 1963 *Van Gend en Loos* judgment. When the Court justified the direct effect of Community obligations in *Van Gend en Loos* on the basis that the Article 169 procedure would be ineffective if it were to be used only after the implementation of a national decision taken contrary to the provisions of the Treaty, the Italian government's unilateral use of safeguards in the *Pork Products* case provided a concrete example of such a scenario. And while this aspect of early Community law is not infrequently overlooked in retrospect, the issue of derogations and safeguards was a salient one in

18 Wenner 1962: 111.

19 Wenner 1962: 111: "*Die Gefahr, die in dem Fehlen einer Vollstreckbarkeit gerichtlicher Entscheidungen gegenüber Mitgliedstaaten für die Vertragsverwirklichung liegt, ist gemindert, soweit dem Vertrag und den Rechtsakten der Organe der Germeinschaft eine unmittelbare rechtliche Wirksamkeit in den nationalen Rechtsordnungen zuerkannt wird.*"

20 Wenner 1962: 111 ft 8 (Art 189), 111 (Art 177), 110 (The logic of the *Pork Products* decision itself is self-evident but it brings attention to questions of the effectiveness of legal control of the member states). Wenner makes no reference to other aspects of the Treaty sometimes used to justify the direct-effect doctrine, such as the wording of the Preamble of the Treaty of Rome. (Wenner's analysis also included an assessment of the circumstances under which Treaty provisions might be given direct effect in the German legal order, noting that the question of whether national law should be inapplicable if it conflicted with Community law [that is, the supremacy question] must be answered by national constitutional law.)

21 Wenner 1962: 112 ft 15, noting the possibility of a case coming to the Court of Justice as a preliminary reference from a Dutch court.

the early 1960s. In judge Lecourt's 1963 description of the Court's role in controlling Community decisions, for example, judgments on "derogations granted to states temporarily excused from Community rules" and on "safeguard measures authorized in case of severe difficulties" provide two of the three types of dispute given as examples.[22]

Among contemporary analyses of European law's approach to safeguards after the Court's *Van Gend en Loos* judgment in 1963, perhaps the most interesting is the 1967 monograph "Safeguard Clauses of the ECSC and EEC Treaties" [*Les Clauses de Sauvegarde des Traités CECA et CEE*] written by Paolo Gori.[23] Gori served as a judge's legal *attaché* – we would now say *référendaire* – first for Italian ECJ judge Catalano and then for his replacement judge Trabucchi. Such a straightforward description may however not do sufficient justice to Gori's role in the early years of the Court of Justice. Among ECJ judges, Trabucchi appears to have played a crucial role, together with Robert Lecourt, in leading a divided Court to declare the direct effect of European law in *Van Gend en Loos*, and Trabucchi in turn appears to have been encouraged by his assistant, Gori. Indeed it is only via Gori himself that we have any hard evidence at all about the Court's internal deliberations in *Van Gend en Loos*, as Gori had kept and later made available a copy of Trabucchi's internal note advocating that Article 12 of the Treaty be granted direct effect. Today Gori is widely recognized as one of the key participants in European law's "revolutionary moment". His prominent contribution

[22] Lecourt 1963: 273. The third was disputes about decisions relating to positions of economic dominance. See also Lecourt's 1970 short description of the tasks of the Commission, which includes "agreeing to any derogatory measures provided for by the Treaties" (Lecourt 1970: 18, safeguards are also mentioned in e.g. Lecourt and Chevallier 1963: 276, Lecourt 1965: 21, Lecourt 1984: 231). Early disputes over safeguards and derogations are likewise mentioned in Lecourt's newspaper articles explaining the development of European law (Lecourt 1966, Lecourt 1967, Lecourt 1968b).

[23] Gori 1967, based it seems on a university course he taught in Luxembourg in 1965. For Gori's close working relationship with judge Trabucchi, see Trabucchi's speech in "Formal Hearings of the Court of Justice of the European Communities 1976", p. 34. For Trabucchi's close working cooperation with Lecourt himself (the "common legal destiny" of "two members of our Court" "with only a difference of a few weeks" associated with the work of the Court over the same period) and his influence on the development of European law, see Lecourt's speech on Trabucchi's retirement from the Court, where he attributes to Trabucchi "some of the most famous grounds of our judgments, which have become classical 'selected passages' of Community law" (Lecourt 1976c: 29, 30).

to the Court of Justice's 50th anniversary celebration of *Van Gend en Loos* was entitled *Souvenirs d'un survivant* – "memories of a survivor".[24]

The major work of scholarship written in the 1960s by this influential employee of the Court addressed a topic at the heart of the legal development of the Common Market – its safeguard clauses. Gori used the *Pork Products* case as the first example of the "very strict" approach adopted by the Court to allowing derogations from the fundamental rules of the Common Market, as an illustration of the temptation of the member states towards unilateral adoption of safeguards even outside any provision of the Treaty, and as a demonstration of the Court's insistence that neither urgency nor seriousness could allow the states to avoid the requirement to apply in advance for permission to impose safeguards as set out in Article 226.[25]

Gori's approach to the safeguard clauses of the Treaty of Rome was explicitly a comparative one. His monograph develops its understanding of the EEC's approach to safeguards by contrast with safeguard mechanisms available in other trade-related treaty systems, above all those provided for within the postwar multilateral trading system, the GATT. Gori emphasized that the essential feature of the safeguard mechanisms provided by the GATT was their unilateral availability to GATT members, while by contrast the essential feature of the safeguard mechanisms provided by the EEC – their *sine qua non* – was the requirement to obtain prior authorization from the European institutions, especially the Commission.[26] Gori noted that derogating measures in the GATT were negotiated between the contracting parties, while the derogating measures in the EEC were decided by the European Commission as an organ independent of the member states. Gori emphasized that in the case of GATT Article XIX safeguard provisions, if the other GATT members did not come to an agreement on a compensatory adjustment, a GATT member was nonetheless free to take protective measures, but the other GATT members could, as a form of countermeasure, in turn suspend equivalent GATT trading concessions benefiting the derogating GATT member.[27] By contrast, where the Commission authorized a

24 Gori 2013. Gori's intervention was introduced by Cremona who described Gori as possessing "uniquely first-hand recollections" of the shaping of the *Van Gend en Loos* judgment (Cremona 2013: 23).

25 Gori 1967: 20, 66, 273.

26 Gori 1967: 38.

27 Gori 1967: 78, also 36. As Gori writes, "The fundamental tendency of the GATT towards a larger liberty of external trade by the contracting parties is evenly counteracted by the

safeguard measure by a state within the Common Market, there was no question of such GATT-style reciprocity, and the obligations of other member states were entirely unaffected.[28]

Gori went on to explain that, despite the important similarities between the safeguard arrangements in Article XIX of the GATT and the EEC safeguards clauses,[29] they remained very different in terms of prior control and the possibility of unilateralism:

> These fundamental differences [between the GATT and the EEC in their approach to safeguards] are strictly tied to the different nature, compared to the EEC and ECSC Treaties, of the 1947 [GATT] Agreement which, although establishing a complex regulation to which all the contracting parties were subjected, as well as an embryo organization, did not give life to a true new legal order [*ordre juridique nouveau*], to a new entity, with its own existence and organization, functioning with a minimum of autonomy from the member states. When these conditions are fulfilled, safeguard clauses can be articulated in a very different way, especially as concerns control in advance, which can then be exercised by a competent organizational organ, without the inconveniences and complications of procedure and of substance which are necessarily involved in any direct consultation between the contracting parties.[30]

As this reference to the Community as "new legal order" demonstrates, with its inescapable allusion to the text of the Court of Justice's famous *Van Gend en Loos* judgment, for Gori the EEC's distinctive approach to safeguards and derogations in general was justified not only by the wording of provisions such as Article 226 of the Treaty, but also, and in a sense more fundamentally, by the essential principles of Community law that were not so explicitly set out in the Treaty but which the judgments of Court of Justice were then, over the 1960s, in the process of establishing. Rejecting Italy's appeal in *Pork Products* to the "ancient idea of the sovereignty of states in international law", Gori wrote that this approach would involve denying the very principles that are at the base of the relationship between Community law and internal law within the scope of Community competences: that is to say, the primacy [*prééminence*] of the rules of Community law, and the obligatory recourse to the

possibility of retaliation [*rétorsions*] provided for by GATT Article XIX 3) a)" (Gori 1967: 80).

28 Gori 1967: 75, 39, similarly 52.

29 Gori 1967: 37–38.

30 Gori 1967: 37–38.

Community method to resolve any conflicts.[31] Similarly, when prefacing his comparison of an extensive list of GATT safeguard mechanisms with the Community approach, Gori notes that while free trade treaties leave intact the sovereign rights and prerogatives of states, a "common market" requires the transfer of certain sovereign rights to this union, including in the EEC's case the direct application of EEC Regulations in the territory of the member states,[32] and adds that the GATT and other trade treaties, unlike the EEC, never addressed themselves directly to private individuals.[33] Gori's book demonstrates how the distinctiveness of the European legal order in its founding years could be explained by an influential lawyer on the staff of the Court using the GATT system as a concrete alternative, indeed using the GATT system of safeguards as a foil to systematically exhibit the detailed features of ordinary trade treaty politics that the EEC rejected.

Gori was not afraid to connect his discussion of safeguard mechanisms with a justification of ambitious interpretative approaches to Community law obligations. His book on safeguards begins with a careful discussion of the correct method of treaty interpretation, arguing that interpreting the Community Treaties in particular requires a rigorous respect of the Treaty text, but that where the text is ambiguous or contains "real lacunas", it may be necessary to go beyond the text to respect its spirit, and emphasizing the danger that a limited approach to interpretation of the Treaties could lead on to the powerlessness of the Communities.[34] In all this Gori distinguishes the European Treaties from more common approaches to interpreting treaties in international law.

Compared to other decisions of the European Court considered in this volume, it is true, *Pork Products* itself may seem a little ordinary. Certainly, this judgment in itself lacks the element of creativity, of "going beyond the provisions of the Treaty", that can be attributed to many of the Court's early landmark decisions. Instead, we may say, in *Pork Products* itself the Court held its nerve on a principle of vital importance – the Community's approach to escape mechanisms – and thus set down a

31 Gori 1967: 20–21.

32 Here Gori notes the "grave perplexities" that the direct application of Community Regulations caused to English legal scholars (Gori 1967: 71 ft 5).

33 Gori 1967: 71–72. Of course, the degree to which the text of the Treaty of Rome addressed itself to private individuals is debatable, but the Court of Justice had by the time of Gori's writing certainly interpreted the Treaty in ways that emphasized and extended the Treaty's direct address to private individuals.

34 Gori 1967: 8, 11.

marker that the European legal system would not accommodate the sorts of unilateral flexibility so central to many trade-related treaty regimes. At the same time, *Pork Products* demonstrated the potentially limited effectiveness of the Article 169 procedure in defending this principle, and thus – as Wenner's use of the *Pork Products* case to advocate for direct effect in 1962 demonstrates – acted as a spur to creative thinking about how this principle might be more effectively vindicated by the Court in its later judgments. And just as Gori connected the Community legal order's approach to safeguards with many of the profound legal principles that the Court had created or developed after its *Pork Products* judgment, so our understanding of those principles – the Community's claim to be a "new legal order", its direct relationship with national courts and private individuals, even its rejection of inter-state reciprocity and countermeasures and the use of the "spirit" of the Treaties, where necessary, to go beyond the Treaty's text – needs to be connected with the Community legal order's efforts to address the very practical problem of obtaining control over states' use of escape mechanisms within the Common Market. And, as we will see, an emphasis on the Community's distinctive approach to safeguard clauses – its insistence on prior authorization by the European institutions – was at the heart of the Court's understanding of the binding nature of European legal obligations, and therefore its doctrines of direct effect and supremacy.

2

Van Gend en Loos, 1963

Direct Effect

The Case before the Court

This case came to the Court of Justice as a request for a preliminary ruling, under the Article 177 procedure, by a Dutch court, the Tariefcommissie, in a dispute over Dutch tariff policies.[1] The Article 177 procedure provided that any court or tribunal of the member states, if it considered that a decision on a question about the interpretation of the Treaty, or about the validity and interpretation of acts of the institutions of the Community were necessary to enable it to give judgment, could request the Court of Justice to give a ruling thereon.

A Dutch firm importing chemicals from Germany claimed that new tariffs adopted by the Netherlands had increased the effective tariffs on intra-Community trade, contrary to the "standstill" requirements set out in Article 12 of the EEC treaty, which obliged the member states to refrain from introducing new customs charges between themselves or increasing those that already applied.[2] The Dutch court requested the Court of Justice's response to two questions. It asked, first, whether Article 12 of the EEC treaty had direct application within the territory of a member state, that is, whether nationals of such a state can lay claim to "individual rights which the courts must protect", and, second, in the event of the first question receiving an affirmative reply, whether the particular increase of import duties in the Dutch case was an unlawful increase within the meaning of Article 12 of the EEC treaty, or whether it was a reasonable alteration of the duty applicable, which should not be regarded as prohibited by Article 12. Note that the Dutch legislation that

[1] Case 26/62 *Van Gend en Loos* v. *Nederlandse Administratie der Belastingen* [1963] ECR 1.

[2] Article 12 of the Treaty of Rome provided that "Member States shall refrain from introducing between themselves any new customs duties on imports or exports or any charges having equivalent effect, and from increasing those which they already apply in their trade with each other."

had led to the alleged increase in import duties was legislation implementing a customs agreement between the Benelux nations – Belgium, the Netherlands, and Luxembourg – and so the conflict in question was between two distinct Dutch laws ratifying treaty obligations, of which the law ratifying the Benelux customs agreement was later enacted than that ratifying the Treaty of Rome.

Several member states intervened in the case. The Dutch, Belgian, and German governments denied that Article 12 had a direct internal effect in that authorities and courts of the member states must apply it directly, arguing that Article 12 imposed "only an obligation on the part of the Member States". The Belgian and Dutch governments also argued that the case was inadmissible in that the Dutch court's reference related not to the interpretation but to the application of the Treaty within the constitutional context of the Netherlands. The solution to the problem whether provisions of the EEC treaty prevailed, before a Dutch court, over other Dutch legislation or other international agreements entered into by the Netherlands and incorporated into Dutch law, therefore fell within the jurisdiction of the national courts, subject to the possible use of the mechanisms provided for by Articles 169 and 170 of the Treaty. The Belgian government further argued that the Court had no jurisdiction on the ground that no answer it could give to the first question posed by the Tariefcommissie could have any bearing on the result of the proceedings brought in that Court. Finally, on the substance of the customs arrangements at issue, the Dutch government argued that the tariffs on the products in question had not in fact been raised at all.

The Advocate General, Karl Roemer, argued that a treaty provision could only be granted direct application by the courts of the participating member states if it clearly provided that individuals were to enjoy such rights. He allowed, for example, that Articles 85 and 86 relating to competition were clearly intended to be incorporated in national law and to modify or supplement it. Article 12, however, only referred to an obligation on the European member states, without any explicit reference to individuals. For that reason, so the Advocate General argued, the Court of Justice should not find that Article 12 enjoyed direct applicability within the territory of the member states.

Furthermore, according to the Advocate General, the provisions of Articles 169 and 171 of the Treaty that specified ways of dealing with breaches of the Treaty indicated that the member states were given a "time limit" to comply with the reasoned opinion of the Commission, and that the member states were required "to take the necessary measures" to comply with the judgment of the Court of Justice. If, however, "it had been intended to make the direct application of the provisions of the Treaty, in the sense that they are to prevail over national law, a fundamental principle, the procedure for enforcing obedience could have been confined to a declaration of the nullity of measures taken contrary to the provisions of the Treaty". The provisions of Article 171, if not also the time limit under Article 169, would then be superfluous.

The Advocate General also argued that the object of Article 12 was "contrary to first impressions . . . very complex". "Judged by its content" Article 12 did not appear to be capable of direct application, because of, inter alia, the difficulties in the exact definition of the concept of "charges having equivalent effect".

Advocate General Roemer also addressed the question of variation in national constitutional law, which was, he claimed, "far from uniform" in regard to the relationship between supranational or international law and subsequent national legislation. "If Article 12 is deemed to have a direct internal effect, the situation would arise that breaches of Article 12 would render the national customs laws ineffective and inapplicable in only a certain number of Member States." That would lead to an uneven development of the law involved in the principle of direct application, the "consequences [of] which do not accord with an essential aim of the Community".

The Advocate General stated that the answer to the second question put by the Dutch court (whether the particular increase of import duties in the Dutch case was an unlawful increase within the meaning of Article 12) ceased to be relevant if his proposed negative answer to the first question (whether Article 12 had direct application) was accepted by the Court. However, in view of the widely conflicting views on the subject, the Advocate General proceeded also to examine the second question, on the hypothesis that the Court's answer to the first question would be that the national court was bound by Article 12.

Here again, the Advocate General drew on the procedures set out in Articles 169 and 170, noting "the danger of circumventing that procedure", and arguing that if the Court dealt with the Dutch court's second question,

> it can only give a general interpretation of Article 12 . . . There must not be a single word in the operative part of the judgment and in the grounds of judgment concerning the conduct of a member state and there must not be any finding that its conduct is compatible with the Treaty, or that it

> constitutes an infringement of it. The Court accordingly does not have to make an assessment, which would only be made under the procedure of Articles 169 and 170.

Enlarging on the distinction between the 169 and 170 procedures and direct effect, the Advocate General argued that "we must conclude that Articles 169 and 170 deal primarily with cases in which a provision of the Treaty is not directly applicable, but contains simply an order addressed to the Member States". As for the substance of the second question, the Advocate General summed up by stating that "Article 12 has an absolute effect in respect of each individual product; it allows no exception either for the elimination of difficulties connected with a rearrangement of nomenclature, or for the benefit of regional unions [such as the Benelux union] within the Community", and that the question of possible increases in duties must be determined according to the "customs tariff applied in fact to each individual product on 1 January 1958."

On 5 February 1963, the European Court of Justice answered the questions of the Dutch court by ruling, first, that Article 12 of the Treaty produced direct effects and created individual rights, which national courts must protect, and, secondly, where, after the entry into force of the treaty, the same product is charged with a higher rate of duty, irrespective of whether this increase arose from an increase of a rate of customs duty or a rearrangement of customs duty classifications, such increase was contrary to Article 12 of the Treaty.

In response to the objections put forward by Belgium and the Netherlands, the Court claimed not to be adjudicating on the application of the Treaty according to the constitutional law of the Netherlands, but only to interpret the scope of Article 12 within the context of Community law and with reference to its effect on individuals. To Belgium's further argument, the Court responded that, while the relevance that a national court attributes to the question in the context of the case before it were not subject to review by the Court, the questions raised by the Dutch court referred to the interpretation of the Treaty, and that the Court therefore had jurisdiction to answer them.

The Court's decision went far beyond its responses to the questions posed by the Tariefcommissie, or the arguments advanced by the member states, however. The Court declared, famously, that the European Economic Community constituted a "new legal order of international law [*nouvel ordre juridique de droit international*] for the benefit of which the states have limited their sovereign rights, albeit within limited fields, and the subjects of which comprise not only the member states but also their nationals". It described the Treaty of Rome as "more than an agreement which merely creates mutual obligations between the contracting states", emphasizing that the Preamble of the Treaty referred not only to governments but also to "peoples".[3] It referred also to establishment of "institutions endowed with sovereign rights", the exercise of which affects member states and also their citizens, and the cooperation of the nationals of the member states in the functioning of the Community through the European Parliament and the Economic and Social Committee. It explained the object of Article 177 as the "uniform interpretation of the Treaty by national courts and tribunals", confirming "that the states have acknowledged that Community law has an authority which can be invoked by their nationals before those courts and tribunals", and found that rights were conferred on individuals "not only where they are expressly granted by the Treaty, but also by reason of obligations which the Treaty imposes in a clearly defined way upon individuals as well as upon the member states and the institutions of the Community".

As regards Article 12 in particular, the Court stated that "The wording of Article 12 contains a clear and unconditional prohibition which is not a positive but a negative obligation", and therefore "the very nature of this prohibition makes it ideally adapted to produce direct effects in the legal relationship between member states and their subjects". The Court continued: "This obligation, moreover, is not qualified by any reservation on the part of States which would make its implementation conditional upon a positive legislative measure enacted under national law."

The Court rejected the argument that Articles 169 and 170 provided an exclusive means of addressing possible violations of the Treaty. It stated that "the fact that Articles 169 and 170 of the EEC Treaty enable the Commission and the member states to bring before the Court a state which has not fulfilled its obligations does not deprive individuals of the right to plead the same obligations, should the occasion arise, before a national court". As the Court explained, there was the risk that recourse to Articles 169 and 170 might be ineffective "if it were to occur after the implementation of a national decision taken contrary to the provisions of

[3] "DETERMINED to lay the foundations of an ever-closer union among the peoples of Europe . . . AFFIRMING as the essential objective of their efforts the constant improvement of the living and working conditions of their peoples."

the Treaty". Therefore, "the vigilance of individuals concerned to protect their rights amounts to an effective supervision in addition to the supervision entrusted by Articles 169 and 170 to the diligence of the Commission and the Member States".

The Court did not respond to Advocate General Roemer's argument that, if the Court decided that Article 12 received direct effect, that would necessarily result in inequalities in application among the various member states according to whether their constitutional law allowed their national courts to directly apply treaty obligations.

Related Cases

Two of the Court's decisions *prior* to February 1963 are often considered relevant to understanding *Van Gend en Loos*. In the 1960 *Humblet* judgment, the Court declared that the Court itself could not annul the legislation of the member states through a finding made under Article 171 of the Treaty of Rome.[4] The competence of the Court was limited to identifying the existence of the Treaty violation, while it was for the member state to take the measures necessary to remove the violation. The limited view of the Article 171 procedure announced in *Humblet* provides an important context for the Court's decision in *Van Gend en Loos*.

The Court had also made an important earlier decision concerning the direct applicability of Community law. In the *Bosch* decision of 1962, the Court was asked to decide on the status of Article 85 of the Treaty of Rome, part of the Treaty's rules on competition.[5] While the Dutch government had argued that these provisions did not apply domestically until Regulations were made by the European institutions, the Commission and the Belgian and German governments all maintained that these provisions were immediately applicable from the date of entry into force

[4] Case 6/60 *Humblet* [1960] ECR 559. *Humblet* itself concerned a dispute under the European Coal and Steel Community Treaty but the judgment included the statement that Article 171 of the EEC Treaty merely attaches "declaratory effect" to the decisions of the Court in cases of failure to comply with the Treaty, albeit obliging the member states to take the necessary measures to comply with the judgment. The Article 171 procedure did not provide for the Court of Justice to annul or repeal legislative or administrative measures adopted by the member states.

[5] Case 13/61 *De Geus en Uitdenbogerd* v. *Robert Bosch* [1962] ECR 45.

of the Treaty.[6] The Court held that in principle Article 85 had been immediately applicable since the date of coming into force of the Treaty. *Bosch* is not best understood as a true forerunner of the principles subsequently announced in *Van Gend en Loos*, however. The Court's decision in *Bosch* did not connect its finding about Article 85 to a broader vision of the status of the Treaty as a whole vis-à-vis individuals in the member states.[7] In the *Van Gend en Loos* proceedings themselves, in fact, Advocate General Roemer had allowed that the competition provisions of Articles 85 and 86 of the Treaty were "clearly intended to be incorporated into national law and to modify or supplement it", and were thus to be given direct effect in line with *Bosch*, while nonetheless maintaining that Article 12 should be considered only addressed to the member states.

As for judgments of the Court *subsequent* to 1963, perhaps they must all be understood as related to *Van Gend en Loos*. As judge Andreas Donner, President of the Court in 1963, wrote in 1968, "[*Van Gend en Loos*] has, as far as one can see, been the fundamental precedent for the entire jurisprudence that followed".[8] Certainly all the other judgments discussed in this book must be understood as related to the Court's judgment in *Van Gend en Loos*.

A line of related cases particularly worth mentioning here are subsequent decisions where the Court expanded the scope of the direct effect of European obligations beyond the limits indicated in *Van Gend en Loos* itself. In *Van Gend en Loos*, after all, the Court had granted direct effect to Article 12 of the Treaty, justifying its application to that Treaty provision in particular on the grounds that Article 12 was "clear", "unconditional", "not a positive but a negative obligation", and that its implementation was not "conditional upon a positive legislative measure enacted under national law". If direct effect of European law had applied only to Community obligations that met these criteria, that scope would have been limited indeed. However, in a series of decisions throughout the 1960s and 1970s, the Court made clear that provisions of the Treaty,

6 Thompson 1962: 725, noting that this argument was supported by the claim that "the constitutional characteristics of the Treaty distinguished it from normal treaties and created a presumption in favour of 'self-executing' rules. They referred to the Spaak Report and other declarations."

7 Rasmussen 2014: 150 ft 87.

8 Donner 1968: 72.

together with other European obligations, that did not so obviously meet these criteria could also be granted direct effect.[9]

In the *Lütticke* decision of 1966, the Court held, first, that Article 95(1) of the Treaty should enjoy direct effect, a provision requiring the member states to maintain an equality between turnover tax on imported goods and those on similar national products, and, second, that a Treaty provision imposing an obligation upon the member states *to act* could be directly enforceable by domestic courts as of the date the states *should have acted*, even though they did not in fact do so.[10] The Court thus moved away from *Van Gend en Loos*'s indications that direct effect was appropriate for "negative obligations" and where the European obligation was not "conditional upon a positive legislative measure enacted under national law".

In the *Molkerei-Zentrale*[11] decision of 1968, the Court found that "the complexity of given situations within a State cannot alter the legal nature of a directly applicable Community provision", given that the national court could resort to the use of the preliminary reference procedure.[12] The Court thus moved away from *Van Gend*'s indication that direct effect could be granted where a European obligation was "clear" in itself.

In the *Reyners* decision of 1974, the Court held that Article 52 on freedom of establishment could be granted direct effect even in the absence of the legislation envisaged by the Treaty.[13] The Court thus, again, moved away from *Van Gend en Loos*'s indication that direct effect could be granted where a European obligation was "clear" in itself, as Article 52 could not be regarded as "complete" and "legally perfect" in the same sense as Article 12. Furthermore, Article 52, and the provisions

[9] This expansion is admirably described in Craig 1992, on which we here rely. See also Hartley 2014: 209–214, for the argument that *Van Gend en Loos* itself suggested that there was a "fairly stringent test" and that direct effect was a rather rare phenomenon, but that the requirements for direct effect were subsequently "cut down", and De Witte 1999: 183–184 for the argument that after *Van Gend en Loos* it seemed that "only very few Treaty provisions would pass the direct effect test", but that the direct-effect doctrine was subsequently extended even to Treaty Articles that did "seem to require national or Community implementing acts and even those granting to the Member States a power to derogate", later continuing to become "ever broader in its scope".

[10] Waelbroeck 1967: 1271, Case 48/65 *Lütticke* v. *Commission* [1966] ECR 19.

[11] Case 28/67 *Molkerei-Zentrale Westfalen-Lippe* v. *Hauptzollamt Paderborn* [1968] ECR 143.

[12] Craig 1992: 461ff.

[13] Case 2/74 *Reyners* v. *Belgium* [1974] ECR 631.

on freedom of establishment, expressly contemplated further action by the legislative organs of the Community and the member states. The Court, again, thus moved away from *Van Gend en Loos*'s indication that direct effect could be recognized where a European obligation was not conditional upon positive legislative measures.[14]

A full description of the expansion of the scope of the direct-effect doctrine by the Court throughout the 1960s and 1970s would require a separate discussion of its own. For our purposes, the point to stress is that aspects of the text of *Van Gend en Loos* appeared to indicate a relatively limited scope for this doctrine, but that is not the way that direct effect was subsequently developed by the Court. One further, and particularly notable, aspect of the Court's extension of the direct-effect doctrine – its application to "Directives" – is discussed in Chapter 6 on the 1974 *Van Duyn* judgment.

Given our focus on safeguard measures within the European legal order, we should also mention the *SpA Salgoil*[15] decision of 1968. Here, the Rome Corte d'Appello asked whether the direct effect of Articles 30, 31, and part of 32 were such as to require the immediate protection of the rights of individuals, or whether the provisions set out in Articles 36, 224, and 226 (the safeguards provision) of the Treaty implied that states could override the interests of individuals if necessary in the national interest. The Court found that the exceptions and potential discretion afforded to states by Articles 36, 224, and 226, "deal with exceptional cases which are clearly defined and do not lend themselves to any wider interpretation". This decision demonstrated that the Court was determined that the preemptory force of direct effect was not to be weakened by enabling the member states to draw on the Treaty articles that provided for safeguards or contained discretion to, for example, prohibit the import of goods on grounds of public policy or public health.[16]

Analysis and Context

The *Van Gend en Loos* judgment and the doctrine of direct effect are, of course, routinely discussed in prominent texts and surveys of the development of European law and in scholarly collections of the Court's

[14] Craig 1992: 465.
[15] Case 13/68 *Salgoil* v. *Ministero del commercio con l'estero* [1968] ECR 453.
[16] Craig 1992: 462–463.

famous judgments.[17] Leading texts define direct effect as meaning that "provisions of binding EU law which are sufficiently clear, precise, and unconditional to be considered justiciable *can be invoked and relied on* by individuals in national courts",[18] "as the capacity of a norm of Union law to be applied in domestic court proceedings",[19] "the doctrine which provides for EU law to be invoked in national courts",[20] and that "[w]here a Treaty provision is directly effective, an individual can invoke European law in a national court . . . This will normally be as against the State."[21] Notably, the Court's judgment made clear both that the Court of Justice itself (not the various national legal orders autonomously) would decide whether provisions of the Treaty granted rights to individuals before the national courts (that is, direct effect), and that provisions of the Treaty of Rome could grant rights to individuals even if they contained neither the word "right" nor the word "individual".[22] *Van Gend en Loos* thus suggested a need for national courts to keep referring preliminary questions to the Court of Justice as to whether a particular European norm had direct effect in the national legal orders or not.[23] Indeed, because the doctrine of direct effect was first elaborated in this judgment, it is far from unusual for *Van Gend en Loos* to be characterized in imposing terms, as "arguably the most important decision ever given" by the European Court, as one of the Court's "most remarkable achievements", even as the judicial decision with by far the most impact in the long history of international courts and tribunals.[24]

Even where there is agreement on the importance of *Van Gend en Loos*, however, it is not uncommon to find reservations about its reasoning, with Schütze describing as "debatable" "all the judicial arguments" marshalled by the Court in *Van Gend en Loos*.[25] The justification of direct effect on the basis of Article 177 in *Van Gend en Loos* can be criticized, writes Arnull, on the basis that a national court might wish to ask the Court of Justice for a preliminary ruling even on provisions of

[17] *Van Gend en Loos* is included as a "basic community case" and as a "classic of EU law" in both Rudden and Rossa Phelan 1997 and Maduro and Azoulai 2010.
[18] Craig and de Búrca 2015: 184 [emphasis in original].
[19] De Witte 2011a: 323.
[20] Chalmers et al. 2014: 291.
[21] Schütze 2016: 87.
[22] De Witte 1999: 181, De Witte 2013: 94.
[23] De Witte 2013: 94.
[24] Chalmers et al. 2014: 16, Weatherill 2014: 81, Weiler 2014: 94, similarly, Arnull 2006: 168.
[25] Schütze 2016: 80.

Community law that are not directly effective, for example where the effect of a provision of national law depends on the validity and interpretation of Community law.[26] Others have disagreed with the way that the Court appears to distinguish itself from general international law, with Weiler rewriting the text of *Van Gend en Loos* to defend the view that the Court's decision to grant direct effect to Article 12 could have been founded on the ordinary interpretative principles of international law, without any of the Court's grandiose references to the European Community as "a new legal order".[27]

Analysis of *Van Gend en Loos* tends to concentrate on the role that this judgment, together with the stream of subsequent decisions that developed and expanded the doctrine of direct effect, created for national courts and individuals to ensure the uniformity and effectiveness of the European legal order. The essential novelty of this decision was the Court's signal that it intended to supplement, and to some extent marginalize, the dispute settlement procedures set out in Articles 169, 170, and 171 of the Treaty of Rome, whereby the European Commission, or a member state, was required to instigate a complaint that a member state had failed to fulfil an obligation under the Treaty. The doctrine of direct effect, as it came to be developed, allowed the instigation of similar complaints – that member states had failed to fulfil their European Treaty obligations – by private individuals, before national courts, even if neither the Commission nor any of the member states had taken any steps to pursue such a claim.

[26] Arnull 2006: 168–170, similarly Hartley 2014: 219–220. De Witte 2013: 95, also 101 refers to a "category of preliminary questions which was, in fact, the 'innocuous' kind that the drafters of the EEC Treaty probably had in mind: when national judges are asked to apply a norm of national law which is of European origin (for example, because it transposes a provision of an EU directive), they may have some difficulty in understanding its meaning and, in such cases, they can ask the Court of Justice for help. This is a mechanism of judicial cooperation which operates quite apart from any possible contradiction between the national and the EU law norm." Such preliminary references are distinct from the two categories of preliminary reference inaugurated by *Van Gend en Loos*: whether an EC law norm had direct effect, and whether a national norm was compatible with EC law. Arnull adds that the Court in *Van Gend en Loos* also failed to acknowledge that the Treaty provided that only one category of the acts of the Community institutions – Regulations – could enjoy direct effect, and that the Court's judgment contained no reference to the procedural guarantees offered to the member states under Articles 169 and 170 [such as the time periods allowed to the member states for taking the necessary measures that were discussed by the Advocate General].

[27] Weiler 2003.

Different aspects of the direct-effect doctrine – the role of individuals, the role of national courts, and the increased intrusiveness and enforcement power of European law – have been taken up by diverse strands of scholarship on *Van Gend en Loos.*

Since 1963 the enforcement role of the private individual has become a distinctive hallmark of the European legal order. Many trade-related treaty systems provide for authoritative dispute settlement arrangements that can only be initiated by state parties to the treaty. Within today's World Trade Organization, for example, only the WTO members themselves – their governments – can activate the procedure set out in the "Dispute Settlement Understanding", so that WTO disputes are described as, for example, the "Brazil–United States cotton dispute" or the "Japan–Korea food products dispute".[28] In the European legal order, by contrast, the countless individuals within the European states can themselves directly access national courts with the mandate to directly enforce many European obligations, and even obtain access to an interpretation of those obligations from the European legal order's authoritative tribunal, the Court of Justice, through the means of a preliminary reference made by the national court. Indeed, the development of many of the European legal order's landmark decisions can be directly traced to the private legal persons – both firms, protecting their economic interests, as in the case of the transportation and distribution company in *Van Gend en Loos*, and citizens, or activist lawyers, seeking to establish legal points of principle or to vindicate rights and liberties.[29] Behind the sometimes colourful cast of characters in landmark cases lies the quotidian part played by many ordinary litigants who have turned to their national courts seeking enforcement of rights guaranteed by European law.

The active role of private individuals in the enforcement of European law is what makes the European legal order work. Private individuals often share an important coincidence of interest in the effective enforcement of European legal obligations with the European institutions that seek to obtain reliable compliance by the European member states. As judge Lecourt explained in his 1976 book, *L'Europe des juges*: "When the individual applies to a judge to ensure that their treaty rights are recognised, they are not acting in their own interest alone, but by this behavior

[28] Brazil–United States, Subsidies on Upland Cotton. DS 264. Japan–Korea, Import Bans, and Testing and Certification Requirements for Radionuclides, DS 495.

[29] E.g. Gubin 2008.

the individual becomes a type of auxiliary agent of the Community."[30] State policy-makers in many trade regimes may be hesitant to press their counterpart policy-makers in other states for rigorous compliance with treaty obligations, as they are aware of the diplomatic costs of doing so, including the possibility that their trading partners may respond by pressing them in turn to fully comply with equally difficult obligations. One of the virtues of the private individual as a litigant in trade-related treaty systems is that to some extent they are ignorant of, or willing to ignore, the economic, political, diplomatic, and constitutional difficulties associated with the treaty obligations they demand to be fulfilled. In that sense it is fair to say that the new doctrines of European law placed the "self-centred individual" at the heart of its new legal order.[31] And because these individuals are often demanding that national courts apply European obligations in place of the law or policy produced by enacted by democratically elected public authorities in the member states, the operation of the direct-effect doctrine has been described as individuals vindicating a personal, private interest against the national public good.[32]

Such is the striking role of the individual litigant in the European legal order that the Court's *Van Gend en Loos* judgment has even been understood, rather grandly, as creating "an incipient form of European citizenship" – understood as a set of rights coupled with a means of participation in authoritative decision-making – for private individuals in the member states.[33] There are traces of this approach even in early commentary, as Jean Robert's 1963 note on *Van Gend en Loos* in *Recueil Sirey* argued that the implicit but clear logic of the judgment was that in return for the abandonment of state sovereignty, each citizen found themselves subjected to a further sovereignty, but acquired all the rights attached to what it was correct to call this "citizenship".[34] This citizenship was, so later scholarship noted, not a "political citizenship" but only a "market citizenship", instrumentally devised to support the

[30] Lecourt 1976a: 260.
[31] Weiler 2014: 103.
[32] Weiler 2014: 103.
[33] Plender 1976. The "incipient form of citizenship" created by *Van Gend en Loos* in 1963 far predated the establishment of "European citizenship" in the Maastricht Treaty in 1994.
[34] "*a acquis tous les droits qui s'attachent à ce qu'il faut bien appeler cette citoyenneté*", Robert 1963: 5.

effectiveness of supranational economic law, but no less extraordinary for all that.[35]

The role of national judges is likewise considered one of the essential distinctions of the European legal order as *Van Gend en Loos* defined and shaped it. Again, within the member states of many trade-related treaty systems, national courts as such have no direct role in the enforcement of treaty obligations, even where treaties possess well-developed dispute settlement systems as does today's World Trade Organization. In the United States, for example, the implementing legislation enacted by the Congress specifies that "no provision of any of the Uruguay Round Agreements [the 1994 agreements establishing the World Trade Organization] . . . that is inconsistent with any law of the United States shall have effect" in US courts.[36] The decisions that arise from US courts (and indeed the domestic courts of many WTO members) are therefore entirely distinct from, and can be fully divergent from, the decisions that arise from the WTO's dispute settlement institutions.

The European legal order is quite different, because national judges have a mandate, derived from the Treaty as the European Court has interpreted it, to apply European obligations in their national courts.[37] Indeed, such is the role of the national courts in the European legal order that the development of many of the European legal order's landmark decisions could also be directly traced to a second set of individual personalities, the judges of the various national courts – such as the Tariefcommissie in *Van Gend en Loos* or the Pretore di Susa in *Costa v. ENEL* – who decided to submit the preliminary reference questions for the Court of Justice to address. And so, just as the development and expansion of European law is often understood as being encouraged by the interests of private individuals seeking to vindicate their European law rights, so too the development and expansion of European law is also understood as being encouraged by the interests of national courts and judges who gained a new role in directly applying European legal obligations in the national legal order. This "judicial empowerment", particularly at the national level, is often considered an essential part of the content and context of *Van Gend en Loos*.[38]

[35] Everson 1995.
[36] Hilf 1996–1997: 337.
[37] Claes 2006.
[38] Weiler 1991: 2426.

Van Gend and its progeny therefore created a new, transformative, role for national courts as direct enforcers of the member states' obligations under the Treaty of Rome. In the words of Maher, the national courts "have acquired a Community mantle and are responsible for the implementation of directly effective Community rights within the national realm".[39] For succinctness, however, one cannot better Lecourt's characterization of the European legal order as *L'Europe des juges* – "The judges' Europe" – a description encompassing both the European and the national judges.[40] The special role of national judges was also recognized in early scholarship on European law, with Delvolve in 1968 portraying the judicial power of the Treaty of Rome as essentially the "diplomacy of judges".[41]

That a Dutch court, of all the courts in Europe, was the first to make use of the preliminary reference procedure and to ask about the direct effect of provisions of the Treaty of Rome was no coincidence, since a series of Dutch constitutional amendments in the 1950s had provided for directly effective treaty provisions to be applied by the Dutch courts.[42] The judgment of the Court of Justice did not rely on these Dutch constitutional provisions, however, but declared instead that the courts of all the member states were obliged to protect the Community law rights of individuals.[43]

That brings us to a third aspect of *Van Gend en Loos*: the combination of the roles of individuals and national courts created by the doctrine of direct effect for provisions of the European treaties and, over time, other acts of the European institutions such as Directives, created a legal system that imposed considerable constraints on state policy in favour of reliable domestic application of European obligations. In line with the doctrine of direct effect, courts of the member states were required to apply European law obligations directly in litigation open to private parties. To the degree that the doctrine of direct effect came to be applied by national courts in practice (and here the associated doctrine of supremacy, set out in the Court's 1964 judgment *Costa* v. *ENEL*, is

[39] Maher 1994: 226.
[40] Lecourt 1976a.
[41] Delvolve 1968.
[42] Van Leeuwen 2012.
[43] Cremona 2013: 27. There was also some wider contemporary state practice allowing that treaty obligations could at times be enforced directly before national courts (Waelbroeck 1969: 161–188).

obviously relevant), European law rights could potentially be vindicated by any interested private party with access to a relevant national court.

By contrast, the dispute settlement arrangements explicitly provided for in the Treaty of Rome itself, to which the objecting member states had referred in their arguments before the Court in *Van Gend en Loos*, provided only a means for the European Commission (under Article 169) or the member states (under Article 170) to obtain a finding by the Court that a member state had failed to fulfil an obligation under the Treaty. To be sure, Article 171 provided that "the State shall be required to take the necessary measures to comply with the judgment of the Court of Justice". But, as many observers pointed out, such a finding of the Court was merely "declaratory", with no specific consequences for the state failing to fulfil its European treaty obligation. Judge Lecourt himself repeatedly emphasized that Article 171 findings by the Court of Justice were not backed by any sanctions vis-à-vis the defaulting state.[44]

In that context, the direct-effect doctrine has often been understood as reinforcing the binding nature of European law by remedying various weaknesses of the dispute settlement provisions set out in Articles 169, 170, and 171 of the Treaty. In the text of *Van Gend en Loos* itself, indeed, the Court had justified the value of the direct application of Community law within the context of the limitations of the Article 169 and 170 procedures, stating that

> there is the risk that recourse to the procedure under these articles would be ineffective if it were to occur after the implementation of a national decision taken contrary to the provisions of the treaty. The vigilance of individuals concerned to protect their rights amounts to an effective supervision in addition to the supervision entrusted by Articles 169 and 170 to the diligence of the Commission and of the Member States.

Commentators have emphasized distinct aspects of the limitations of the Article 169 and 170 procedures – prominently, and above all, the delays inherent in such a system, but also the reliance of private actors affected by treaty violations on the willingness of the Commission, or the member states, to pursue legal actions before the Court. The most

[44] Lecourt 1979: 90, Lecourt 1976a: 262 "an essentially moral sanction", by contrast with national court enforcement, Lecourt 1984: 226 condemnation by the Court of Justice implied "only a moral sanction", Lecourt and Chevallier 1963: 276 distinguishing the EEC Treaty from the reprisals that could be authorized under Article 88 of the ECSC Treaty - see Chapter 6 on *Van Duyn*, also Lecourt 1991 discussed later in this chapter. See also e.g. Wenner 1962, Weiler 1991: 2421.

compelling scholarly discussions of the Court's direct-effect doctrine view it as *complementary* to Article 169 and 170 procedures. On the one hand, the direct-effect doctrine harnesses the incentives of adversely affected private interests to the strengthening of the treaty system as a whole, allows the pursuit of smaller legal claims (perhaps below the interest of the Commission or the member states, but not below the interest of economic actors themselves so affected),[45] and provides European obligations with the enforcement authority associated with national court systems within European democracies.[46] On the other, the Article 169 and 170 procedures allow the European Commission (in particular) to develop legal principles through strategic litigation over time, as well, of course, as pressing for member-state compliance with important European obligations that are not sufficiently clear and precise so as to enjoy direct effect in the national legal orders. The doctrine of direct effect therefore has not so much replaced the enforcement provisions explicitly set out in the Treaty as alleviated various of their weaknesses, and created a much more intrusive and binding enforcement environment. As Lecourt explained, "the reason why it is fairly rare for Member States to fail to fulfil their obligations is that their courts, which are responsible for applying Treaties and regulations to individuals, make Member States themselves observe their provisions".[47]

Through a combination of the above factors, therefore, and over time of course, the Court of Justice's *Van Gend en Loos* judgment can be understood as creating a "new legal order" that moved the enforcement of European treaty obligations away from a reliance only on direct actions before the Court by the Commission, or between the member states, and towards a decisive and more effective role for individuals and domestic courts in cooperation with the Court of Justice. The enforcement of European treaty obligations therefore appears to have been largely separated from the old realm of state interests and granted instead to the new world of private individuals.

The approach of this book, however, is to situate the great judgments of the Court of Justice in the context of treaty provisions and state practices in other trade-related treaty regimes, above all those related to

[45] Judge Lecourt noted in *L'Europe des juges* that the Commission would only pursue a violation through the Article 169 procedure if it involved a certain degree of seriousness, to avoid dissipating the activities of its staff (Lecourt 1976a: 33).

[46] Weiler 1991: 2421.

[47] Lecourt 1974–1975: 27.

the enforcement of, and escape from, demanding treaty obligations. From that perspective, *Van Gend en Loos* must also be understood as the basis for creating a specific and profound new relationship *between the states* of the European Community. That is to say, *Van Gend en Loos* altered the relationship between France and Germany, between Italy and the Netherlands, and of course between Ireland, Poland, Spain, and Denmark, and so on, as the Community has been enlarged. We must begin by describing the wider range of mechanisms by which international legal obligations, particularly international trade obligations, are often enforced in other treaty systems, and in general international law, to set the stage for a better understanding of how *Van Gend en Loos* transformed the possible operation of those mechanisms in the context of the Treaty of Rome.

In general international law, international legal obligations are commonly enforced within the context of the availability of inter-state countermeasures, that is to say, by the possibility of self-help forms of retaliation by one treaty state against another, in line with international law's rules on state responsibility. As the Arbitral Tribunal in a dispute between France and the United States in 1978 explained: "If a situation arises which, in one State's view, results in the violation of an international legal obligation, the first State is entitled . . . to affirm its rights through countermeasures."[48] "Countermeasures" is perhaps the term most commonly used in contemporary scholarship, but other expressions such as "reciprocal measures" or even the ancient expression "reprisals" continue to be in use. To be sure, the principles of general international law tend to require that states give other states notice of any such complaints, subject their complaint to any agreed dispute settlement mechanism, and allow other states sufficient time and opportunity to change their policy to remove any alleged inconsistency with their treaty obligations, before any use of countermeasures may be attempted.[49] Such mechanisms are nonetheless particularly relevant as a last resort where a participating state whose policies have been found inconsistent with their treaty obligations persists nonetheless in maintaining them. That is certainly the point at which such countermeasures are authorized in, for example, the Dispute Settlement Understanding of today's WTO.

In general international law, the right to adopt countermeasures permits a state to adopt policies that would generally be contrary to that

[48] *France* v. *United States* 18 RIAA 417.
[49] Zoller 1984, Elagab 1988.

state's international legal commitments, for example as contrary to that state's treaty obligations, on the grounds that their treaty partner state had already failed to fulfil such obligations. Similarly in a trade-related treaty regime, such as today's WTO, a trading state may be authorized to impose trade restrictions, themselves otherwise contrary to that WTO member's obligations, in response to a failure of one of their trading partners to fulfil their own trade-related obligations, even after an adverse finding by dispute settlement institutions. Such trade sanctions are often referred to as the "suspension of concessions", or by similar expressions. The trade restrictions imposed by the United States against the EU in WTO disputes over trade in bananas and beef provide well-known instances of this way of enforcing trade treaty obligations, and of course there are many other examples, both within the WTO and other trade treaty systems.[50]

It is widely acknowledged that the enforcement of treaty obligations by the threat or imposition of such "self-help" countermeasures brings its own set of difficulties. After all, the possibility of such inter-state countermeasures imbues every allegation that a state has failed to fulfil their treaty obligations with the potential for retaliation by one trading partner against another. Even leaving aside the tensions this may produce in diplomatic relationships, such a mechanism produces continual uncertainty about trading opportunities for firms and individuals, since all access to the markets of another state may be potentially subject to retaliatory restriction as part of dispute settlement processes. So even the latent possibility of inter-state countermeasures creates a pervasive environment of risk and uncertainty about all trading opportunities, over and above any limitations on trade actually imposed as the results of disputes.

The right of states to impose countermeasures against other states on the grounds that they have failed to fulfil their treaty obligations is nonetheless profoundly important. If state policy-makers within a treaty regime with demanding obligations can persist in failing to fulfil those obligations without putting at risk the benefits they reciprocally obtain from other states, they may have few incentives to fulfil their obligations. The possibility that other states will, in retaliation, reduce their own fulfilment of obligations that benefit trading firms and individuals in the defaulting state acts as a powerful motive against such behaviour.

[50] Devereaux et al. 2006.

After all, a finding that a state has failed to fulfil its treaty obligations, even where the finding is made by a treaty-based dispute settlement tribunal such as the European Court of Justice, is merely "declaratory". If a state persists in such behaviours even after such an authoritative finding, what else can be done? The resort by other states to self-help retaliatory countermeasures has the considerable advantage that – unlike such declaratory judgments, or even obligations to pay a monetary penalty – they may be imposed on a target state even if the later does not cooperate in the acceptance of the penalty.

Now let us return to *Van Gend en Loos*. What the Court created, in this judgment and those that developed and confirmed it, was not just a mechanism to ensure the uniformity of the application of Community obligations across the member states, or to prevent delays in the detection or remedying of violations of Community obligations if legal action had been restricted to the use of the Article 169 and 170 procedures provided by the Treaty of Rome. In *Van Gend en Loos*, the Court of Justice announced a mechanism – the direct effect of European law – that acts as an alternative to the use of inter-state countermeasures as enforcement mechanisms within the European legal order.

To understand why, recall the moment at which the imposition of inter-state countermeasures becomes most relevant in general international law. Such mechanisms are most relevant as a last resort, where a participating state, authoritatively found to have failed to fulfil its treaty obligations by treaty-based dispute settlement institutions, fails nonetheless to change its policies to make them consistent with their treaty obligations. In such a scenario, the findings of dispute settlement institutions are merely declaratory, and states whose policy-makers then decline to remedy the violations so identified may prompt policy-makers in other states to consider imposing inter-state countermeasures in retaliation. In the European legal order, however, as shaped by *Van Gend en Loos*, the judgments of the dispute settlement institution – the European Court of Justice – are not, however, merely declaratory. Rather, via the preliminary reference procedure, or the possibility of its use, the interpretation of Community law by the European Court is passed down into the relevant national legal order to inform the decision-making of the national courts. National court application of Community obligations, within the context of the preliminary reference procedure and the other duties falling on national courts as the Court of Justice's jurisprudence defined them, therefore fills exactly the gap that is elsewhere occupied by the mechanism of inter-state countermeasures in trade-related treaty regimes.

The possibility of resort to such inter-state reciprocity and retaliation mechanisms had not been ruled out by the provisions for enforcement established in Articles 169, 170, and 171 of the Treaty of Rome. After all, these procedures could only lead to a declaratory judgment by the Court, and so the fundamental problem remained as to how to address the possible situation where a member state persisted in non-compliance notwithstanding a contrary judgment of the Court. The Treaty was silent on how to address such a scenario, and not a few scholars encouraged the Court to allow (or declared the states could adopt) various forms of retaliation in such conditions.[51] Moreover, it is in just such circumstances that many treaty systems envisage the use of such retaliatory mechanisms, and indeed it is in just such circumstances that states do at times resort to such mechanisms even apparently contrary to treaty provisions if no other effective means of enforcing the obligations of their treaty partners is provided for.[52]

The change in inter-state relations produced by the *Van Gend en Loos* judgment has been obscured for a variety of reasons. Within the Court's decision itself, there is no mention at all of the function of the direct-effect doctrine as a substitute for general international law-style inter-state reciprocity or countermeasures. The *Van Gend* judgment does state that the Treaty was "more than an agreement that merely creates mutual obligations between the contracting states". However, this claim by the Court is commonly understood only in relation to the Court's justification of the ability of individuals to vindicate their Community law rights before the national courts, in conjunction with the preliminary reference procedure provided for in Article 177 of the Treaty, and thus to supplement enforcement through the infringement procedures provided by

[51] E.g. Däubler 1968, see also references in Chapter 4 on *Dairy Products*.

[52] Gradoni 2008: 70 contains a discussion of how retaliatory practices emerged in the GATT in response to the ineffectiveness of the mechanisms provided for the enforcement of GATT obligations, despite GATT rules that appeared to some to require that GATT members needed to consent to retaliation against themselves. As the representative of the United States explained in GATT discussions held in 1989, "Wherever it could, the United States would challenge unfair practices under the dispute settlement provisions of the General Agreement or the Tokyo Round Codes, but where other contracting parties prevented or impeded that process or blocked efforts to ensure that their practices were covered by multilateral disciplines, the United States would act to protect its interests. If such action was considered unilateral, it should nevertheless be recognized as [a] perfectly justifiable, responsive action necessitated by the failure of bilateral or multilateral efforts to address a problem." *Discussion on Unilateral Methods Held in the GATT Council on 8–9 February 1989*, C/163, p. 4.

Articles 169, 170, and 171. As the Court stated, "The fact that these articles of the Treaty enable the Commission and the member states to bring before the Court a state which has not fulfilled its obligations does not mean that individuals cannot plead these obligations, should the occasion arise, before a national court." This is of course a vital aspect of *Van Gend en Loos*, but it certainly does not capture its full impact on relationships between the member states.

The nature of the parties to the dispute in *Van Gend en Loos* also tends to obscure its impact on inter-state relationships. After all, the litigation was brought by a Dutch company against the Dutch government, complaining about Dutch barriers to the import of goods from Germany. If the European states had organized their relationships according to a WTO-style dispute settlement system, the dispute might have been known as the "Germany–Netherlands chemicals dispute", with the German government initiating the complaint against the Dutch government, in pursuit of removing barriers to the export of German goods to the Netherlands, and the same German government then possibly threatening retaliation against the Netherlands if Dutch policy-makers persisted with policies found by the Court to be inconsistent with their treaty obligations.[53] But of course in the actual *Van Gend en Loos* litigation, the German government's legal representative supported the Dutch government's position! Obviously, in those circumstances, the German government was not likely to begin threatening the Dutch government with countermeasures if they failed to accept the Court of Justice's new interpretation of Article 12 of the Treaty of Rome. With such a jumbled jigsaw, it is no wonder that few observers have appreciated all of *Van Gend en Loos*'s most important implications for the development of the European legal order.

The complementarity of the direct-effect doctrine, as first set out by *Van Gend en Loos*, and the dispute settlement procedures contained in Articles 169, 170, and 171 of the Treaty therefore goes beyond the issues that are most often referred to in discussions of interrelationship of such procedures. In terms of the most profound distinctions and novelties of

[53] Thus trade-related litigation by private parties through the mechanism of direct effect within the European legal order can be matched to a hypothetical legal action between European states, in much the same way as legal action against the EU as a member of the GATT, now WTO, by another GATT member can be matched with real or hypothetical litigation by private parties attempting to use the doctrine of direct effect to enforce GATT obligations or WTO dispute settlement outcomes within the European legal order. For examples of such litigation, see Chapter 5 on *International Fruit*.

the European legal order compared to other trade-related treaty systems, the central contribution of *Van Gend en Loos* is that it provided a mechanism that allowed the member states to give up the use of inter-state retaliation and reciprocity mechanisms to enforce European treaty obligations.

This book takes the view that the great judgments of the European Court of Justice can be better understood both by comparisons with alternative means of enforcing trade-related treaty obligations and through the writings of influential ECJ judge Robert Lecourt. Both these perspectives support the view that the direct-effect doctrine of European law, as first set out in *Van Gend en Loos*, should be understood as a substitute for inter-state countermeasures or reciprocity mechanisms within the European legal order.

One way to appreciate the impact of direct effect on the enforcement of trade-related treaty obligations is to look at the way that this doctrine is understood by lawyers involved in other trade treaty systems. Perhaps the best example of this sort is provided by Jan Tumlir, an official in the GATT's secretariat as well as a theorist of international economic law.[54] In a series of essays published in the early 1980s Tumlir expressed his dissatisfaction with the GATT's persistent emphasis on inter-state reciprocity and retaliation, and argued instead for the enforcement of treaty obligations by the domestic courts of trading states. In his 1983 article "Need for an Open Multilateral Trading System", Tumlir set out the argument with clarity:

> There was a fault in the very foundation of the multilateral trading system. It consisted in the failure to state the case for free (liberal) trade fully and rigorously; that is, to make clear that trade liberalization benefits the liberalising country first and foremost. From this failure developed the notion of "concessions" and "counter-concessions" which nourished the lingering mercantilism of the belief that each national economy benefits primarily from the liberalising action undertaken by its trading partners. The operation of the system was dominated by insistence of reciprocity in this narrowly technical sense. Today that notion of reciprocity may be seen operating in reverse, enabling any member country to use a failure of its trading partners to live up to the rules for justifying its own protectionist sins.
>
> Broadly speaking, the debate [over the multilateral trading system] was between two camps, which may be called the "internationalists" and the

[54] See Slobodian 2018 for more on Jan Tumlir's views on international economic law.

> "sovereigntists". . . . The sovereigntists are saying that the rules can only be administered and interpreted diplomatically, on the basis of reciprocity, and can only be enforced as international law has always been enforced, by threats of retaliation. On the historical and practical level it is a very strong argument.
>
> The main flaw in the sovereigntist argument is . . . ultimately one of inattention to individual rights. . . . An effort at rational reform would therefore aim at bringing the international rules. . . to bear on national legislatures. . . . In a governmental system of divided powers, the [domestic] courts are the agency which can bring the internationally-agreed rules to bear on legislative decisions.[55]

For Tumlir then, allowing international economic treaty obligations to be enforced by private parties as individual rights in domestic courts is an instrument to tackle an overemphasis on reciprocity between trade treaty partners, and to prevent countries justifying their own failures to fulfil treaty obligations on account of the failure of their trading partners. Looking on from his position outside the European Community, as an official of the GATT world trade system, Tumlir saw the impact of the enforcement of international economic law by private parties in national courts from a more comparative perspective than that emphasized in a great deal of scholarship on *Van Gend en Loos*.

A similar perspective on national court enforcement of treaty obligations was, however, also advanced by one of most influential judges then serving on the Court – Robert Lecourt. Thanks to the "new historians" of European law, it is now understood that Lecourt played an essential part in bringing about the Court's *Van Gend en Loos* judgment in 1963.[56] It appears to have been Lecourt, together with judge Trabucchi, who pressed for the Court to find the direct effect of Article 12 of the Treaty against the initial opposition of both the *juge-rapporteur* and the then

[55] Tumlir 1983b: 397, 399, 400–401, 406–407. Similarly, Tumlir 1983a, criticizing the postwar trading system for enabling countries to use any failure of their trading partners to justify "their own protectionist sins" and for its disproportionate emphasis on reciprocity (75), while advocating that "the closer adjustment of international and national economic order can only be brought about by securing a firmer grounding in national law for the economic–political engagements that governments undertake internationally" (80), of which the most radical example [Tumlir was willing to accept more modest steps in this direction] was provided by the European Community: "The Treaty of Rome has constitutional standing and its three basic principles – freedom of trade and factor movements, undistorted competition and non-discrimination – create, through directly effective provisions, private rights (and obligations) which national courts must protect (enforce)" (81).

[56] Rasmussen 2008: 94–95, 98, also Gori 2013.

President of the Court Andreas Donner. Without the nomination of Lecourt as a judge in May 1962, therefore, the Court would likely have refused to declare the direct effect of European law in *Van Gend en Loos* in 1963.[57] We also know that Lecourt, in particular, seems to have become highly influential on the Court as time went on, culminating with his own election to the Presidency of the Court from 1967 to 1976.[58] Another prominent judge, Pierre Pescatore, who joined the Court of Justice in 1967, even talked of the "jurisprudential miracle" of the Court's "Lecourt years" from 1962 onwards.[59]

As we have explained, Lecourt wrote no memoirs and appears to have arranged for his private papers to be destroyed before his death. His surviving public writings, however, sometimes indicate unexpected rationales for the Court's decisions. In his contribution to a 1991 *Festschrift* for European law scholar Jean Boulouis, for example, judge Lecourt, then long in retirement from the Court of Justice, addressed the vital question, "What would Community law have been without the decisions of 1963 and 1964?"[60] His answer was largely the conventional story of how the Court of Justice's most famous two decisions – *Van Gend en Loos* and *Costa* – transformed European law, making it more effective, granting rights to individuals, and so on, combined with a criticism of the delays, and reliance on goodwill of the Commission, associated with the Article 169 procedure. Towards the end of the article, however, appears a discussion of considerable significance. Lecourt wrote that the problems of delayed justice were not the only weakness of the Article 169 procedure.[61] As Lecourt explained:

> Delay is however not the only defect of the [Article 169] procedure. There is another, less apparent but legally more serious [*moins apparent mais juridiquement plus sérieux*]. It concerns the case where, despite an ECJ decision finding that it had failed to fulfil its obligation, the State does not take any effort to take measures to execute the judgment of the Court as provided for Article [171].[62] That provision is, it is true, particularly laconic. It neither specifies what measures may be required by the Court nor within what period of delay they must be adopted, nor what sanction

[57] Rasmussen 2008: 98.
[58] Edward 2001: 180.
[59] Pescatore 2005: 595.
[60] Lecourt 1991. The first discussion by this author of Lecourt's 1991 book chapter appeared in the *International Journal of Constitutional Law*, on which this section draws (Phelan 2016c).
[61] Lecourt 1991: 358.
[62] Lecourt writes Article 170, but it is clear in context that he refers to Article 171.

> might apply to a State failing a second time. It does not arm the Court with legal, economic, or financial coercive measures.
>
> As a result, despite a legally condemned failure to fulfil its obligations, doubled by the lack of execution of the Court's decision, nothing prevents a defaulting State from continuing to enjoy all the advantages of the Treaty. It is not without the ability, after long delays of procedure, to continue the irregularity of its situation even after the Court decision which is charged with putting an end to it. . . .
>
> If this situation did not become alarming, it is because, as well as the remedies available to the Commission against the member States, economic actors made use of all the legal means available to ensure the application of the rules of the Treaty. Dark indeed would have been the outlook if, without all means of direct access of individuals and all primacy for these rules, the only means for ensuring respect for the Treaty was recourse to Article 169.
>
> The risk of ineffectiveness of [the Article 169 procedure] would be all the more worrying because the principle of reciprocity between the member States depends on the exact implementation of the Treaty by each one. None of them can hide behind the failure of another State to justify its own irregularities. This essential principle might be put at risk if the shortcomings of Article 169 infringement procedure were to have co-existed with the absence of any right of legal action by private individuals [through the Article 177 procedure].[63]

The key to understanding this passage is the expression "None of them can hide behind the failure of another State to justify its own irregularities". In more common forms of international law, as Tumlir explained, states can indeed, on the basis of "reciprocity", hide behind the failures of another state to justify their own non-compliance with treaty commitments. Read with an awareness of the enforcement mechanisms of general international law therefore, Lecourt's 1991 article straightforwardly connects European law's direct-effect doctrine with the European legal order's rejection of the weaknesses of many international trade regimes that operated on the basis of inter-state reciprocity.[64]

[63] Lecourt 1991: 358–359.

[64] Lecourt also mentions that without *Van Gend* and *Costa* the Treaty would have become a simple convention organizing reciprocal cooperation between states (Lecourt 1991: 360). Lecourt's chapter in the *Festschrift* for Jean Boulouis is well-known, and many authors have used it to mark the claim that European law would not have become what it is now without the Court's judgments in 1963 and 1964. As far as I am aware, however, no

Understanding *Van Gend en Loos*, and the direct effect of Community law before national courts, as directly related to the removal of inter-state reciprocity and retaliation mechanisms within the European legal order is therefore supported by comparative analysis. It is supported by contrasts with the provisions of other trade-related treaty systems, and with the organizing principles of general international law, in both of which reciprocity and retaliation mechanisms are recognized as playing an essential role. It is supported by analysis of the processes created by the direct effect itself, which intervenes in the dispute settlement processes just at the point where inter-state reciprocity and retaliation mechanisms might otherwise become most salient. It is supported by scholarship looking to the reform of other trade treaty systems, which regularly recognize the enforcement of treaty obligations by private parties before national courts as straightforward substitutes for reciprocity and retaliation principles. Finally, and not least, it is an understanding of *Van Gend en Loos* that finds support in the writings of judge Lecourt, one of the essential promoters of the *Van Gend en Loos* judgment in the internal deliberations of the Court.

Thus direct effect, the Court of Justice's important doctrinal innovation, often celebrated for its creation of a legal role for the private individual, is intimately connected with inter-state trade politics, and derived from efforts to address the practical realities of enforcement within trade treaty regimes. It is direct effect that has allowed the European legal order to do without threats of inter-state retaliation, and it is also direct effect that has allowed the European legal order over time to develop an effective means of control against the unilateral adoption of "safeguard" mechanisms by the European states, which the Article 169 procedure alone would have been unable to secure.[65] And, as we shall go on to show, many of the other early landmark judgments of the Court of Justice can be understood as demonstrating a similar logical connection between self-help, safeguards, and individual rights.

previous author has recognized that Lecourt's chapter specifies relatively precisely what European law would have become without the Court's judgments of 1963 and 1964, i.e. a system based on inter-state reciprocity, like so many trade treaties, in the case of a failure of states to comply with an Article 171 judgment. For Lecourt's further discussion of this theme, see our discussion of Lecourt's 1965 article connecting *Van Gend en Loos*, *Costa* v. *ENEL*, and the rejection of self-help by the European states, in Chapter 4 on *Dairy Products*, and Lecourt and Chevallier's 1963 article discussing national court enforcement of European law in the context of Directives in Chapter 6 on *Van Duyn*.

65 See our discussion of *Pork Products* in Chapter 1.

3

Costa v. *ENEL*, 1964

Supremacy

The Case before the Court

This case came to the Court of Justice as a request for a preliminary ruling, under the Article 177 procedure, by an Italian court, the Giudice Conciliatore in Milan, in a dispute over the compatibility with the Treaty of the nationalization of the electricity company ENEL by the Italian government.[1]

An individual, Flaminio Costa, complained that the Italian nationalization law, enacted subsequent to the Italian law ratifying the Treaty of Rome, was contrary to various provisions of that Treaty, and, on the basis of that allegation, the Italian court made a reference to the Court of Justice, containing the allegation that the Italian laws in question infringed Articles 102, 93, 53, and 37 of the Treaty.

After the Italian court had made a reference to the Court of Justice but before the European Court had made a decision, the same dispute was heard before the Italian Constitutional Court. The Constitutional Court decided the case on 24 February 1964, finding that a subsequent Italian law conflicting with prior treaty obligations remained valid within Italy, although that result could give rise to state responsibility at the international level. The Italian Constitutional Court's judgment focused on the question of the status granted to Italian statutes executing treaty obligations by Article 11 of the Italian Constitution, which allows for limitations of sovereignty:

> Article 11 is here prayed in aid in so far as it states that Italy agrees, under conditions of parity with other States, to such limitations of sovereignty as are necessary for the establishment of an order that will ensure peace and justice among nations; and it will promote and favour international organisations for that purpose.

[1] Case 6/64 *Costa* v. *ENEL* [1964] ECR 585, [1964] CMLR 425.

> This means that, given certain circumstances, it is possible to stipulate treaties as a result of which we accept certain limitations to our sovereignty and it is quite lawful to give effect to such treaties by means of an ordinary Law; but . . . Article 11 did not confer a greater effect upon the ordinary Law that gives effect to a treaty. . . .
>
> Article 11 . . . in as much as it is a permissive provision, ascribes no particular significance to a Law giving execution to an international treaty as opposed to any other Law.
>
> Nor is there any validity in the other argument, according to which the State, once it has agreed to limitations to its own sovereignty, could not pass any Law withdrawing such limitations and restoring its freedom of action without contradicting the Constitution. Against this can be set our foregoing remarks, from which we are led to believe that the violation of a treaty, even if it results in responsibility by the State at international level, does not detract from the validity of any conflicting Law.
>
> There is no doubt that the State is bound to honour its obligations, just as there is no doubt that an international treaty is fully effective in so far as a Law has given execution to it. But with regard to such Law, there must remain inviolate the prevalence of subsequent laws in accordance with the principles governing the succession of laws in time; it follows that any conflict between the one and the other cannot give rise to any constitutional matter.
>
> From the foregoing we reach the conclusion that for present purposes there is no point in dealing with the character of the E.E.C. and the consequences that derive from the Law giving effect to the Treaty creating the E.E.C.; nor is it necessary to question whether the Law that is being attacked before us has violated the obligations undertaken by virtue of the Treaty aforesaid. It follows from this that the question regarding the remission of the file to the Court of Justice of the European Community, and the relevant question of jurisdiction, does not even arise.
>
> For all these reasons this Court declares that any question upon the constitutional legality of the Law [creating the electricity company ENEL] . . . is unfounded.[2]

Following this decision of the Italian Constitutional Court, the Italian government argued before the Court of Justice that the request of the Guidice Conciliatore for a preliminary ruling was absolutely inadmissible, in that a national court that was obliged to apply a national law could not avail itself of the Article 177 procedure.

[2] [1964] CMLR 425, 430–436.

The opinion of Advocate General Maurice Lagrange was divided into two parts. The first part dealt with the question of the use of the Article 177 procedure by the Italian court, and the related objections by the Italian government, and the second part considered the Articles of the Treaty in question, offering an assessment as to whether each of them had "such a self-executing character" to enable it to be enforced by national courts at the instance of individuals.

The first part began with the Advocate General carefully pointing out that while the Italian court's reference referred to the allegation that the Italian law constituting ENEL had "infringed" Articles 102, 93, 53, and 37 of the Treaty, the Court itself was limited by the Article 177 procedure to offering an interpretation of those Treaty provisions, without offering a finding as to whether national laws had in fact infringed those provisions. As Lagrange stated "What must be avoided – and this is a danger which becomes apparent as cases under Article 177 multiply – is that this Court, under the guise of interpretation, might more or less substitute itself for the national court which, let us not forget, retains jurisdiction to apply the Treaty and the regulations of the Community which have been incorporated into national law by ratification."

The Advocate General then went on to discuss the claim by the Italian government that the question referred to the Court was "absolutely inadmissible" because in this dispute "the court merely has to apply a domestic law of the Italian state" while, on the other hand, "an examination of the possible infringement by a member state of its Community obligations through a domestic law can only take place in accordance with the procedure laid down in Articles 169 and 170 of the Treaty in which individuals have not, even indirectly, any standing". In those circumstances, in the words of the Italian government included by Lagrange in his opinion, "the rules of law remain valid even after the judgment of the Court, until such time as the State, in pursuance of the general obligation undertaken under Article 5, itself takes the necessary measures to comply with such judgment".

The Advocate General first addressed the objection that infringement of the Treaty by a subsequent domestic law that conflicts with the Treaty can only be pleaded under the procedure for a finding of default by a member state laid down in Articles 169 to 171, "which does not affect the validity of the impugned law until it has been finally repealed following a judgment of the Court declaring its incompatibility with the Treaty". "In fact", said Lagrange, "that is not the problem; it is that of the *coexistence of two opposing legal rules* (as a hypothesis) *which both apply to the domestic system*, one deriving from the Treaty or the Community institutions, the other from the national legislature and institutions: which must predominate until such time as the conflict is resolved? That is the real problem."

To answer this question, the Advocate General stated that he would forgo "recourse to legal theory", and "without taking sides between 'Federal Europe' and 'the Europe of Countries', or between the 'supranational' and the 'international'", "the Court can only consider the Treaty as it is", but that "the Treaty establishing the European Economic Community" "creates its own *legal system* which, although distinct from the legal system of each of the member states, by virtue of certain precise provisions of the Treaty, which bring about a *transfer of jurisdiction* to the Community institutions, partly replaces the internal legal system". It was universally conceded, Lagrange told the Court, that the EEC treaty contains "a certain number of provisions" that are "directly applicable in a domestic legal system . . . In deciding that Articles 12 and 31 of the EEC treaty *produce direct effects and create individual rights which national courts must protect*, you yourselves have declared that they are, to use the hallowed expression, 'self-executing'." Lagrange noted that provisions of the Treaty that were not of direct effect could enter the domestic legal system through two different ways, either by Regulations where the Treaty provided the power to issue them, or where this is not the case, in pursuance of Recommendations or Directives where "the Treaty only becomes part of the domestic legal system as a consequence of national measures adopted by the competent organs of the State in question". It therefore follows that two classes of provisions are directly applicable: "The provisions of the Treaty which are considered as 'self-executing'" and "Those which have been the subject of implementing Regulations". Lagrange continued, "Thus, we cannot avoid the problem which results from the coexistence within each Member State of two systems of law, domestic and Community, each operating in its own sphere of competence, nor can we avoid the question what sanction should follow the encroachment by one into the sphere of competence reserved to the other."

"For encroachments on the part of national authorities", the sanction "must be available not only at the instance of states but also in favour of individuals when the latter derive individual rights from the Treaty or Community regulations. As the Court has said, the protection of these rights falls upon the national courts. The question then arises, in what circumstances must such courts exercise their control and, in particular, apply the self-executing provision of the Treaty or the Community regulations duly adopted, when they conflict with a national law?" Here Lagrange emphasized the difficult scenario related to a national act adopted by the national legislature (not merely an administrative act, say) in conflict with a self-executing provision of European law and coming into force after the Treaty or after the relevant Community Regulation has been adopted. In such circumstances, allowed Lagrange, "one is inevitably confronted with a constitutional problem".

The Advocate General then briefly discussed the various national constitutional arrangements on this topic in the various member states, starting with the "most satisfactory" system in the Netherlands where national laws that were inconsistent with treaty provisions of a self-executing character could be found illegal in the national courts, before coming finally to Italy the member state involved in this particular dispute. Here he described the 24 February–7 March 1964 decision of the Italian Constitutional Court in the *Costa* dispute, where the Italian court had claimed that the adoption of a domestic law contrary to the provisions of the Treaty of Rome "was not relevant except as regards the responsibility of the State as international level". "Since the Treaty was ratified by an ordinary law, a later inconsistent law should have effect in accordance with the principles that govern the succession of laws in time, from which it follows that [in the Constitutional Court's words] 'there is no need to inquire whether the law at issue infringes the obligations assumed by virtue of the Treaty'".

At this point, the Advocate General cautiously stated that "It is patently not for me to criticize this judgment". "But what I would insist upon," he went on, "are the disastrous consequences (and I do not think this expression is too strong) that such a precedent, if it is maintained, would risk having as regards the functioning of the system of institutions established by the Treaty and, as a consequence, the very future of the Common Market." He continued:

> If it happened that the constitutional court of one of the Member States, possessed of its full jurisdiction, felt bound to acknowledge that such a result cannot be achieved within the framework of the constitutional rules of its own country – for instance, as regards the possibility that ordinary national laws, contrary to the Treaty, might prevail against the Treaty itself without any court (not even the constitutional court) having the power to stop their application, so that they could only be repealed or modified by Parliament – such a decision would create an indissoluble conflict between the two legal systems and would undermine the very foundations of the Treaty.

> For not only could the Treaty not be applied under the conditions envisaged in it, within the country concerned, but, as a chain reaction, it could not even be applied within the other countries of the Community; certainly this would be so in those Member States of the Community (such as France) where the precedence of international treaties is only granted "on condition of reciprocity".

The Advocate General concluded this section of the argument by suggesting that in such a circumstance there would be only two courses of action to such a state: to amend their constitution or to renounce the Treaty itself.

Before moving on the questions raised by the Italian Court, the Advocate General noted that that court was obliged by national law to consider whether to submit the question of the legality of the ENEL nationalization law with European law to the Italian Constitutional Court. This raised an interesting question for Lagrange:

> The only problem which could possibly arise is whether, in the case of a law, a court might be justified in refusing to apply it in those cases where, pursuant to the interpretation given by the Court of Justice, it would be bound to reach the conclusion that such a law was contrary to the Treaty. In other words, do Italian courts, other than the Constitutional Court, have the right to decide on the plea of unconstitutionality or are they bound, in any event, to refer the matter to the Constitutional Court? Otherwise, there is no doubt that the court should have referred the matter to the Constitutional Court leaving it to such court to call upon you to interpret the Treaty. But that is a matter relating to the division of internal jurisdiction between the Courts of a member state, a question with which you do not have to concern yourselves.[3]

These preliminary points of principle thus addressed, the Advocate General then proceeded to assess each of the provisions of the Treaty in question as to whether it should be considered self-executing and thus enforceable by individuals in the national courts.

The first provision to be considered was Article 102, which required the member states to consult the European Commission in advance where it planned to adopt laws, regulation, or administrative action when there was reason to fear that these might lead to a distortion of the Common Market. It appeared that the Italian government had failed to consult the Commission in this way prior to the adoption of the law

[3] The Court would in fact later concern itself with this question in its 1978 *Simmenthal* judgment (see Chapter 7).

concerning the nationalization of ENEL. Considering whether the failure of a member state to comply with the formalities prescribed by Article 102 should result in the automatic invalidity of the measure in relation to the Treaty so that national courts are bound to disregard it, the Advocate General answered in the negative. To allow national courts to decide at the instance of individuals that Article 102 had been infringed, would involve national courts having the power to appraise the necessary "fear"of distortion, "involving a more or less delicate value-judgment which cannot reasonably be made without the intervention of the organs of the Community, particularly the Commission". He concluded that the infringement by a member state of its obligations under Article 102 could only be raised pursuant to the procedure of Articles 169 to 171.

The Advocate General gave a similar opinion as regards the second provision, Article 93, which provided for review by the Commission of systems of aid within the member state to ensure they are compatible with the Common Market. He argued that sanctions for failures by the member states to fulfil this obligation were only to be imposed under the Articles 169 to 171 procedures, and that the provisions of Article 93 should not be considered self-executing. Assessing whether systems of aid within the member states were compatible with the Common Market, so Lagrange explained, "implies here again a delicate value-judgment, requiring a balancing of the political and economic interests of the State concerned with the requirements for a common market. This judgment cannot possibly be left to the sole appraisal of the national courts without any intervention by the Community organs or by governments."

The third provision under consideration was Article 53, which provided that the member states "shall not introduce any new restrictions on the right of establishment in their territories of nationals of the Member States, save as otherwise provided in this Treaty". Here, by contrast with the previous two provisions discussed, Lagrange submitted that Article 53 was a self-executing provision: "The provision is clear, precise, and, it would appear, requires no preliminary examination by the Commission and the governments, nor any value judgment: we are much closer to the provisions such as those in Article 12 or in Article 31 concerning the standstill in matters of customs duties or quantitative restrictions." Nonetheless, interpreted in the light of Article 52, which provided that "freedom of establishment" included the right to take up and pursue activities as self-employed persons "under the conditions laid down for its own nationals by the law of the country where such establishment is effected", the Advocate General indicated that to comply with Article 53 it was sufficient to show that no new restrictions should be introduced that bring about *discrimination* between the nationals of different member states. So nationalizations – as in the case of the Italian electricity company ENEL – will not be contrary to Article 53 if the conditions of access to the exercise of the activity at issue are restrained or suppressed in the same manner as regards nationals of the country and without any discrimination whatsoever against non-nationals.

The final provision considered by the Court was Article 37, requiring the member states to progressively adjust any "State monopolies of a commercial character" to the Common Market, and in particular in Article 37(2) required that "Member States shall refrain from introducing any new measure which is contrary to the principles laid down in paragraph 1 or which restricts the scope of the Articles dealing with the abolition of customs duties and quantitative restrictions between Member States." Lagrange first rejected the view put forward by the Italian government that ENEL had the character of a "public service" and therefore should be considered outside the ambit of Article 37's reference to "State monopolies of a commercial character".

Lagrange then went on to consider whether provisions of Article 37 were self-executing. Finding that many aspects of Article 37 should not be considered self-executing, by contrast the Advocate General found that in relation to 37(2), "We find here again the rather drastic wording of Articles 12 and 31: 'The Member States shall refrain' ... which has been interpreted by the Court as not preventing a direct application by national courts."

Lagrange set out a distinction between the first and second parts of Article 37(2). The first part of Article 37(2) required that the member states "shall refrain from introducing any new measure which is contrary to the principles laid out in paragraph (1)". Such a "more or less difficult and subjective" appreciation, so claimed the Advocate General, cannot reasonably be made outside the framework of the discussions between the Commission and the member state or states that are immediately concerned, and therefore the possible infringement of the first part of Article 37(2) cannot be raised except under the procedure laid down in Articles 169–171. By contrast, the second part of Article 37 involved a "more direct application of the rule on standstill" in the matters of customs duties and quotas. It is true that "a certain margin of appraisal remained" in relation to restrictions on the "scope of the Articles", but that cannot in itself prevent the application of a sanction by national courts in favour of interested parties, so concluded Lagrange, "because the rule of standstill is in such cases directly affected and its infringement may adversely and directly affect the rights of individuals and private legal relationships".

On 15 July 1964, the Court of Justice addressed the Italian court's questions about particular Articles of the Treaty of Rome, finding that Articles 102 and 93 did not contain provisions capable of creating individual rights that national courts must protect, while Articles 53 and 37 did contain provisions capable of creating individual rights that national courts must protect. Article 53(3) is satisfied, explained the Court, "so long as no new measure subjects the establishment of nationals of other member states to more severe rules than those prescribed for nationals of the country of establishment", while in the case of Article 37(1), the Court pointed out that it did not "prohibit the creation of any state monopolies", but merely those "of a commercial character", and then only in so far as they tend to introduce discrimination regarding the conditions under which goods are procured and marketed between nationals of the member states. The Italian court was to make its own assessments in the dispute before it in light of the Court's interpretation of the provisions of the Treaty of Rome.

The Court of Justice's judgment also discussed the purposes and effect of the Article 177 procedure. The Court denied that the Article 177 procedure allowed the Court to "decide upon the validity of a provision of domestic law in relation to the treaty, as it would be possible for it to do under Article 169". Rather, "a decision should be given by the Court not upon the validity of an Italian law in relation to the treaty, but only upon the interpretation of the above-mentioned Articles [i.e. those Articles of the Treaty of Rome which, it had been alleged, the Italian nationalization law had violated] in the context of the points of law stated by the *Giudice Conciliatore*".

As regards the claim of the Italian government that a national court that was obliged to apply a national law cannot avail itself of the Article 177 procedure, the Court of Justice stated, famously, that:

> By contrast with ordinary international treaties, the EEC treaty has created its own legal order which, on the entry into force of the treaty, became an integral part of the legal systems of the member states and which their courts are bound to apply.
>
> By creating a community of unlimited duration, having its own institutions, its own personality, its own legal capacity and capacity of representation on the international plane and, more particularly, real powers stemming from a limitation of sovereignty or a transfer of powers from

> the states to the community, the member states have limited their sovereign rights, albeit within limited fields, and have thus created a body of law which binds both their nationals and themselves.
>
> The integration into the laws of each member state of provisions which derive from the community, and more generally the terms and the spirit of the treaty, make it impossible for the states, as a corollary, to accord precedence to a unilateral and subsequent measure over a legal system accepted by them on a basis of reciprocity. Such a measure cannot therefore be inconsistent with that legal system. The executive force of community law cannot vary from one state to another in deference to subsequent domestic laws, without jeopardizing the attainment of the objectives of the treaty set out in Article 5(2) and giving rise to the discrimination prohibited by Article 7.

Two detailed aspects of the Treaty were referred to by the Court in support of its understanding of its terms and spirit. The first was the severe limitations that the Treaty placed on unilateral action by individual member states, including the requirement for prior authorization by the European institutions in the case of safeguard actions or derogations from the European treaties:

> The obligations undertaken under the Treaty establishing the Community would not be unconditional, but merely contingent, if they could be called in question by subsequent legislative acts of the signatories. Wherever the Treaty grants the states the right to act unilaterally, it does this by clear and precise provisions (for example Articles 15, 93(3), 223, 224 and 225). Applications by member states for authority to derogate from the treaty are subject to a special authorization procedure (for example Articles 8(4), 17(4), 25, 26, 73, the third subparagraph of Article 93(2), and 226) which would lose their purpose if the Member States could renounce their obligations by means of an ordinary law.

The second was the provision that the Treaty made for the creation of Regulations by the European institutions:

> The precedence of Community law is confirmed by article 189, whereby a Regulation "shall be binding" and "directly applicable in all member states". This provision, which is subject to no reservation, would be quite meaningless if a state could unilaterally nullify its effects by means of a legislative measure which could prevail over Community law.

From these observations, the Court concluded:

> It follows from all these observations that the law stemming from the treaty, an independent source of law, could not, because of its special and original nature, be overridden by domestic legal provisions, however

> framed, without being deprived of its character as community law and without the legal basis of the community itself being called into question.[4]
>
> The transfer by the states from their domestic legal system to the community legal system of the rights and obligations arising under the treaty carries with it a permanent limitation of their sovereign rights, against which a subsequent unilateral act incompatible with the concept of the community cannot prevail. Consequently Article 177 is to be applied regardless of any domestic law, whenever questions relating to the interpretation of the treaty arise.

As regards the various provisions of the Treaty at issue, the Court's decisions as to their direct effect in the national legal orders largely followed the outcomes suggested by the Advocate General. In relation to the requirement for prior consultation contained in Article 102, the Court said:

> Member states have limited their freedom of initiative by agreeing to submit to an appropriate procedure of consultation. By binding themselves unambiguously to prior consultation with the Commission in all those cases where their projected legislation might create a risk, however slight, of a possible distortion, the states have undertaken an obligation to the community which binds them as states, but which does not create individual rights which national courts must protect. For its part, the Commission is bound to ensure respect for the provisions of this article, but this obligation does not give individuals the right to allege, within the framework of community law and by means of Article 177 either failure by the state concerned to fulfil any of its obligations or breach of duty on the part of the Commission. In relation to the monitoring of the systems of aid in the member states under Article 93, the Court said that "the states have entered into an obligation with the Community, which binds them as states but creates no individual rights except in the case of the final provision of article 93(3), which is not in question in the present case.

In relation to the prohibition on restrictions on the "freedom of establishment" under Article 53, the Court said:

4 The French-language version of the *Costa* judgment describes the Treaty as an "autonomous" rather than "independent" source of law: *attendu qu'il resulte de l'ensemble de ces elements, qu' issu d' une source autonome, le droit ne du traité ne pourrait donc, en raison de sa nature specifique originale, se voir judiciairement opposer un texte interne quel qu'il soit, sans perdre son caractere communautaire et sans que soit mise en cause la base juridique de la communauté elle-même.*

> the obligation thus entered into by the states simply amounts legally to a duty not to act, which is neither subject to any conditions, nor, as regards its execution or effect, to the adoption of any measure either by the states or by the Commission. It is therefore legally complete in itself and is consequently capable of producing direct effects on the relations between member states and individuals ... Article 53 is therefore satisfied so long as no new measure subjects the establishment of nationals of other member states to more severe rules than those prescribed for nationals of the country of establishment, whatever the legal system governing the undertaking.

In relation to the requirements on the member states to progressively adjust any State monopolies of a commercial character to the Common Market under Article 37, the Court stated that

> Article 37(2) contains an absolute prohibition: not an obligation to do something but an obligation to refrain from doing something. This obligation is not accompanied by any reservation which might make its implementation subject to any positive act of national law. This prohibition is essentially one which is capable of producing direct effects on the legal relations between member states and their nationals.

The Court concluded, differing here from the Advocate General,

> Article 37(2) is in all its provisions a rule of Community law capable of creating individual rights which national courts must protect.

Related Cases

Prior to *Costa*, the Court of Justice's 1960 *Humblet* judgment had insisted that if the Court decided that a legislative or administrative act produced by the authorities of the member states was contrary to Community law, then the state was obliged to rescind the measure and make reparation for any unlawful consequences.[5] This is in many ways a classic restatement of the supremacy of treaty obligations over domestic law. Compared to *Humblet*, however, the Court of Justice in *Costa* was addressing itself to the choice that the *national judge* was obliged to make when

[5] In the French-language version, the Court of Justice stated that the Treaty "had the force of law in the member states and prevailed over internal law": *Qu'en effet, si la cour constate dans un arrêt qu'un acte législatif ou administratif émanant des autorités d'un état membre est contraire au droit communautaire, cet état est obligé, en vertu de l'article 86 du traité C.E.C., aussi bien de rapporter l'acte dont il s'agit que de réparer les effets illicites qu'il a pu produire; que cette obligation résulte du traité et du protocole qui ont force de loi dans les états membres à la suite de leur ratification et qui l'emportent sur le droit interne.*

facing conflicts between national law and Community law, requiring the national judge to adopt the same position as the Court of Justice in recognizing the supremacy of European law inside their own national legal order.[6]

Since *Costa* the Court of Justice has consistently maintained that national judges must resolve any conflicts between directly effective European obligations and national legal obligations by applying the European obligations. In Chapter 7 of this book we will consider the 1978 judgment *Simmenthal*, where the Court maintained that the duty to apply European legal obligations even in the presence of newly enacted and conflicting national legislation was a duty that applied to all national judges, even if national constitutional arrangements restricted the right to declare national legislation unconstitutional to the national constitutional court, as well as the 1970 judgment *Internationale Handelsgesellschaft*, where the Court maintained that possible conflicts with fundamental rights protected by national constitutional law could not prevent the application of European legal obligations in the national legal orders (see Chapter 9).

There are of course many other cases where the Court has defended, or extended, European law's supremacy doctrine in various different scenarios. In the 1971 case *Politi*, for example, the Court maintained that the effect of a Regulation made under Article 189 of the Treaty was to prevent the implementation of any incompatible national legislative measure, even if enacted subsequently.[7] In the 1987 case *Albako*, the Court explained that "by virtue of the principle of precedence of Community law", as laid down in *Costa*, national courts must refrain from applying any national provision that would hinder the implementation of a Decision made under Article 189 of the Treaty.[8] In the 1999 case *Kreil*, finally, the Court found that a general rule of the German Constitution prohibiting women from performing armed service did not exclude the application of a Directive on equal treatment for men and women as regards access to employment, which required that derogations from

[6] Stein 1965: 24, De Witte 1986: 258. De Witte argues overall that even internal supremacy of treaty obligations already had a latent existence in international law, but that the Treaty of Rome's preliminary reference procedure allowed the Court of Justice to intervene in national courts' deliberations to promote the recognition of this internal supremacy within the national legal orders.

[7] Case 43/71 *Politi* v. *Ministero delle finanze* [1971] ECR 1039.

[8] Case 249/85 *Albalko* v. *B.A.L.M.* [1987] ECR 2345, cf. Lenaerts 1992: 98 ft 20.

equal access to employment be justified by the specific nature of the posts in question or specific activities being carried out.[9]

Analysis and Context

The *Costa* v. *ENEL* decision, and the "supremacy", or "primacy", doctrine of European law are regularly discussed in prominent texts and surveys on the development of European law as well as in scholarly collections of the Court's great judgments.[10] Leading texts define supremacy as meaning that "when EU law has identified a conflict between it and national law, it should take precedence over national law";[11] that, according to the Court of Justice, "any norm of EU law takes precedence over any provision of national law, including the national constitutions";[12] that, for national courts, "respecting the principle of primacy means that, when an EU rule applies in a given case, any conflicting national norm should be *set aside*";[13] that the European legal order insists that its law prevails over all national law, including national constitutions;[14] and that it is a basic rule of European law that "a directly effective provision of [European] law always prevails over a provision of national law. This rule, which is not found in any of the Treaties but has been proclaimed with great emphasis by the Court, applies irrespective of the nature of the [European] provision … or that of the national provision".[15] *Costa* is also sometimes mentioned as the Court's first recognition of the Community's international legal personality (one of the Court's justifications for the supremacy doctrine was to refer to the Community's "capacity of representation on the international plane") and as an example of a case where the question posed in the preliminary reference from the national court was not very clearly stated.[16]

[9] Case C-285/98 *Kreil* v. *Bundesrepublik Deutschland* [2000] ECR I-69.

[10] *Costa* is included as a "basic community case" and as a "classic of EU law" in both Rudden and Rossa Phelan 1997 and Maduro and Azoulai 2010.

[11] Chalmers et al. 2014: 208.

[12] Craig and de Búrca 2015: 266.

[13] Craig and de Búrca 2011: 341.

[14] Schütze 2016: 120.

[15] Hartley 2014: 243.

[16] Craig and de Búrca 2011: 219, Rasmussen 1986: 480. *Costa* v. *ENEL* was also mentioned in *L'Europe des juges*, where Lecourt emphasizes doubt as to whether the electricity was a commercial product that would affect cross-border exchange and that the Court of Justice therefore left this question to the national judge (Lecourt 1976a: 71–72).

Different aspects of *Costa* v. *ENEL* – its relationship to the Court's 1963 decision in *Van Gend en Loos*, the nature and quality of the justification for the supremacy doctrine advanced by the Court, and what can only be described as the judgment's ambition – have been extensively discussed in scholarship.

Costa's relationship with *Van Gend en Loos*, and, more generally, the supremacy doctrine's relationship with the direct-effect doctrine, has always been a focus of scholarly debate. *Costa* is frequently paired with *Van Gend en Loos* as the twin foundations of the European legal order,[17] and, for many, *Costa* is an obvious consequence of *Van Gend en Loos*. As Boulouis explained, "primacy is the necessary complement to direct effect at the national level", and given the benefits of the "vigilance of individuals concerned to protect their rights" before national courts (as *Van Gend en Loos* explained), the primacy of European law gives the national judge before whom individuals appear "the means to overcome obstacles created by its own national law".[18] *Van Gend en Loos* and *Costa* are therefore often seen as an inseparable "pair" at the foundation of the European legal order.[19]

Claims for such a compelling logical connection between the two cases can certainly be questioned, however. As Diarmuid Rossa Phelan correctly writes, *Van Gend en Loos* would not have "become meaningless" "if Case 6/64 *Costa* had not happened":

> [Certainly] the effect of Case 26/62 *Van Gend en Loos* would have been lessened. But without Case 6/64 *Costa* the European Community law right would still exist, just as a right under the European Convention of Human Rights and Fundamental Freedoms still exists even when it is denied. It might not be uniformly applied until, for example, Italy and any other Member State which denied the right changed its law *sua sponte* or following a declaration by the Court of Justice in an action brought by the Commission pursuant to Article 169 ... or by a Member State

17 Chalmers et al. 2014: 199, 201, Dashwood et al. 2011: 37, 235, 284, Weatherill 2014: 70.

18 Boulouis and Chevallier 1978: 139ff, 142–143.

19 Subsequent scholarship has raised the question of whether the supremacy of European law, by itself and without being "triggered" by the presence of a directly effective European norm, is capable of producing legal effects in the national legal systems, such as the setting aside of contrary national rules (e.g. Dougan 2007, with a focus on 1990s judgments of the Court of Justice concerning unimplemented Directives). The classic supremacy doctrine scenario, however, and the one originally addressed in *Costa* itself, relates to the resolution of conflicts between directly effective European law and national law in favour of the former.

> pursuant to Article 170 . . . This ought to result in uniformity, at least in theory. So Case 6/64 *Costa* did not "have to" happen as a matter of usual legal reasoning.[20]

From an internal Court document later made available by former legal *attaché* Paolo Gori, we do know, however, that members of the Court did consider the question of the supremacy of European law over contrary national law during the deliberations on *Van Gend en Loos* itself. Judge Trabucchi recommended that the Court avoid addressing this issue "*pour le moment*", presumably to return to advance this proposition when the time appeared right.[21]

Because the supremacy doctrine protected the role that the direct-effect doctrine had created for private individuals and national courts in the enforcement of European law, so, just as with *Van Gend en Loos*, *Costa* can be considered as appealing to the interests of private individuals and national courts to support the creation and development of the European legal order. For national courts, in particular, the supremacy of European law created new possibilities for judges, particularly those in "lower" national courts, to control national legislation that might otherwise not have been subject to their judicial review.[22] Thus the supremacy doctrine in *Costa* was an essential part of the "judicial empowerment" that the developing European legal order offered to national judges.

The reasons that the Court provided for its decision in *Costa* v. *ENEL* have often been carefully assessed. The essential point, noted by many authors, is that the Court's argument can be described as a "functionalist" or "consequentialist" one.[23] In Gaudet's words, the legal and political system adopted by the member states necessarily implies priority for Community law, without which it will not function,[24] or, as Boulouis explained it, the Court's argument is based on necessity, not on federalism.[25] The Court's argument has similarities to the functionalist argument for the priority of European law over national law advanced by German law professor Hans-Peter Ipsen at a 1964

20 Rossa Phelan 1997: 102–103.

21 Azzalini and Sandei 2008: 223. Cf. Rasmussen 2012: 390. The document was made available by Trabucchi's legal *attaché* at the time of *Van Gend en Loos*, Paolo Gori.

22 Weiler 1991: 2426.

23 Rudden and Rossa Phelan 1997: 43.

24 Gaudet 1965: 203.

25 Boulouis and Chevallier 1978: 139ff, 140.

conference attended by several European Court judges shortly in advance of the *Costa* decision.[26]

The other aspect of the *Costa* decision that often draws attention is the open ambition of the Court's judgment, above all its frank contrast between the European Economic Community and "ordinary international treaties".[27] Indeed, the Court's emphasis on the "autonomy" of European law, its "special and original nature", and its distinction from ordinary international law, may have been designed to facilitate the acceptance of the supremacy doctrine by national courts, who were not therefore necessarily being asked to alter long-standing approaches to resolving conflicts between national law and international law other than Community law.[28] The grandiose wording of the Court's text also made clear that *Van Gend en Loos* was not an isolated decision, in a treaty system where only a few treaty provisions would be expected to be granted direct effect. Even though the *Costa* decision itself was perhaps cautious in its assessment of whether the particular treaty provisions at issue should enjoy direct effect, the tone and mood of the judgment indicated that the scope of direct effect in Community would likely be far-reaching.

Nicola Catalano, then recently retired as judge of the Court of Justice, wrote a detailed commentary on *Costa* in 1964 that emphasized the differences between the reasoning of the Advocate General's opinion and that of the Court's judgment.[29] Both the Advocate General and the Court, of course, found in favour of the supremacy of European law. The Advocate General's account, however, appeared to Catalano to confirm the view that directly applicable European norms would constitute the exception within the system of the Treaties, while in the Court of Justice's version, within the limits of Community competences, "the exception is, by contrast, the reserve competence of the member states".[30] One can also see this, perhaps, in the Advocate General's repeated concern to

[26] Ipsen 1964–1965, Ipsen 1965. "If I have to choose one principle as a guiding light, let it be that of *ensuring the Communities capacity to function*" (Ipsen 1964–1965: 393), emphasis in the original.

[27] As ECJ judge Donner noted a few years later, the Court expressed itself so plainly in *Costa* in order to give national judges some support in deciding the problem of the priority of Community law over national law (Donner 1968: 81).

[28] De Witte 1986: 274–275.

[29] Catalano 1964.

[30] Catalano 1964: 3.

avoid the result that domestic court judges should be placed in a position requiring them to make sensitive value-judgments, a concern that the Court itself did not appear to share so strongly.

The judgment contains other noteworthy aspects. The Court describes the limitations by the member states of their sovereign rights as "permanent" (in French *definitive* or "final") and thus apparently irreversible. The Court also describes the European Community as constituting "a legal order of its own" (in French, *un ordre juridique propre*), a somewhat different expression than the "new legal order of international law" the Court had employed in *Van Gend en Loos*.

Given the proliferation of debates about the supremacy of European law in all its various aspects over the decades, it is worth underlining that the practical problem addressed by *Costa* was the possibility of conflicts between directly effective European obligations and *subsequently enacted national statutes*. Because many of the member states, among both the original members and the later adherents, had given domestic force to the obligations of the Treaty of Rome by means of an ordinary statute (a statute enabled by a national constitutional provision to be sure in both Italy and Germany, but nonetheless it was the statute, rather than the constitutional provision, that actually introduced European legal obligations into the domestic legal order),[31] then by ordinary rules for the solution of conflicts between obligations contained in different national statutes, the obligations contained in the more recently enacted statute would prevail, according to the maxim *lex posterior derogat legi priori*. In *Costa* itself, for example, the conflict was between various provisions of the Treaty of Rome, which might have been suitable for direct application in the national courts, and the subsequently enacted Italian statute providing for the creation of the nationalized energy monopoly ENEL. The *Costa* decision, and European law's supremacy doctrine in general, was designed above all to address what may be called the "*lex posterior* problem" potentially facing many European obligations in the national legal orders.[32]

The vitality of European law's *lex posterior* problem was recognized both in the *Costa* litigation itself, where the Advocate General's discussion draws attention to this scenario in particular, and much contemporary

[31] Phelan 2010.
[32] Phelan 2010.

commentary during the early years of European legal integration.[33] In later scholarship however, discussions of the supremacy doctrine, including discussions of its historical development, have tended to focus on potential conflicts between European obligations and other national legal obligations, above all fundamental rights protected by national constitutional provisions. An understanding of the most important achievements of the supremacy doctrine in general, and of the *Costa* decision in particular, requires a maintenance of focus on the *lex posterior* problem itself, that is to say, the potential conflicts between European law and the continuing stream of ordinary national legislation being enacted by national parliaments.[34]

Costa can therefore be understood as a foundation stone of the European legal order, as an essential pair with *Van Gend en Loos*, as a declaration of a supremacy doctrine justified largely by the functionalist considerations, as an example of the supremacy doctrine's essential connection with the *lex posterior* problem, and as a marker of the Court's great ambition. *Costa*'s relationship with national court decisions and doctrine within the member states has also been much discussed.[35]

The approach of this book, however, is to situate the great judgments of the Court of Justice in the context of treaty provisions and state practices in other trade-related treaty regimes, above all those related to the enforcement of, and escape from, demanding treaty obligations. From that perspective, two different aspects of *Costa* are particularly relevant. The first is the Court's often overlooked emphasis on the Treaty of Rome's approach to safeguard mechanisms in the *Costa* judgment. The second is the essential contribution made by the Court's 1963 and 1964 direct effect and supremacy doctrines, as a pair, to the relationship between the member states.

The Court's decision in *Costa* was of course a creative one, in that the Treaty had not explicitly provided for the supremacy of European obligations over conflicting national law. Only two detailed aspects of the Treaty of Rome were called upon by the Court in support of its judgment. The first were the very limited circumstances under which the Treaty provided for unilateral behaviour by the member states, including the

[33] E.g. Ipsen 1964–1965, Gaudet 1965, Lecourt 1970: 45. Lecourt's speech on his retirement from the Court in 1976 refers to the basic principle that Community law takes precedence over all national laws "even those subsequently enacted" (Lecourt 1976b: 49).

[34] Phelan 2014.

[35] E.g. Eisemann 1996.

fact that the various safeguard and derogation provisions provided for throughout the Treaty were controlled by the European institutions. As the Court explained, "Applications by member states for authority to derogate from the treaty are subject to a special authorization procedure." These procedures, claimed the Court, "would lose their purpose if the Member States could renounce their obligations by means of an ordinary law". The second was that Article 189 of the Treaty provided that Regulations adopted by the European institutions "shall be binding" and "directly applicable in all member states". The Court claimed that this provision would be "quite meaningless" if a state could "unilaterally nullify its effects" by national legislation.

In short, of the Court's justifications in *Costa* that relied on detailed provisions of the European Treaties – which was only one element of the Court's reasoning, to be sure, as the Court also called upon various more general features including Articles 5 and 7 – the Court relied first and foremost on the fact that the derogation procedures such as that contained in Article 226 of the Treaty were not unilaterally available to the member states but were instead subject to prior Community control. Thus it becomes clear that a leading part of the reasoning behind the supremacy doctrine was the principle that the Court had stoutly defended in its 1961 *Pork Products* decision.

At the time of the Court's judgment, this aspect of *Costa* was sometimes readily acknowledged. As we have seen, former judge Catalano wrote an analysis of the *Costa* judgment in 1964, which carefully distinguished between the rationales for the supremacy provided by the Advocate General, on the one hand, and the "more solid" rationale put forward by the Court of Justice itself, on the other.[36] His analysis of the premises of the main decision in *Costa* are just as interesting. The Court, noted Catalano, started from a recognition of an original division of competences between the European Community and its member states, citing "the provisions which permit the States to act unilaterally, not committing to underline that, even in these circumstances, a procedure of authorization is at times set out".[37] "From this premise", wrote Catalano, "the Court did not hesitate to affirm that the transfer undertaken by the Court in favour of the Community legal order implied a limitation of their sovereign rights; from this fact, all subsequent unilateral acts, incompatible with the system of the Community, would be

[36] Catalano 1964: 2.
[37] Catalano 1964: 2.

completely deprived of effect."[38] By contrast with many later analyses, Catalano's analysis of the way that the Court addressed the "central problem" in *Costa* does not emphasize the direct applicability of Regulations as provided for in Article 189, or for that matter the preliminary reference procedure, the Preamble of the Treaty, or the Article 5 obligation on the member states. Catalano saw the Court's decision in *Costa* as straightforwardly derived from Treaty provisions such as the Article 226 safeguard mechanism.[39]

In more recent discussions of *Costa* and the supremacy doctrine, however, this part of the Court's reasoning is often downplayed or omitted. In an extensive and interesting monograph on the supremacy doctrine, for example, Claes writes,

> Indeed, in *Van Gend en Loos* and *Costa* v. *ENEL*, the Court referred to Article 5 of the EEC Treaty, and Articles 177 and 189 of the EEC Treaty, as grounds for the supremacy of Community law. It follows from the authoritative interpretation of those provisions, according to the Court, that Community law is to take precedence over conflicting legislation even before the domestic courts.[40]

As the reader will note, the Court's references in *Costa* to Article 226 and the other provisions of the Treaty that restrict the unilateral adoption of safeguards by the member states have been overlooked in this account. In fact, in Claes's monograph the only mention of the Court of Justice's connection of supremacy doctrine with the specific procedures provided for derogating from the Treaty occurs when a detailed discussion of the text of *Costa* itself requires it to be mentioned in passing.[41] By contrast, the role of Articles 5, 85, 177, and 189 each receive both their own separate considerations as well as continuing references throughout Claes's book.[42] This sort of approach is far from unusual. Both scholarly and

[38] Catalano 1964: 2.

[39] Catalano 1964: 2 (*le problème central*...), Catalano does mention the preliminary reference procedure in relation to the discussion of admissibility, where the Court had "completely followed" the reasoning of the Advocate General.

[40] Claes 2006: 209. Similarly, Temple Lang answers the question, "why are national courts involved with Community law at all?" by referring to the direct application of Regulations and the preliminary reference procedure provided for by Arts 189 and 177 of the Treaty (Temple Lang 1997: 4).

[41] Claes 2006: 90. Even there it is quickly left behind, as this aspect is omitted in the comparison with the supremacy of non-Community Union law in the passage that follows.

[42] Claes 2006: 53–57.

textbook accounts of *Costa* frequently "trim" the Court's text to remove the judgment's emphasis on the Treaty's distinctive pre-authorization procedures for derogations, and omit or downplay this aspect when discussing justifications for the decision.[43] No wonder then that the connection between the supremacy doctrine and the Treaty's distinctive approach to safeguards and derogations is not commonly appreciated. By keeping a focus on the text of the Court's decision itself, however, and on the wider context of the unilateral availability of safeguards within many trade-related treaty systems, we will get a better understanding of the practical issues of trade and treaty politics that the *Costa* decision was addressing.

That brings us towards an important way in which the Court's 1963 and 1964 direct effect and supremacy doctrines, as a pair, acted to change the relationship between the member states.

Recall that the *Costa* dispute had already been heard by the Italian Constitutional Court in late February/early March 1964. In that decision, the Constitutional Court denied that directly effective provisions of the European treaties could be enforced by Italian courts where these conflicted with subsequently enacted Italian legislation, given that European obligations entered the Italian legal order by virtue of an ordinary Italian statute from which a later Italian statue could derogate. Such a "violation of a treaty, even if it results in responsibility by the State at international level, does not detract from the validity of any conflicting Law" internally, so the Italian Constitutional Court declared. The Italian government insisted further that even after any finding by the European Court that Italy had failed to fulfil its European obligations through the Article 169 to 171 procedures, such national legislation remained valid in Italy until the Italian legislature had taken action to remove or replace it.

What is clearer therefore in the Italian Constitutional Court's decision together with the Italian government's arguments before the Court of Justice than in the decision of the Court of Justice itself is that the obvious alternative to the creation and acceptance of the supremacy of European law within the national legal orders was the mechanisms of "responsibility by the State at international level", as in more common forms of international law.

[43] Among many examples, see e.g. Rossa Phelan 1997: 107–108, 113–114, Dashwood et al. 2011: 237–238, Kaczorowska 2013: 242, Hartley 2014: 206, Craig and de Búrca 2015: 267–268.

Now for any international treaty, discussion of scenarios that incur the international responsibility of states must be straightforwardly related to scenarios where widely accepted principles of international law may authorize the threat or imposition of countermeasures or reprisals against a defaulting state. That is why Weiler describes the doctrine of state responsibility as having "concomitant principles of reciprocity and countermeasures", and why De Witte directly links state responsibility with the possibility of "international sanctions".[44] The scenario first set out by the Italian Constitutional Court, and completed in the arguments put forward by the Italian government as described by the Advocate General, describes almost perfectly a scenario that would straightforwardly prompt threats of inter-state retaliation in many other treaty regimes. Certainly, a member of today's WTO, which unilaterally "restored their freedom of action" (to use the Constitutional Court's expression) by legislating contrary to their WTO obligations in this way could expect that their national legislation would remain valid internally regardless of being found incompatible with WTO obligations by WTO dispute settlement institutions, but at the cost, of course, of the risk of the imposition of retaliatory trade restrictions by other WTO members. Thus the discussion of ordinary forms of "state responsibility" in the Italian Constitutional Court's decision, together with the Italian government's open discussion of states continuing with treaty-inconsistent policies even after their condemnation under the Article 169 procedure, demonstrate how easily and straightforwardly the issues at stake in the *Costa* litigation can be connected to the possible use of inter-state retaliation and reciprocity mechanisms between the various European states.

Although of course many important variants can be generated, the scenario discussed by the Italian Constitutional Court can also be used to illustrate the change brought about by European law's supremacy doctrine. Under those circumstances, treaty obligations enter the national legal order via the national legislation implementing a treaty as authorized by the national constitutional provisions permitting "limitations of sovereignty", but because the national courts recognize the supremacy of directly effective European law even when in conflict with subsequently enacted national legislation, it is no longer possible for the state to "restore its freedom of action" by enacting new and contrary legislation. Thus the scenario where state responsibility would have been incurred, as

[44] De Witte 1986: 262–263, Weiler 1991: 2422.

described by the Italian Constitutional Court, and thus the possibility of inter-state countermeasures would have been raised, is effectively suppressed by the doctrine that the Court of Justice announced in *Costa*.[45]

This point can be further elaborated. For a demanding trade-related treaty system that seeks to comprehensively rule out any use of inter-state retaliatory enforcement mechanisms by the use of domestic court enforcement of treaty obligations, a doctrine of direct effect of treaty obligations is itself insufficient. Placing domestic courts in participating states under an obligation to ensure the domestic application of treaty obligations is insufficient because it does not address the situation where domestic courts in the participating states are also under other obligations deriving from their national legal orders, a situation that is most acute when those conflicting obligations are derived from subsequently enacted national legislation. If, in those circumstances, the national legal obligation is permitted to continue to be applied in place of the directly effective treaty obligation, then other treaty states cannot continue in those circumstances to rely on domestic court enforcement as an alternative to ordinary forms of inter-state retaliation. It is not therefore the doctrine of direct effect that is the true substitute for any use of such retaliatory enforcement mechanisms – it is the doctrine of direct effect *contrary national legal obligations notwithstanding* that is the full substitute for any use of such retaliatory enforcement mechanisms between trading states. That is in fact the most compelling reason why *Costa* must be considered the essential and logical pair to *Van Gend en Loos*, as both doctrines are necessary if the purpose is to reject any use of inter-state retaliation or reciprocity mechanisms as enforcement mechanisms within the European legal order.[46]

Judge Lecourt's discussions of the supremacy doctrine at times bring out this aspect very plainly. The chapter on the supremacy of European law in his 1976 book *L'Europe des juges* begins with a short section addressing the "Community logic" (*logique communautaire*) of supremacy.[47]

[45] De Witte's discussion of *Costa* states straightforwardly that the application by national courts of the *lex posterior* doctrine in favour of national law in conflict with prior treaty obligations serves to violate international law and thus incurs the international responsibility of that state and exposes it to the possibility of international sanctions (De Witte 1986: 262–263). On the same logic, the supremacy doctrine of European law serves to block this path towards state violations of European treaty obligations and thus reduces the role to be played by international sanctions.

[46] Cf. Rossa Phelan 1997: 102–103.

[47] Lecourt 1976a: 284–285.

The logic of supremacy, so Lecourt explained, is directly connected to the suppression of self-help and unilateral use of safeguard mechanisms by the European states. On self-help, so Lecourt went on, "as elementary as it seems, the principle according to which no one can take the law into their own hands is the foundation of the Community, as it is of any authentic civilization". (Lecourt used the expression *nul ne peut se faire justice à lui-même*, wording that recalls the rejection of self-help set out at length in Lecourt's doctoral dissertation, as well as the text of the Court of Justice's 1964 *Dairy Products* judgment, which will be discussed in the next chapter.[48]) Referring then to the many decisions where the Court had opposed unilateral measures adopted by the member states, Lecourt explained, "the Community jurisdiction did not deny the reality of the difficulties which the member states wanted to address, but rejected the way that in doing so they had acted by themselves, outside the Community mechanisms".[49] The expression "difficulties" is a common feature of the safeguard provisions of the Treaty of Rome, most prominently in Article 226, which begins "If, during the transitional period, difficulties arise...".[50] The "Community mechanisms" to which Lecourt refers are therefore the mechanisms for requesting authorization of safeguards and derogations under provisions such as Article 226. Lecourt's explanation of the logic of supremacy in *L'Europe des juges* therefore overwhelmingly emphasizes its connection with Community law's prohibition of unilateral safeguards, as the Court had already set out in *Pork Products* in 1961, and Community law's prohibition of self-help, which the Court would go on to establish in *Dairy Products* in 1964.[51] Given the prominence and accessibility of *L'Europe des juges*, and Lecourt's frank emphasis there on

[48] Lecourt 1931. Lecourt's description of the prohibition of self-help as "the foundation of the Community, as it is of any authentic civilization" in *L'Europe des juges* closely recalls his description of the desirability of the prohibition of self-help in international law in his doctoral dissertation: "This principle is so essential to the life of society, it is so much the foundation of all law, that it is the object today of a considerable expansion in international law. ... Where the Law extends to a new area, this principle appears as a foundation. Its extension is so great and so visible that although once limited to conflicts between private interests it now constantly tends to apply to disputes between peoples" (Lecourt 1931: 284–285).

[49] Lecourt 1976a: 285, see also mention of "except for derogations provided by the Treaties" in the discussion of supremacy in Lecourt 1970: 42.

[50] Lecourt and Chevallier list several of the Treaty's safeguard/derogation mechanisms that use the expression "difficulties" in their 1963 article (Lecourt and Chevallier 1963: 276).

[51] The third aspect mentioned in Lecourt's discussion is the direct applicability of Regulations as set out in Article 189 of the Treaty.

the supremacy doctrine's role in preventing unilateral use of safeguards or use of self-help enforcement measures by the European states, it is perhaps a little surprising that many subsequent discussions of the logic of European law's supremacy doctrine make no reference to such matters at all.

To conclude, therefore, we can see how the *Costa* decision can be linked to the Community's distinctions from other trade-related treaty systems: the supremacy doctrine was justified by the Court in *Costa* by explicit connection with the Community's requirement that national safeguard measures be subjected to prior approval by the European institutions; the discussion of the *Costa* dispute by the Italian Constitutional Court combined a rejection of the supremacy of European law with an acknowledgment that such a result could give rise to Italy's "state responsibility" at the international level, a description that raises the possibility that the other European states might be justified in imposing countermeasures against Italy in such a scenario; the logical necessity of combining direct effect with supremacy if direct effect was to serve as a secure substitute for inter-state retaliation; and, we may finally add, recalling Wenner's discussion of the supremacy question in his 1962 commentary on *Pork Products*, the necessity of combining direct effect with supremacy if direct effect was securely to prevent the unilateral adoption of safeguards in violation of the Treaty of Rome's requirements for prior authorization by the European institutions. Thus the relationship between the supremacy doctrine of European law and the practical issues of enforcement and escape in international trade politics is demonstrated by both the text of the Court's judgment and the scenarios under discussion in the case before the Court. It was recognized too in Lecourt's discussion of the logic of supremacy in *L'Europe des juges*. And, as we will see in the next chapter, writings by judge Lecourt demonstrate his recognition of a logical connection between the doctrines of direct effect and supremacy, on the one hand, and the Court of Justice's *Dairy Products* judgment rejecting of any form of inter-state retaliation within the European Community, on the other.

4

Dairy Products, 1964

No Inter-State Retaliation

The Case before the Court

This case came to the Court of Justice as a consequence of the Article 169 procedure, which provided that if the Commission considered that a member state had failed to fulfil an obligation under the Treaty, then the Commission could bring the matter before the Court.[1]

One of the provisions establishing a customs union between the member states, Article 12 – the same provision as at issue in *Van Gend en Loos* – required that the "Member States refrain from introducing between themselves any new customs duties on imports or exports or charges having equivalent effect, and from increasing those which they already apply in their trade with each other." This was the so-called stand-still clause of the Treaty of Rome. However, in November 1958, both Luxembourg and Belgium, operating within the framework of the Belgo-Luxembourg economic union, had enacted new duties on imports of a number of dairy products, including powdered milk, condensed milk in tins, and various cheeses, soft and blue. The Commission, after various consultations with the member state governments, in April 1963 delivered a reasoned opinion alleging that these customs duties infringed Article 12 of the Treaty, and the case was brought before the Court.

The Luxembourg and Belgian governments argued that the case was inadmissible on various grounds: first, that they had declared themselves ready to abolish the measures complained of as soon as it was possible to work out with the Commission solutions for replacing the existing system; second, that, at the time that proceedings were started, it was reasonable to expect that a Community-wide organization of the milk

[1] Cases 90 & 91/63 *Commission* v. *Luxembourg & Belgium (Dairy Products)* [1964] ECR 625.

market would be introduced and that this would substantially correspond with the Belgian and Luxembourg system being complained of; third and finally, that a Resolution of the Council of April 1962 had stated that it was necessary to set up a common organization of the market for milk by July 1962, with compensatory levies to take effect by November 1962 at the latest, and therefore that the Commission would not have had any reason to bring proceedings against Luxembourg and Belgium if the Resolution of the Council had been acted on.

As to the substance, in essence, the Luxembourg and Belgian governments admitted that the introduction of these duties on dairy products had the effect that Article 12 of the Treaty of Rome sought to prohibit, but argued in effect that Article 12 was not applicable to agriculture, as the Treaty explicitly provided that national market organizations for agricultural products were to continue in operation until Community-level market organizations were established, and that included the ability to vary the measures adopted in relation to particular products as market circumstances changed.

The Advocate General, Karl Roemer, disagreed with the arguments advanced by Luxembourg and Belgium. Roemer pointed out the Court had already, in *Pork Products*, decided that a declaration of willingness by a member state to abolish measures complained of as soon as a solution to replace the current system had been worked out with the Commission did not exclude the possibility of an action by the Commission under the Article 169 process. The member states could exclude the admissibility of such an action only if they took steps to actually end the situation complained of. He argued, notwithstanding that a common market organization for milk had been adopted by the Council of Ministers in February 1964, that the case raised issues of fundamental importance, relevant to similar situations as long as no comprehensive common organization of agricultural markets had been established. On the final argument about admissibility raised by the member states, Roemer conceded that the Resolution of the Council was not acted on in due time, and therefore that "an obligation based on the Treaty was not observed". "But", he went on, "I think it is a mistake to conclude from this that the cases are inadmissible, using the argument from international law or civil law of '*tu quoque*'." Roemer pointed out that the terms of the Council's Resolution were "vague" and lacking detail, and that the infringement of the Treaty by the member states went back to a time "long before" the adoption of the Resolution by the Council. Roemer added, finally,

> Maybe in international law an *ultima ratio* permits taking the law into one's own hands when no other procedure exists for protecting legitimate interests. In Community law, however, other Community channels exist for solving the difficulties which arise. For example as regards the law on agriculture there is the application of the rules on minimum prices . . . or finally the application of the general safeguard clauses in the Treaty. These ensure that the Community keeps a check on internal acts, and guarantee that the measures taken will not go beyond what is strictly necessary. It does not seem to me to have been proved that recourse to the remedies under Community law would not have made possible a satisfactory solution to the Belgian and Luxembourg question. Therefore to my mind the negligence of the Council does not constitute a justification of the attitude of the two Member States.

As for the substance, Roemer first denied that a market organization for these milk products, as defined by the Treaty, existed in Luxembourg and Belgium when the Treaty of Rome entered into force, and that allowing the "potential existence" of certain measures to constitute a market organization as defined by the Treaty would dangerously weaken that concept. Furthermore, even if it was allowed that the Belgian and Luxembourg system for products derived from milk in fact constituted a market organization in the terms of the Treaty, the Advocate General nonetheless denied that the member states were "free to amend at will" this system to maintain its effectiveness. Here Roemer drew on the *Pain d'épices*[2] judgment to argue that when considering the relationship between general provisions of the Treaty, such as the Article 12 "stand-still" clause, and the special provisions relating to agriculture, the later must always be interpreted strictly, with the consequences of exceptions limited to the absolute minimum necessary. Therefore "what is decisive is that at the time when the Treaty entered into force no import duties of the type in question in this case were being levied".

On 13 November 1964, the Court rejected the arguments put forward by Luxembourg and Belgium. On the questions raised as to admissibility, it began as follows:

[2] Cases 2 & 3/62 *Commission* v. *Luxembourg & Belgium (Pain d'épices)* [1962] ECR 425, where the Court had stated: "It follows, then, from the clarity, certainty and unrestricted scope of Articles 9 and 12, from the general scheme of their provisions and of the treaty as a whole, that the prohibition of new customs duties, linked with the principles of the free movement of products, constitutes an essential rule and that in consequence any exception, which moreover is to be narrowly interpreted, must be clearly stipulated."

> The defendants, arguing that the application is inadmissible, complain that the Community failed to comply with the obligations falling on it by reason of the Resolution of the Council of 4 April 1962, and was thus responsible for the continuance of the alleged infringement of the Treaty, which should have ceased before the issue of the reasoned opinion under Article 169. In their view, since international law allows a party, injured by the failure of another party to perform its obligations, to withhold performance of its own, the Commission has lost the right to plead infringement of the Treaty. However, this relationship between the obligations of parties cannot be recognized under Community law.
>
> In fact the Treaty is not limited to creating reciprocal obligations between the different natural and legal persons to whom it is applicable, but establishes a new legal order which governs the powers, rights, and obligations of the said person, as well as the necessary procedures for taking cognizance of and penalising any breach of it. Therefore, except where otherwise expressly provided, the basic concept of the Treaty requires that the Member States shall not take the law into their own hands. Therefore the fact that the Council failed to carry out its obligations cannot relieve the defendants from carrying out theirs.

It is these words – "the basic concept of the Treaty requires that the Member States shall not take the law into their own hands" or, even more so, the original French, "*l'économie du traité comporte interdiction pour les états membres de se faire justice eux-mêmes*" – that constitute the most famous and oft-repeated extract from the *Dairy Products* judgment.

The Court went on to emphasize that the Resolution of the Council to take a decision on rules for milk products by July 1962 at the latest did not create time limits having the same effect as those laid down in the Treaty. The Resolution was not a binding measure within the meaning of Article 189 of the Treaty, and therefore the Council "did not infringe the treaty" when it failed to observe the time limits set out in the Resolution. Furthermore, the disputed decrees of Luxembourg and Belgium were made before both the Council's April 1962 Resolution and the time limits laid down therein.

As to the substance, the Court emphasized that "Article 12 constitutes a fundamental rule and any possible exception, which in any event must be strictly construed, must be clearly laid down". Furthermore, Articles 39 to 46, concerning the setting up of the common agricultural policy, "contain nothing conferring exemption from Article 12". The Court went on to say that "the argument that prohibition on the use of new measures must gradually lead to national market organizations losing their effectiveness . . . is unfounded. The Treaty expressly provides means and special procedures for remedying the difficulties in question under the supervision of the Community authorities or with their approval." (By "means and special procedures", the Court was understood to be referring to the safeguard mechanisms provided for in Article 226 and similar provisions of the Treaty.[3]) The Court concluded that "Article 12 applies also to measures taken within the framework of a national market organization in so far as they constitute customs duties or charges having equivalent effect". The Court therefore found that the Luxembourg and Belgian governments, by introducing a special duty leviable upon the issue of import licences of dairy products, had failed to comply with the obligations laid down in Article 12 of the Treaty of Rome.

Related Cases

The *Dairy Products* case was the first, and foundational, judgment of the European Court to reject any use of self-help reciprocity and retaliation mechanisms by member states within the European legal order. An earlier hint of the Court's approach in *Dairy Products* can be found in the December 1962 *Pain d'épices* case. There the two member states had unilaterally adopted an import duty on import licences of gingerbread (*pain d'épices*), and, upon the Commission initiating an action under Article 169, requested the authorization of protective measures under, inter alia, Article 226. They then complained before the Court that the Commission had improperly demanded the suspension of the measures criticized before deciding upon the various requests for derogations. In the *Pain d'épices* case, the Court stated that "any wrongful act or default on the part of the Commission – which would have to be decided upon in an action especially brought on this point – would not in any way affect the proceedings for the infringement of the Treaty . . ."[4], without however also making the wide-ranging declarations about the logic of the Treaty that the Court included in the *Dairy Products* judgment.

[3] E.g. Kapteyn 1964–1965: 243. The Advocate General had referred to the possibility of Belgium and Luxembourg applying "the general safeguard clauses in the Treaty" as an alternative means of addressing their difficulties.

[4] Case 2 & 3/62 *Commission* v. *Luxembourg & Belgium (Pain d'épices)* [1962] ECR 425. Judge Pescatore later discerned in the text of the *Pain d'épices* judgment, decided on 14 December 1962 with Lecourt (for the first time) as *rapporteur*, the earliest manifestation of the fundamental trend of the new case law that would include *Van Gend en Loos* and *Costa* v. *ENEL* – the energetic defence of Community law against attempts by governments to circumvent its provisions (Pescatore 2005).

There have been many subsequent Court decisions that have developed and reinforced the principle first established in *Dairy Products*. In *Germany* v. *Commission*,[5] the Court rejected a claim by the German government that its actions were justified by alleged misuses of the Commission's powers, stating that "Any possible failure by the Commission to fulfil its obligations towards other member states cannot exempt one of them from performing the obligations which are legimately placed upon it by measures taken in application of the Treaty." In *Commission v. Italy*,[6] the Court responded to a claim by the Italian government that the time allowed for the implementation was "too short", as "demonstrated by the fact that no Member State was successful implementing the Directive" by the required date, by declaring that "any delays there may have been on the part of other Member States in performing obligations imposed by a Directive may not be invoked by a Member State in order to justify its own, even temporary, failure to perform its obligations". In *Steinike*,[7] the Court declared that "any breach by a Member State of an obligation under the Treaty in connexion with the prohibition laid down in article 92 [restricting state aid] cannot be justified by the fact that other Member States are also failing to fulfil this obligation". In *Essevi*,[8] the Court had responded to a claim by the Italian government that it had no intention of altering its contested system of alcohol taxation "until the national monopolies existing in Germany and in France were modified", by declaring that "above all, it must be pointed out that in no circumstances may the Member States rely on similar infringements by other Member States in order to escape their own obligations under the provisions of the Treaty".

In *Commission v. Germany*,[9] a case concerning duty-free shopping cruises, the German government had claimed that "the Commission, by requiring the Federal Republic of Germany alone to terminate these exemptions, was not complying with [a prior judgment of the Court], since ... the problem must be examined in relation to all the Member States and in relation to all types of maritime transport". The Court however declared that "As the Court has already held, a Member State cannot, in any circumstances, plead the principle of reciprocity and rely

[5] Cases 52 & 55/65 *Germany* v. *Commission* [1966] ECR 159.
[6] Case 52/75 *Commission* v. *Italy* [1976] ECR 277.
[7] Case 78/76 *Steinike und Weinlig* v. *Germany* [1977] ECR 595.
[8] Case 142 & 143/80 *Amministrazione delle Finanze dello Stato* v. *Essevi* [1981] ECR 1413.
[9] Case 325/82 *Commission* v. *Germany* [1984] ECR 777.

on a possible infringement of the Treaty by another Member State in order to justify its own default. Nor, therefore, can a Member State rely on the principle of reciprocity to contest the admissibility of an action brought against it for failure to fulfil its obligations."[10] In *Guy Blanguernon*,[11] in response to a claim by M. Blanguernon that "certain Member States had not adopted measures to implement the [Directive requiring publication of annual accounts]", placing French companies at a disadvantage, the Court declared that

> A Member State may not rely on the fact that other Member States have also failed to perform their obligations in order to justify its own failure to fulfil its obligations under the Treaty, since in the legal order established by the Treaty, the implementation of Community law by the Member States cannot be made subject to a condition of reciprocity, and Articles 169 and 170 of the Treaty provide the appropriate remedies in cases where Member States fail to fulfil their obligations under the Treaty ... It follows that the national law of a Member State giving effect to a Community directive must have full force, even if the directive in question has not yet been transposed and implemented in the legislation of other Member States.[12]

In *Hedley Lomas*,[13] a case where the United Kingdom had restricted export to Spain of live animals for slaughter, on the ground that their treatment in Spanish slaughterhouses was contrary to Community law obligations, the Court declared that "the Member States must rely on trust in each other to carry out inspections on their respective territories and one Member State may not unilaterally adopt, on its own authority, corrective or protective measures designed to obviate any breach by another Member State of rules of Community law".[14] In *Commission* v. *Italy*, the Court declared that "a Member State cannot plead failure to

[10] The Court referred to Case 232/78 *Commission* v. *France (Sheep Meat)* [1979] ECR 2729 as the reference for this prior rejection of reciprocity. The Court's *Sheep Meat* judgment does not use the word "reciprocity", however.

[11] Case C-38/89 *Ministère Public* v. *Guy Blanguernon* [1990] ECR I-83.

[12] Similarly in Case C-146/89 *Commission* v. *United Kingdom* [1991] ECR I-3533, the Court declared that "a Member State cannot justify its failure to fulfil obligations under the Treaty by pointing to the fact that other Member States have also failed, and continue to fail, to fulfil their own obligations. ... Articles 169 and 170 of the Treaty provide suitable means of redress for dealing with the failure by Member States to fulfil their obligations under the Treaty."

[13] Case C-5/94 *The Queen* v. *Ministry of Agriculture ex parte Hedley Lomas* [1996] ECR I-2553.

[14] The Court referred to its prior decisions in *Dairy Products* and *Sheep Meat.*

observe the principle of reciprocity or rely on a possible infringement of the Treaty by another Member State to justify its own default".[15]

Another prominent case addressing retaliatory behaviours between the European states, the 1979 *Sheep Meat* judgment,[16] will be discussed in Chapter 8 of this volume.[17]

Of course, if the principle declared in the *Dairy Products* case is understood as one of the essential foundations of the European legal order, then almost any decision made by the Court after November 1964, as well as all the major judgments of the European Court discussed in this book, must be considered related to the Court of Justice's *Dairy Products* decision.

Analysis and Context

The *Dairy Products* decision is rarely included in prominent texts and surveys of the development of European law, or in scholarly collections of the Court's famous judgments.[18] At times it may be briefly referred to as the basis of European law's rejection of international law-style reciprocity,[19] but, most often, if it is included at all, *Dairy Products* is discussed as merely one of a catalogue of defences by the member states in Article 169 actions that have been rejected by the Court.[20] Approaches such as these leave *Dairy Products* largely disconnected from the great judgments of the Court of Justice in the years that preceded and followed it.

The *Dairy Products* decision is also sometimes noted as the first occasion on which the Court "edited" its famous declaration in *Van Gend*

[15] Case C-131/01 *Commission* v. *Italy* [2003] ECR I-1659.

[16] Case 232/78 *Commission* v. *France (Sheep Meat)* [1979] ECR 2729.

[17] An even wider range of related issues could be included, including scenarios related to whether breaches of Community law could justify countermeasures affecting legal relationships "outside" Community law, and whether breaches of "outside" rules of international law may be answered by countermeasures affecting Community law (Simma 1985: 124). We omit any discussion of these secondary scenarios here.

[18] *Dairy Products* is omitted entirely in e.g. Craig and de Búrca 2011, Chalmers et al. 2014, Weatherill 2014, Craig and de Búrca 2015. *Dairy Products* is not included as a "basic community case" or a "classic of EU law" in either Rudden and Rossa Phelan 1997 or Maduro and Azoulai 2010.

[19] Kaczorowska 2013: 116, 379, Schütze 2016: 57, 373.

[20] Arnull 2006: 45, Dashwood et al. 2011: 144, Hartley 2014: 326, Woods and Watson 2014: 254, Foster 2016: 200. E.g. Case 7/61 *Commission* v. *Italy (Pork Products)* [1961] ECR 317, Case 77/69 *Commission* v. *Belgium* [1970] ECR 237, Case 7/71 *Commission* v. *France* [1971] ECR 1003, Case 101/84 *Commission* v. *Italy* [1985] ECR 2629.

en Loos that the European Economic Community constituted a "new legal order of international law", substituting the terser description that the EEC constituted a "new legal order" *tout court*. The new, shorter description may have been prompted by judges on the Court who wished to further distance the Court's description of the European legal order from ordinary forms of international law.[21]

The *Dairy Products* judgment is moreover used as justification for the claim that the decision-making procedures provided for by the Treaties must be correctly followed if the decisions of the European institutions are to be granted binding legal effect.[22] In later debates about the legal implications of the 1966 "Luxembourg compromise", for example, scholars pointed to the *Dairy Products* decision as denying that any legal consequences should be derived from the "political" declarations by the member states indicating that decision-making in the Council would continue to require unanimity among themselves even though the Treaties themselves specified a move to qualified majority decision-making.[23] That strand of thinking about the authority of *Dairy Products* is also present in more recent debates, buttressing claims that the European Treaties can only be modified by means of the amendment procedure provided for in the Treaties themselves.[24]

Like the other foundational judgments of the European Court in its early years, however, the significance of *Dairy Products* may best be understood in the context of treaty provisions and state practices in other

[21] In *Van Gend en Loos* the Court described the European Community as a "new legal order of international law". In *Costa* v. *ENEL*, the Court described the European Economic Community as possessing "its own legal order". In *Dairy Products*, the Court used the expression "new legal order", dropping the phrase "of international law" (Rossa Phelan 1997: 48, 71–72). Judge Lecourt, writing in 1970, explained that the "innocent words" referring to international law in *Van Gend en Loos* had encouraged some too rapidly [*trop rapidement*] to identify Community law with the "international order", but that all reference to the international character of the Community legal order had subsequently disappeared from the judgments of the Court (Lecourt 1970: 65).

[22] As the Court explained in *Dairy Products*: "[T]he resolution of the Council to take a decision under article 43 by 31 July 1962 at the latest, so that the rules for milk products would enter force by 1 November 1962 at the latest, does not create time-limits having the same effect as those laid down in the Treaty. The intention of the authors of the measures is clear from the fact that they adopted it under a style and form which are not those of the binding measures of the council within the meaning of article 189 of the Treaty. Therefore the Council did not infringe the treaty when it failed to observe the time-limits which it had set itself in its resolution of 4 April 1962."

[23] Bellanger 1968: 195 ft 28.

[24] "Editorial" (2014) 51 CML Rev 1, 3–4.

trade-related treaty regimes, above all those related to the enforcement of, and escape from, demanding treaty obligations. As we have explained, the possibility that inter-state retaliation – "reprisals", "countermeasures", "reciprocal measures", "suspension of equivalent concessions" – may be authorized as a mechanism to encourage states to fulfil their obligations is a common feature of many international trade regimes. They are available, for example, within the NAFTA (North American Free Trade Area), the Mercosur (The Common Market of the South), and the Andean Community (The Andean Community of Nations).[25] They are also available to states within many other regional or bilateral trade treaties.[26]

The WTO's dispute settlement procedures, set out in the "Dispute Settlement Understanding" agreed as part of the "Uruguay Round" trade negotiations concluded in 1994, can be taken as a paradigmatic example of a well-developed state-to-state dispute settlement system that relies on the possible authorization of inter-state retaliation.[27] It makes no attempt to remove all use of inter-state countermeasures within the world trading system. Instead, the WTO's Dispute Settlement Understanding seeks to control and tame such inter-state retaliations by restricting their authorization until the end of an extensive legal procedure; that is, to circumstances where a WTO member has authoritatively been found by a Panel, or the Appellate Body as the case may be, to have adopted "measures" inconsistent with their WTO obligations, but nevertheless, after a "reasonable period of time" has been allowed, failed either to replace the "measures" in question with policies consistent with WTO obligations, or alternatively to have come to an agreement on compensation or an agreed alternative solution with the WTO member that had initiated the complaint.

To be sure, the actual imposition of such retaliatory measures is relatively rare within the WTO but the possibility of their use is widely

[25] NAFTA: Enforcement by Retaliation: Hufbauer et al. 2003: 29, Jensen 2011: 46–47. Mercosur: Enforcement by Retaliation: Article 31 of the Protocol of Olivos, Vinuesa 2005: 440. Andean Community: Enforcement by Retaliation: Article 27 of the Treaty Creating the Court of Justice of the Cartagena Agreement (Amended by the Cochabamba Protocol), Secretaría General 2006: 26, Phelan 2015a.

[26] Chase et al. 2013: esp 36ff, Froese 2014.

[27] "Understanding on Rules and Procedures Governing the Settlement of Disputes", Annex 2 of WTO Agreement. The full set of procedures involved in the settlement of disputes between WTO members is of course more extensive than is set out here in brief, and the reader is referred to the Understanding for a complete account.

agreed to be essential to incentives for WTO members to comply with their obligations.[28] As self-help measures adopted by other states, trade retaliation can be imposed on a defaulting state within a trade regime, and thus prevent it from benefiting from a treaty violation, even if the state in question does not cooperate in accepting a penalty, as would be required by a merely declaratory finding of fault by a treaty-based tribunal or even by an obligation to pay a financial penalty or fine. That is the essential reason why retaliatory restrictions in trading opportunities have had a long-standing role in international trade politics and why contemporary international trade regimes most often attempt only to limit and guide, rather than eliminate, such instruments. After all, they offer a mechanism for enforcing international legal obligations that may be of significant importance when other mechanisms fail. The "last resort" availability of such countermeasures is then a latent presence even in the operation of other aspects of treaty-based dispute settlement processes.

The widespread acceptance that a role for trade retaliation between treaty partners may be a necessary part of trade treaty systems is but the parochial version of a wider debate on the role for retaliatory self-help between treaty states in general international law. Of course, the literature on self-help by states in international law is vast and cannot possibly be summarized here. We will limit ourselves to three aspects. The starting point is that the concept of state responsibility in general international law may authorize a state that has been injured by the failure of another state to fulfil its treaty obligations to take countermeasures by way of reciprocity or reprisal.[29] There is therefore the presumption that states have the right to respond to the internationally wrongful act of another state by countermeasures, subject to various requirements such as proportionality, prior notice, compatibility with the UN Charter's restrictions on the use of armed force, etc.[30] Second, however, treaties can provide arrangements that restrict this general right to adopt countermeasures,

[28] Bown 2009, Davis 2012.

[29] Gradoni and Tanzi 2008: 41. See the Report of the International Law Commission on "Responsibility of States for Internationally Wrongful Acts", *Yearbook of the International Law Commission*, 2001, Vol. II (Part 2).

[30] The presumption is such that the silence of a treaty cannot be interpreted as implying the exclusion of a right that has its source in general international law (see discussion in Gradoni and Tanzi 2008: 44–45).

subjecting it to detailed procedural or substantive limitations.[31] Third and finally, however, limitations imposed by treaties on the right of states to respond with countermeasures to the failure of their treaty partners to fulfil their treaty obligations are themselves understood to be dependent on the actual *effectiveness* of such treaty arrangements, so that a reversion or "fall back" on inter-state countermeasures remains a possibility where treaty procedures prove ineffective.[32]

All three of these elements can be observed in a 1978 arbitration decision concerning the 1946 Air Service Agreement the United States and France.[33] The first passage demonstrates both the presumption that states have the right to employ countermeasures where other states are infringing their treaty obligations and the possibility that this right be restricted by treaty rules:

> Under the rules of present-day international law, and unless the contrary results from special obligations arising under particular treaties, notably from mechanisms created within the framework of international organisations, each State establishes for itself its legal situation vis-a-vis other States. If a situation arises which, in one State's view, results in the violation of an international obligation by another State, the first State is entitled, within the limits set by the general rules of international law . . . to affirm its rights through "counter-measures".

The second passage illustrates the contingent relationship between dispute settlement procedures – in this case a tribunal – and the role of

[31] Gradoni and Tanzi 2008: 43. Per Article 55 on the International Law Commission's draft Articles on State Responsibility, the applicability of general rules may be set aside "where and to the extent that the conditions for the exercise for an internationally wrongful act or the content or implementation of the international responsibility of a State are governed by special rules of international law". *Yearbook of the International Law Commission*, 2001, Vol. II (Part 2).

[32] As Simma writes, "States contract out of the general rules on the consequences of treaty violations on the expectation that these regimes will work to their *mutual* benefit. If the balance thus foreseen appears to them to be later destroyed, the principles of *inadimplenti non est adimplendum* or of the *clausula rebus sic stantibus* will work as strong rationales for a fall-back to the general regime" (Simma 1985: 136) [emphasis in original]. Also Gradoni and Tanzi 2008: 42. The possibility of such "fall back" has been extensively discussed in the context of work on draft articles on State responsibility by the International Law Commission, e.g. "[Special *Rapporteur* Arangio-Ruiz's] perception was that treaty regimes . . . could fall back on [the general rules of state responsibility] for whatever was not provided, or in case of the malfunctioning of the system established" (Gianelli 2004: 760–761, *Fourth Report, Yearbook of the International Law Commission*, 1992, Vol. II, Part 1, p. 42).

[33] *France* v. *United States* (1978) 18 RIAA 417.

inter-state countermeasures: the effectiveness of dispute settlement procedures provided by treaties may suppress the right of states to employ countermeasures:

> To the extent that the tribunal has the necessary means to achieve the objectives justifying the counter-measures, it must be admitted that the right of the Parties to initiate such measures disappears.[34]

This contingent relationship also holds contrariwise, as the right of the parties to initiate countermeasures may be resuscitated by the ineffectiveness of treaty-provided dispute settlement procedures.

To be sure, there is considerable debate about all of these elements of the law of state responsibility in international law, along with divergent views about the importance of the availability of countermeasures in encouraging states to fulfil their international obligations. Many scholars agree that the threat of reprisals, retaliation, and so on between states is an unappealing means of encouraging compliance with international law, further disrupting as it does the operation of the treaty in question for states and private actors that rely on it, and patently being more readily available to larger and more powerful states. The necessity of the potential availability of countermeasures is nonetheless insisted on by many, however, who are unwilling to definitively sever states' incentives to fulfil difficult treaty obligations from the expectation that they must do so in order to avoid their treaty partners from reciprocally reducing their own fulfilment in reply.[35]

Both the enduring role of inter-state retaliation in international trade regimes and the oft-limited ambitions for how it can be reformed were on vivid display in a 1947 speech by US Ambassador Wilcox during discussions over draft enforcement provisions of the then proposed "International Trade Organization":

> There are many commitments in the Charter, some of them general, some of them specific. But if any of these commitments are violated, there is only one sanction that can be applied. And that, in its crudest terms, is retaliation by another State. Now this sanction was not invented by the framers of the Charter. It has existed from time immemorial. It exists today. It will exist tomorrow, even though the Organization that we have conceived is never brought to life. What, then, have we done in Article 35?

[34] Cf. Dero 2006: 48.
[35] E.g. Simma 1994.

> We have introduced a new principle into international economic relations. We have asked the nations of the world to confer upon an international organization the right to limit their power to retaliate. We have sought to tame retaliation, to discipline it, to keep it within bounds. By subjecting it to the restraints of international control, we have endeavoured to check its spread and growth, to convert it from a weapon of economic warfare into an instrument of international order.[36]

Ambassador Wilcox was accurate when he foresaw that "retaliation by another State" would continue to exist in international trade even if the proposed International Trade Organization then under discussion did not come to life – in fact, that agreement failed to be ratified by the US Congress and was replaced by the less-ambitious GATT multilateral trade system. "Retaliation by another state" continues to thrive, however, within many of today's trade treaty regimes, as part of the solution to the basic international collective action problems of trade politics and law. This is not the case in today's European Union, however, where the Court of Justice has comprehensively rejected such mechanisms, first and above all in its 1964 *Dairy Products* judgment.

It is precisely because the possible use of such countermeasure and retaliation mechanisms appears so vital in trade regimes such as the WTO, and in general international law, yet has been so firmly and consistently rejected by the European legal order, that scholarship has at times elevated this aspect of the European legal order to one of its defining features. As Weiler, for example, writes,

> [O]ne may speculate about the most profound difference between the Community legal order and international law generally. The combined effect of [European law doctrine and remedies] results, in my view, in the removal from the Community legal order of the most central legal artifact of international law: the notion (and doctrinal apparatus) of exclusive state responsibility with its concomitant principles of reciprocity and countermeasures. . . . Without these features, so central to the classic international legal order, the Community truly becomes something "new".[37]

The importance of the principle announced in the *Dairy Products* judgment is therefore prominently if intermittently acknowledged in

[36] *Verbatim Report of the Sixth Meeting of Commission A Held on 2 June, 1947, Second Session of the Preparatory Committee of the United Nations Conference on Trade and Employment*, E/PC/T/A/PV/6, 2 June 1947, p. 4. Ambassador Wilcox's speech was brought to our attention by Gradoni 2008: 68 ft 47.

[37] Weiler 1991: 2422. Weiler supports this claim with reference to the Court of Justice decisions *Essevi*, *Dairy Products*, *Sheep Meat*, and *Guy Blanguernon*.

theoretical discussions of the European legal order, and has in fact inspired a scholarly literature focusing specifically on this judgment and the related cases where the Court of Justice repeated and extended its principles.

Two contributions particularly stand out. First and foremost is Simma's analysis of treaty regimes that have excluded, to a greater or lesser extent, the application of the general legal consequences of wrongful acts, in particular the application of the countermeasures normally at the disposal of an injured party.[38] Simma's terse discussions of the European Economic Community within this framework in the 1985 *Netherlands Yearbook of International Law* are among the most influential passages of scholarship ever written on Community law. The other outstanding contribution is scholarship by Gradoni, above all his book "'Regime Failure' in International Law" (*"Regime failure" nel diritto internazionale*).[39]

These scholars have much in common. Both consider that the *Dairy Products* judgment contains one of the most profound and distinctive principles ever declared by the Court of Justice. Simma's assessment of the European legal order in light of the rules of general international law provides citations to just two judgments of the Court, the *Dairy Products* and *Sheep Meat* cases.[40] Gradoni, writing with Tanzi, describes the outcome of *Dairy Products* as "revolutionary", and argues that it would be difficult to overestimate its judicial, political, and psychological importance for the subsequent development of Community law.[41]

Second, and even though their answers to this question differ, both of these scholars concentrate their analysis on the question of whether, and if so under what circumstances, the European member states might revert, or "fall back", on the possible use of self-help, retaliatory, enforcement mechanisms against other member states for failing to fulfil their European obligations. Simma starts from the premise that the *Dairy Products* case had rejected as inadmissible within the Community the

[38] Simma 1985: 117, Simma and Pulkowski 2006, and Simma and Pulkowski 2010: 152–155, the latter maintaining the possibilty of "fall back on the general rules of State responsibility" even after the introduction of the 'suspension of membership' procedure introduced by the Treaty of Amsterdam.

[39] Gradoni 2008, also Gradoni and Tanzi 2008. Among other scholarship on the *Dairy Products* judgment, we have particularly benefited from the thorough and interesting Dero 2006.

[40] Simma 1985: 126 ft 60. Only *Dairy Products* is discussed in the text.

[41] Gradoni and Tanzi 2008: 50, 67. For our own discussions along these lines, see Phelan 2011b, Phelan 2012, Phelan 2013.

principle of international law that recognizes that a party affected by a failure of another party to comply with its obligations has the right not to fulfil its own obligation, and then sets out his argument as follows:

> Thus, a member State affected by a breach of Community obligations by another member State would have to seek relief by instituting proceedings according to Article 170 EEC. The alternative would be an analogous procedure initiated by the Commission in accordance with Article 169. Both approaches would lead to a judgment declaring that the member State against whom the action has been brought has or has not failed to fulfil its obligations under the treaty. If the former is the case, "the State shall be required to take the necessary measures to comply with the judgment of the Court of Justice" (Article 171). If the defaulting State prefers not to do so, the member affected by such persistent non-compliance would again have to bring the matter before the Court, this time with the aim of obtaining a judgment declaring that the member guilty of the first breach has added another violation by not fulfilling the earlier judgment. The EEC treaty does not answer the question of what may happen if the violator, despite such cumulative condemnation, does not desist from its course of action. According to what is probably the leading view in literature, however, measures of reprisal or *exceptio non adimpleti contractus* . . . would not become admissible even at this point. . . .
>
> But despite all misgivings and the unparalleled "density" of both the original content and the further concretization of the Community treaties by secondary legislation and jurisprudence, it cannot be denied that these treaties have been concluded as (and remain) treaties under international law. The exclusion of the legal systems created by them from the general law of treaties and State responsibility goes as far as the six original members intended to go. An intention to exclude the applicability of the general legal consequences of internationally wrongful acts to the Community treaties under all circumstances can hardly be established through accepted methods of treaty interpretation, however. . . . [I]f and when the remedies provided within this regime definitively fail to put an end to persistent violations of Community law, the situation may reach the point where further fulfilment of community obligations towards a defaulting member State would simply become an intolerable burden on the injured party or parties. Through such a fundamental change of circumstances any treaty system excluding the applicability of certain general legal consequences and/or countermeasures will fall back on the general regime.[42]

[42] Simma 1985: 126–127. Simma indicates that such countermeasures would have to avoid infringing on the rights of other member states not guilty of a breach (Simma 1985: 128). See Dero 2006: 61 for the proposal to amend the Treaties to allow for inter-state sanctions

Gradoni, while equally starting from the presumption that in general international law, every state has the right to enforce their own legal rights, using countermeasures or other forms of self-help,[43] in the absence of clear treaty arrangements to the contrary,[44] and agreeing with Simma and others on the limited effectiveness of the declaratory judgments of the Court of Justice,[45] nonetheless firmly rejects the possibility of any "fall back" on inter-state countermeasures within the European legal order.[46]

Gradoni effectively criticizes the sufficiency of many possible justifications advanced for the principle declared in the *Dairy Products* case, including arguments based on the Article 5 obligation on the member states to take all appropriate measures to ensure the fulfilment of their Treaty obligations, on the Article 219 undertaking by the member states not to submit a dispute concerning the interpretation or application of the Treaty to any method of settlement other than as provided by the Treaty, and on the impact on private individuals who might be affected by any such countermeasures.[47] He also rejects the argument that the

controlled by the Court following the failure of a state to comply with the Court's judgment of non-compliance within a reasonable delay.

43 Gradoni and Tanzi 2008: 41.

44 Gradoni argues that the *Dairy Products* judgment appeared to be wrong in the light of the law of the time, in that the Court set aside important principles of general international law in the absence of an express derogation in the Treaty, or at least a derogation derived from the Treaty in line with customary canons of interpretation.

45 Gradoni 2008: 235.

46 Gradoni 2008, Gradoni and Tanzi 2008.

47 Obligation to take all appropriate measures (Article 5): Gradoni and Tanzi 2008: 55 ft 77 (contra Dero 2006: 420ff): a state taking effective action with the aim of persuading another state to desist from violating the Treaty, after a violation has been identified by the Court of Justice, does not appear to be jeopardizing the attainment of the Treaty's objectives. Gradoni 2008: 240: in addition, the Article 5 obligation for solidarity between the member states would not extend to a solidarity with "outlaws". Exclusive jurisdiction of the Court (Article 219): Gradoni and Tanzi 2008: 49, 55ff: (contra e.g. Hartley 2000: 14) the exclusive jurisdiction of the Court would be compatible with the Court's exclusive competence to assess the existence of violations of treaty obligations without any renunciation by the states as to their use of self-help as a means of holding their counterparty state responsible. The Treaty did set out an ambitious compulsory procedure for the assessment of violations, but was silent on the connected question of sanctions. It is plausible therefore that the states intended to retain their right to employ self-help according to the rules of general international law, and thus that the Community could have evolved in a very different direction. Gradoni 2008: 239–240: in addition, the use of self-help mechanisms is not really a "method of settlement" to which the member states would "*submit* a dispute" [emphasis in Gradoni]. Importantly, the Court itself did not rely on Article 219 to justify the rejection of international law-style reciprocity either in *Dairy Products* or later. Similarly, Simma and Pulkowski 2006: 518: the scenarios

Community's rejection of self-help by its member states gains its binding power through the judgment of Court of Justice alone.[48] Instead, the best way to understand the impact of the *Dairy Products* judgment, according to Gradoni, is to recognize that the Court used the decision to invert the interpretative presumption that states could employ self-help to secure their legal rights absent any rule to the contrary, substituting instead a rejection of such self-help unless expressly provided for. Here Gradoni emphasizes the Court's phrase "except where otherwise expressly provided" as the preface for its famous claim "the basic concept of the Treaty requires that the Member States shall not take the law into their own hands", noting of course that the Court over the years never did permit such behaviours and has consistently rejected them.

Thus the decision of the Court of Justice on 13 November 1964 can be seen as the initial moment in the invention of a particular customary rule to which the member states have not objected and which indeed over time they have come to accept.[49] In contrast therefore with Simma's argument that, in the case of the ineffectiveness of the Article 169 procedure and in the absence of express provisions of the Treaty, the principle of effectiveness indicates that states would recover their self-help facilities under general international law, Gradoni claims that with the acceptance of this rule by the member states, the rejection of such inter-state countermeasures has become binding on the European states, who, even where the Article 169 procedure is ineffective, must play by those rules or withdraw from the Community.[50] Gradoni therefore has his own distinct perspective, but, just as for Simma, the possibility of "fall back" is the central focus of his analysis.

envisaged for the possibility of fall back on inter-state countermeasures take due account of the Court's central role, since these actions are reserved for cases of non-compliance with the Court's decision. Impact of rights of individuals: Gradoni 2008: 243–245: (contra Weiler 1991: 2422 ft 42) not all Community obligations involve individual rights, and even when interference between self-help and the rights of individuals is inevitable, the temporary suppression of these rights can be justified in the name of a higher public interest, as a public policy exception in the interest of bringing a persistent violation of Community law to an end. Simma and Pulkowski 2006: 519 note that the violation of Community law against which self-help measures may be directed may also violate the rights of individuals (although Gradoni 2008: 245 ft 50 argues this point is not decisive from a legal perspective).

48 Gradoni 2008: 235.

49 Gradoni 2008: 249–250, Gradoni and Tanzi 2008: 51–52.

50 Consistent with this view, Gradoni adds that it cannot be ruled out that the Court of Justice itself might reopen the door to self-help within the European Treaties (Gradoni 2008: 277, Gradoni and Tanzi 2008: 70).

Third, both of these scholars address the importance of the *Dairy Products* case within the context of a truncated consideration of the other early judgments of the European Court. Simma's assessment of whether the European member states might revert to the use of countermeasures against each other does refer to "the direct effect of Community law before national courts" as one of several legal and political institutions and procedures through which breaches of the EEC treaty "can be countered in an effective and constructive manner", without however any further deliberation on this point.[51] Gradoni also offers little engagement with the other new doctrines of European law. *Costa* v. *ENEL*, for example, is referred to but once in Gradoni's monograph; *Van Gend en Loos* is absent.[52] As for the role of direct effect and thus national courts in the enforcement of Community law, Gradoni briefly states that the problem reemerges, and thus remains conceptually intact, when this form of spontaneous compliance with Community rules is less than adequate.[53]

Here we will take a new approach to *Dairy Products*. In full agreement with these distinguished scholars, and – we are happy to admit – under the influence of their arguments, we accept that the European legal order must be understood in a comparative context, particularly by contrast with the vital importance of inter-state countermeasure mechanisms in general international law and in other international trade treaty systems. The *Dairy Products* judgment was a profound, even revolutionary decision. We disagree, however, with the insistent focus of this scholarship on the possible "fall back" on such countermeasures by the European member states vis-à-vis each other. We are more interested in the European legal order's "leap forward" – how it developed without the availability of such mechanisms in the first place. We also argue for the close integration of *Dairy Products* with the other landmark early judgments of the Court of Justice, including those rejecting the unilateral availability of safeguards as well as those establishing and developing the direct effect of European law.

The Treaty of Rome itself, of course, did not contain any provision ruling out the use of self-help countermeasures by the member states.

[51] Simma 1985: 125.

[52] *Costa* is mentioned only in relation to Advocate General Lagrange's discussion of the possibility of a "chain reaction" by other member states to Italy's rejection of the supremacy of European law (Gradoni 2008: 253 ft 72).

[53] Gradoni 2008: 259 ft 90 (*Il problema però riemerge – e resta quindi concettualmente intatto – quando viene meno questa forma di adesione spontanea alla regola comunitaria*). There is no detailed discussion of the direct effect or supremacy of European law in the shorter account contained in Gradoni and Tanzi 2008.

Neither did it contain any provision explicitly providing for the Court to authorize such countermeasures between the European states, or between the European states and the European institutions. The Treaty of Rome differed in this respect from the earlier Treaty of Paris, which had established the European Coal and Steel Community, which provided in Article 88(3) that the High Authority could, subject to control by the Court of Justice, authorize the other member states to adopt trade barriers or discriminatory measures towards a member state deemed to be delinquent with its ECSC Treaty obligations.[54] The Treaty of Rome was silent on this most important of issues, and *Dairy Products* was therefore a creative judgment of the first importance, as the Court could have decided otherwise.[55] For many years after the signing of the Treaty of Rome there was a widespread understanding that the infringement procedures set out in Articles 169, 170, and 171 could, if necessary, lead to the authorization of countermeasures against a European member state by the other member states, or that resort to inter-state countermeasures might be possible should Community mechanisms prove ineffective.[56] Indeed, scholars at times bluntly criticized the *Dairy Products*

[54] Article 88 of the Treaty of Paris reads in part: "If the State has not taken steps for the fulfilment of its obligation within the period fixed by the High Authority, or if its appeal has been rejected, the High Authority may, with the concurrence of the Council acting by a 2/3 majority: (a) suspend the payment of sums which the High Authority may owe to the State in question under the present Treaty; (b) adopt measures or authorize the other member States to adopt measures involving an exception to the provisions of Article 4 [which prohibited e.g. "import and export duties" in the coal and steel market], so as to correct the effects of the delinquency in question. An appeal to the Court's plenary jurisdiction may be brought against the decisions taken in application of paragraphs (a) and (b) within two months following their notification."

[55] Gradoni and Tanzi 2008: 42, 48, 56, Simma 1985: 126. On traditional presumptions of interpretation, therefore, the silence of the Treaty of Rome would suggest that general international law would continue to govern the relationship between the member states in this area (Gradoni and Tanzi 2008: 48). As we will discuss in Chapter 6 on *Van Duyn*, judge Lecourt himself, writing in 1963 and thus before *Dairy Products*, floated the possibility of falling back on classical reciprocity methods of enforcing treaties in the scenario where a state failed to fulfil its EEC obligations after an Article 171 finding by the Court of Justice, preferring however instead to advocate alternative means of making the Treaty effective, particularly litigation by private individuals before national courts (Lecourt and Chevallier 1963: 276). A reversion to the use of inter-state reciprocity within the EEC was therefore "thinkable", although not advocated, by one of the Court's leading judges.

[56] For a discussion in a leading textbook, see Kapteyn and VerLoren Van Themaat 1973: 27: "Thus from the availability of the procedures necessary for determining and adjudicating violations of the Treaty the Court has derived a *prohibition of self-help* for the Member states except for those cases in which the Treaty expressly permits it [citation to *Dairy Products*]. In this context, however, it is to be noted that the traditional international

judgment for appearing to rule out the use of such measures. Däubler, for example, wrote in 1968 that the Court of Justice "had not seen the problem in full clarity" [*der Gerichtshof hat diese Problematik nicht in voller Schärfe gesehen*] when in *Dairy Products* the Court appeared to rule out any role for reprisals by states against Treaty violations, arguing that this would allow non-compliant states to benefit from their behaviour [*ja der Verletzerstaat würde von seinem Verhalten sogar profitieren*].[57]

As the principles of the *Dairy Products* case were confirmed again and again in other judgments, however, over time it came to be relatively widely accepted that the European legal order comprehensively rejected any use of self-help enforcement mechanisms by the European member states. In *Dairy Products* itself, the Court's decision had gone far beyond what was necessary to reject the claims by Belgium and Luxembourg.[58] After all, the failure by these states to comply with the European obligations in question began well in advance of the failure by the European institutions to meet their self-imposed deadline to introduce a European market organization. Furthermore, the self-imposed deadline adopted by the Council was more in the way of a political commitment than a binding legal obligation. As such, the exact situation under consideration in *Dairy Products* was far from being the strongest scenario under which self-help retaliatory measures by a member state might have been

doctrine of self-help may be resuscitated again if these procedures, *e.g.* those of Articles 169 or 170 of the EEC Treaty, have produced no result, since as the Treaties stand the Community cannot take proceedings against the Member States to enforce a judgment. Against the Member State which fails to fulfil its obligation under Article 171 of the EEC Treaty and refuses to act upon a decision of the European Court of Justice, the Community as such or the Member States may make reprisals, *i.e.* measures which *per se* are unlawful, but which are justified as a defence against the unlawful act of another state. Self-help as a possible extension of the procedure of Articles 169–171 on the margin of the Community legal order does, however, form a more acceptable means for obtaining justice than is usually the case outside it in the weakly organized or unorganized society of states. In the first place the Court will already have objectively established the infringement of the Treaty, so that the parties' subjective opinion about the facts no longer plays a part in the conflict. Moreover, the Court will also be in a position to examine the justice of the measures taken, in so far as they set aside EEC law..." [emphasis in original] (similarly, Kapteyn and VerLoren Van Themaat 1989: 39–40, Kapteyn and VerLoren Van Themaat 1998: 80). This view was only abandoned by Kapteyn et al. in their 2008 edition, on grounds of the new sanctioning mechanism introduced by the Treaty of Amsterdam (Kapteyn et al. 2008: 74). Also e.g. Kapteyn 1964–1965: 242–243, Reuter 1968: 685, Reuter 1969: 439, and the extensive references to literature on this question in e.g. Simma 1985, Dero 2006, and Gradoni 2008.

[57] Däubler 1968: 331 ft 54.

[58] Gradoni 2008: 233, Gradoni and Tanzi 2008: 49.

justifiable. Even an international dispute settlement system that did allow for the authorization of self-help measures in the most obvious scenario – where, for example, a member state persisted in policies inconsistent with binding treaty obligations after an authoritative contrary finding by a tribunal – would likely have rejected the arguments put forward by Belgium and Luxembourg in this particular case.

The importance of the *Dairy Products* judgment does not therefore rest on the Court's finding that Belgium and Luxembourg had, in these particular circumstances, violated the Treaty, but rather on the much wider rejection of international law-style reciprocity that was set out in the judgment. The Court's decision was much stronger than Advocate General Roemer's opinion which, in stating that "it does not seem to me to have been proved that recourse to the remedies under Community law would not have made possible a satisfactory solution to the Belgian and Luxembourg question", perhaps raised the possibility of a scenario where the remedies under Community law would *not* provide a satisfactory solution.[59] By calling on "the basic concept of the Treaty" to justify its rejection of international law-style reciprocity and self-help mechanisms, the Court's decision pointed to this issue as a fundamental principle of Community law as the Court intended to develop it. That was a strong signal that the Court would also reject any use of such retaliatory mechanisms by one member state against another member state even in a scenario that much more closely resembled a clear case where the use of countermeasures would be justified by general international law, or within other trade-related treaty regimes.[60] This scenario was certainly addressed in later cases, of course, including *Essevi*, for example, where the Court of Justice declared that "in no circumstances may the Member States rely on similar infringements by other Member States in order to escape their own obligations under the provisions of the Treaty".[61]

If the Court, in *Dairy Products* and its related cases, announced that the European legal order comprehensively rejected any use of self-help reciprocity and retaliation by the European member states, then we are confronted with the question of how this was possible. If the availability of such inter-state countermeasures appears so important in general international law, and inescapable in many international trade regimes, how was the European legal order able to do without them?

[59] Similarly, Gradoni and Tanzi 2008: 60 ft 97.

[60] Gradoni 2008: 233, Gradoni and Tanzi 2008: 49.

[61] Cases 142 & 143/80 *Amministrazione delle Finanze dello Stato* v. *Essevi* [1981] ECR 1413.

A common answer to this question is that the use of inter-state countermeasures by the member states is ruled out because of the infringement procedure mechanisms provided for in Articles 169, 170, and 171 of the Treaty by which a member state may bring another member state, or (in practice, much more often) the European Commission may bring a member state, before the Court of Justice.[62] As De Witte writes,

> A famous example of [the European Community's] particularity is the Court's early affirmation that the general international rule allowing states to retaliate in the event of non-compliance by other parties to the same treaty (*inadimplenti non est inadimplendum*) did not apply in the context of EC law. This innovative characteristic was deduced by the Court from a specific feature of the EEC Treaty itself, namely the power of the independent Commission to bring infringement actions against non-complying states [with citation here to the *Dairy Products* judgment].[63]

And similarly, Dehousse:

> The Court has moreover held that the existence of these legal avenues in the treaty [that is, Articles 169 and 170] divests the member states of all possibilities to resort to the arsenal of unilateral countermeasures provided for in international law. The breach of Community law by other countries cannot serve as an excuse for a state to ignore its Community obligations. (Joined cases 90 and 91/63, *Commission* v. *Luxembourg and Belgium*.)[64]

And ECJ judge Da Cruz Vilaça:

> It was on the basis of Article 169 that the Court of Justice ruled, in Joined Cases 90 and 91/63, *Commission* v. *Luxembourg and Belgium* [1964] ECR 625, that, by establishing a new legal order which governs the powers, rights and obligations of the natural and legal persons to whom it is applicable, as well as the necessary procedures for taking cognizance of and penalising any breach of it, the Treaty is not limited to creating reciprocal obligations between the said persons. On the contrary, as the Court stated, the basic concept of the Treaty requires that Member States shall not fail to carry out their obligations and shall not take the law into their own hands.[65]

[62] Case C-38/89 *Ministère Public* v. *Guy Blanguernon* [1990] ECR I-83.
[63] De Witte 2011b: 39. Similarly, Dero 2006: esp 43ff, 49.
[64] Dehousse 1998: 20.
[65] Da Cruz Vilaça 2014: 23 ft 42.

Such an interpretation can be supported by decisions such as the 1990 case *Guy Blanguernon* where the Court of Justice stated:

> It must first of all be pointed out that, as the Court has consistently held, a Member State may not rely on the fact that other Member States have also failed to perform their obligations in order to justify its own failure to fulfil its obligations under the Treaty... In the legal order established by the Treaty, the implementation of Community law by the Member States cannot be made subject to a condition of reciprocity. Articles 169 and 170 of the Treaty provide the appropriate remedies in cases where Member States fail to fulfil their obligations under the Treaty.[66]

This understanding of the logic of *Dairy Products*, and the basis for the removal of retaliatory countermeasures within the European legal order, is not however a convincing one. The Article 169, 170, and 171 procedures could produce only a declaratory judgment, a finding – in the words of Article 171 – that "a Member State has failed to fulfil an obligation under this treaty". To be sure, Article 171 continues, the State "shall be required to take the necessary measures to comply with the judgment of the Court". But no solution was provided for the scenario where a State failed to "take the necessary measures" so required, as Simma, Gradoni and many others accurately stress.[67] It is in just such a scenario – where a state persists in failing to change their policy even after it has been condemned by authoritative dispute settlement procedures – that the possibility of justified use of countermeasures would ordinarily become salient in general international law and many international trade regimes.

Thus the Article 169, 170, and 171 procedures cannot provide an effective substitute for the possible use of countermeasure mechanisms within the European Treaties, any more than, say, allowing WTO members to be brought before the WTO dispute settlement institutions by other WTO members (or even, hypothetically, the WTO Secretariat) would be an effective substitute for the possible use of countermeasure mechanisms within the WTO system *after* a finding by those institutions that a WTO member is in default.[68] On these grounds, the Court's

[66] Case C-38/89 *Ministère Public* v. *Guy Blanguernon* [1990] ECR I-83.

[67] Similarly, Lecourt and Chevallier 1963.

[68] As the above examples demonstrate, brief discussions of the *Dairy Products* judgment in scholarly overviews of the European legal order sometimes tend to justify the principle contained in the Court's decision on the basis of the Article 169 and 170 compliance procedures, while the specialist and detailed scholarship on *Dairy Products*, more convincingly, comprehensively rejects the view that the availability of the Article 169 and 170 mechanisms could act as an effective substitute for the function of self-help

description, in *Dairy Products*, that the European legal order provided "the necessary procedures for taking cognizance of and penalising any breach of it" has been critically dissected: the Treaty of Rome did indeed provide "the necessary procedures for taking cognizance of" any breach, through a finding by the Court itself. The Treaty did not, however, appear to provide the necessary procedures for "penalising any breach of it". Gradoni and Tanzi go so far as to declare that the Court, in *Dairy Products*, referred to a "phantom" penalty mechanism – a penalty mechanism that did not then exist.[69]

Whatever the wording of *Guy Blanguernon* in 1990, however, the careful reader may have noted that the 1964 *Dairy Products* judgment itself did not justify the European legal order's rejection of international law-style self-help mechanisms associated by an explicit reference to the Article 169, 170, and 171 infringement procedures. In *Dairy Products*, the Court stated simply that the Treaty "establishes a new legal order which governs the powers, rights, and obligations of the said person, as well as the necessary procedures for taking cognizance of and penalising any breach of it. Therefore, except where otherwise expressly provided, the basic concept of the Treaty requires that the Member States shall not take the law into their own hands." It is readers of the Court's decision that have projected a restricted meaning of these words onto the text of the 1964 judgment. The "procedures for taking cognizance of and penalising any breach of" the Treaty that the "new legal order" had started to develop prior to November 1964, are often, and correctly, understood to go well beyond the infringement procedures set out in Articles 169, 170, and 171. The foundation of the European legal order's

countermeasures in enforcing treaty obligations. Lecourt and Chevallier's discussion of this issue in 1963, considered in Chapter 6 on *Van Duyn*, supports the view that the Article 169 and 170 procedures were no substitutes for inter-state reciprocity, but (in the absence of direct effect) would rather have prompted possible recourse to inter-state reciprocity mechanisms (Lecourt and Chevallier 1963). As for the wider literature on dispute resolution in international trade politics outside the European legal order, such as proposing reforms to the WTO, this author is unaware of any scholarship that argues that the necessity for a "last resort" recourse to inter-state retaliation as an enforcement mechanism could be eliminated by introducing mechanisms similar to those contained in Articles 169, 170, and 171 of the Treaty of Rome.

69 Gradoni and Tanzi 2008: 59. This observation was also made in immediate commentary on *Dairy Products*: see Kapteyn 1964–1965: 243.

rejection of any use of self-help countermeasures by the member states may be better found elsewhere.[70]

What other explanations can be advanced for the European legal order's rejection of any use of self-help countermeasures by the member states? Two tempting possibilities must swiftly be set aside. The first is the ability of the European Court, under the revision of the Article 171 procedure as provided for by the Treaty of Maastricht, to allow the Court to impose financial penalties, i.e. "fines", on member states that fail "to take the necessary measures to comply with the judgment of the Court".[71] In relation to wider discussions of the role of self-help countermeasures in general international law and international trade politics, it should be said that fines are frequently considered ineffective substitutes for the possibility of countermeasures because the payment of fines, unlike the imposition of inter-state countermeasures by other states, requires the cooperation of the target state, which may not always be forthcoming.[72] In relation to the European Economic Community in any event, the availability of such a fining mechanism cannot be considered a substitute for the possibility of self-help countermeasures because the fining mechanism was only introduced in 1994, and only applied for the first time in 2001, while the Court of Justice ruled out any use of international law countermeasures several decades earlier, in the *Dairy Products* decision of 1964.

The second tempting explanation would be that the use of self-help countermeasures within the European legal order can be considered ruled out by the entry into force of the Treaty of Amsterdam, which

[70] Judgments such as *Van Gend en Loos* itself demonstrate that the Court of Justice was certainly capable of explicitly referring to the Article 169 and 170 procedures when it so wished. The Court did not do so when discussing "procedures for taking cognizance of and penalising any breach of" Community law in *Dairy Products*. Instead it made a much more general statement about the European legal order. Similarly, the scope of the Court's judgment in *Dairy Products* should not be limited to our understanding of the legal options that may have been available to Luxembourg and Belgium in this particular dispute, that is to say an action against the Council or the Commission. Again, the Court made a much more general statement about the European legal order.

[71] From the text of the revised article: "If the Member State concerned fails to take the necessary measures to comply with the Court's judgment within the time limit laid down by the Commission, the latter may bring the case before the Court of Justice. In so doing it shall specify the amount of the lump sum or penalty payment to be paid by the Member State concerned which it considers appropriate in the circumstances. If the Court of Justice finds that the Member State concerned has not complied with its judgment it may impose a lump sum or penalty payment on it."

[72] See the discussion of the NAFTA Side Agreements later in this chapter.

provided that the member states could agree to suspend the Treaty rights of a member state that has committed "a serious and persistent breach" of the principles of "liberty, democracy, respect for human rights and fundamental freedoms, and the rule of law".[73] This mechanism, unlike the declaration that financial penalties must be paid, can be considered a "true" countermeasure, one that can be imposed on a state by its treaty partners even without the cooperation of a targeted state.[74] There must be some question over whether this "nuclear option" mechanism could provide an effective substitute for the proportionate countermeasures usually envisaged by general international law or the "suspension of equivalent concessions" retaliation mechanisms provided for in many international trade regimes. In relation to the development of the European Economic Community in any event, this mechanism cannot be considered a substitute for the possibility of self-help countermeasures because it was only introduced in 1999, while, again, the Court of Justice first ruled out any use of international law-style countermeasures some thirty-five years earlier, in the 1964 *Dairy Products* judgment. It is for these reasons that Gradoni has argued that the Court banned the use of international law-style countermeasures in the European legal order long before the European legal order was furnished with the adequate sanctioning systems to replace them, and that the Court in its *Dairy Products* decision therefore "wagered on the spontaneous observance of the rules".[75]

We must mention one final alternative sometimes referred to in the literature. That is the argument that the European legal order must reject the use of self-help countermeasures because these would adversely affect individuals within the European states. As Weiler writes:

[73] Articles 7 TEU and 309 EC provide the Council with the power of sanctioning member states for serious and persistent violations of one or more of the principles mentioned in Article 6(1) TEU, i.e. "the principles of liberty, democracy, respect for human rights and fundamental freedoms, and the rule of law" (e.g. Simon 2000: 281–282). It is open to doubt whether this mechanism was established as, or could successfully function as, a routine compliance procedure for European law obligations vis-à-vis the member states, as opposed to a procedure to respond to the deterioration or collapse of democratic institutions within a member state, but a full discussion of this issue is outside the scope of this book.

[74] Thus with these provisions of the Treaty of Amsterdam, the Community has finally obtained a form of countermeasure, the coercive instrument that the Court had in 1964 ordered the states to set aside (Gradoni and Tanzi 2008: 59, similarly, Kapteyn et al. 2008: 74).

[75] Gradoni and Tanzi 2008: 59.

> Even in an extreme case in which a Member State failed to execute a judgment of the European Court, the recourse to countermeasures would inevitably affect individuals removed from the dispute, militating against the very notion of a "new legal order of international law. . . the subjects of which comprise not only the Member States but also their nationals".[76]

This sort of argument relies heavily on the unwelcome consequences attendant on any possible use of self-help countermeasures within a demanding trade-related treaty system. Examples of such countermeasures affecting "individuals removed from the dispute" are of course not hard to find in other trade regimes, whether traders in pastries and prepared soups caught up a Peruvian–Bolivian dispute over trade in bananas in the Andean Community, or traders in catfood and dishwashing machines caught up in a US–Mexican dispute over cross-border trucking services in NAFTA.[77] For that very reason, however, they do not provide a convincing answer to our question. After all, the problem of damage to the interests of unrelated individuals is widely acknowledged as an important drawback in the use of such mechanisms in international dispute settlement mechanisms more generally.[78] These methods are nevertheless resorted to *faute de mieux*, in full awareness of these problems, because no other mechanism provides an effective substitute, particularly for the most difficult situation where a state has clearly failed to fulfil their treaty obligations, even after a declaratory finding of failure to comply has been produced by authoritative treaty-based dispute settlement mechanisms.[79] A solution to the problems arising from the use of reciprocal or retaliatory countermeasures as an enforcement mechanism must demonstrate how the interests of state actors who would otherwise have incentives to resort to such instruments can be sufficiently effectively vindicated without the availability of these mechanisms.

[76] Weiler 1991: 2422 ft 42.

[77] Phelan 2015a: 850 ft 19, Phelan 2018.

[78] Discussion of the problems of the WTO's dispute settlement process are often motivated by damages to "innocent" "retaliation victims" in industries unrelated to the original dispute, e.g. Thies 2013: 1, Ruiz Fabri 2014: 165. Retaliatory measures imposed by the US against products imported from the EU in the WTO dispute over bananas have targeted such items as bath preparations, handbags, paperboard boxes, bed linen, and coffee makers (Thies 2013: 1, ft 4).

[79] Put another way, avoiding damage to the interests of individuals "removed from the dispute" can be considered a luxury item in trade-related dispute settlement. It can only be obtained where states have alternative means of effectively requiring their trading partners to fulfil their obligations that do not involve such damage.

There is, however, a straightforward answer to our question: how was the European legal order able to do without self-help countermeasures? The answer is that the direct effect and supremacy of European treaty obligations, and the sufficiently reliable automatic application of treaty obligations by national courts at the suit of private parties that has over time been derived from those doctrines, provides an instrument for the enforcement of treaty obligations that can allow states to comprehensively forgo any use of inter-state retaliation mechanisms.

Granting direct effect to treaty obligations addresses the problem that otherwise appears can only be addressed by the possibility of inter-state countermeasures. Recall that the most obvious scenario where inter-state countermeasures may be justified is one where a state persists in failing to change their policy even after it has been condemned by authoritative dispute settlement procedures. However, in the European legal order by virtue of the doctrine of direct effect, however, many judgments of the European Court are enforced by national courts, in litigation initiated by private parties within the context of the availability of the preliminary reference procedure. More generally, where national courts will reliably act to directly apply a treaty obligation in their national legal order, it removes the requirement for a state's compliance with its treaty obligations to be supported by threats of retaliation by the state's trading partners, because the decisions of treaty-based dispute settlement tribunals are no longer merely declaratory but instead embedded within the internal legal orders of the participating state.[80]

This argument can be supported in various ways. Let us start with a discussion of quite a different treaty regime in another continent. The North American Free Trade Agreement – NAFTA – is the regional trade and integration regime incorporating the United States, Canada, and Mexico.[81] The original trade agreement came to be supplemented by

[80] The essential relationship between the rejection of inter-state retaliation and individual rights in European law is not therefore that inter-state retaliation is rejected because it would damage the rights of individuals removed from the dispute, but rather that inter-state retaliation is rejected because the enforcement of European law obligations through the mechanism of individual rights before national courts, that is to say through direct effect, provides sufficient control over the internal policy-making of the member states that inter-state retaliation (with its associated disadvantages) is unnecessary to ensure the enforcement of demanding obligations.

[81] The first discussion by this author of the similarities between the European legal order and enforcement of the NAFTA Side Agreements by Canadian domestic courts appeared in an article the *European Law Journal*, on which this section draws (Phelan 2015c).

two Side Agreements containing obligations to "effectively" enforce their national laws in the areas of the environmental and labour respectively. The requirement for "effective" enforcement of national laws was potentially a demanding one, as it allowed international dispute settlement institutions to make an independent finding as to whether such national environmental or labour laws were being "effectively" enforced in the three NAFTA states, and further to specify a detailed "action plan" requiring a NAFTA state to remedy any defects identified. The obligations of these Side Agreements can be enforced through an international dispute settlement procedure, which culminates, should disagreements persist, in the possibility of a dispute settlement panel authorising the "loss of benefits" – that is, the imposition of trade retaliation – between one NAFTA member and another.[82]

That is, at least, the Side Agreements' dispute settlement procedure as it applies to complaints against the United States or Mexico. However, in the case of complaints against Canada, a different bargain was reached. Throughout the negotiations, Canadian policy-makers refused to accept any possibility that the Side Agreements would lead to any increased opportunities for the United States to impose trade sanctions against Canada. Instead they proposed, and United States policy-makers came to accept, that, on the one hand, the results of international dispute settlement under the Side Agreements would be enforced directly by Canada's Federal Court, and on the other, the United States would lose the right to impose trade sanctions as an enforcement mechanism. As Mayer writes, "The United States and Mexico agreed that in extreme cases of failure to enforce national law [in the manner required by the treaties], an international dispute panel could authorize trade sanctions. Canada, unwilling to allow the possibility, however remote, that international trade sanctions could be used against them . . . agreed instead to make the decisions of the international dispute panel enforceable in Canadian courts."[83] Domestic court enforcement of the Side Agreements in Canada was therefore an explicit intergovernmental bargain to remove enforcement through inter-state retaliation.

The role of domestic court enforcement as a means to remove self-help enforcement by states themselves was also noted in the early years of European legal integration. In early 1965, just a few months after the *Dairy Products* decision, then ECJ judge Robert Lecourt published a

[82] Hufbauer et al. 2003: 29.
[83] Mayer 1998: 166.

short paper entitled "The Judicial Dynamic in the Building of Europe" [*La Dynamique Judiciaire dans l'Édification de l'Europe*].[84] This analysis appeared in *France-Forum*, a Christian Democrat publication or "journal of ideas" affiliated with the *Mouvement Républicain Populaire* political party of which Lecourt had been a leading member. In this analysis, Lecourt offered an explanation and assessment of the development of the European legal order including the various judgments of the Court of Justice, drawing on comparisons of the role of law in the unification of states in France and Germany.

Starting by noting that the Treaty had not provided the European Community with a system of arbitration or a classical international court,[85] Lecourt offered the following justification of the Court of Justice's new and ambitious decisions, developing the logic step by step, and stitching passages drawn from the Court's judgments into his narrative:

> Therefore the Court was led to conduct a sort of x-ray analysis of the Treaties to discover the solution to certain legal cases. If it [the Court] therefore claimed that "contrary to ordinary international treaties" the Treaty of Rome had "instituted its own legal order, integrated into the judicial system of the member states", it was to observe that the Treaty imposes its obligations on all without exception (decision of 15 July 1964). . . . The result of this is that individuals can invoke a direct right to ensure the respect of the directly applicable provisions of the treaties. This right was disputed. But the Court finally observed that in instituting certain obligations in relation to individuals the Common Market should also inevitably confer on them "rights that enter into their judicial patrimony" (decision of 5 February 1963) and which should be protected by national courts.
>
> But a delicate problem emerged which would engage the future of the Community: *what is then the authority of the community law*[86] *in the face of national law?* The question is one of importance. To refuse the priority to community law would be to allow the possibility that courts would give preference to national law over it, which would then permit a simple national rule to deprive the treaties of their substance. By contrast, to affirm the superiority of the community law would lead to the question of

84 Lecourt 1965. The first discussion by this author of Lecourt's 1965 writing in *France-Forum* appeared in an article in the *International Journal of Constitutional Law*, on which this section draws (Phelan 2016c).

85 Lecourt 1965: 20.

86 In this context the expression "*loi commune*" used here by Lecourt refers to "community law", and we have translated it as such to avoid confusion with other meanings of "common law".

the legal value of a contrary national law. The future of Europe would depend on the Court's solution to this serious problem.

> ... To decide such a finding in respect of the Treaty, it was necessary to analyze its terms and spirit. That is what the Court did, in judging that the texts "make it impossible for the states, as a corollary, to accord precedence to a unilateral and subsequent measure over a legal system accepted by them on a basis of reciprocity". Otherwise the law derived from the Treaty would not be able to "vary from one state to another" without provoking prohibited discriminations or even putting the goals of the Treaty itself in danger". The law common to six states "could not be overridden by domestic legal provisions, however framed, without being deprived of its character as Community law and without the legal basis of the Community itself being called into question". No unilateral legal act of a state "can prevail against the Treaties" (decision of 15 July 1964) because the States "have renounced the ability to take self-help action to enforce their legal rights" (decision of 13 November 1964).[87]

The "decision of 15 July 1964" is *Costa* v. *ENEL*, the "decision of 5 February 1963" is *Van Gend en Loos*, and the "decision of 13 November 1964" is, of course, the *Dairy Products* judgment.

By linking passages from these Court judgments in this way, Lecourt's analysis did not merely suggest that these are three important decisions by the Court of Justice, or even that they constituted the three "most important" decisions that the Court had made by early 1965 – although that may perhaps be implied by Lecourt's discussion of these three judgments and no others. Rather Lecourt said something much more specific: the national courts must directly apply European legal obligations (*Van Gend en Loos*) and allow these to prevail over conflicting national law (*Costa*) *because* the member states have given up "self-help" forms of treaty enforcement (*Dairy Products*). Thus while leading scholarship often justifies *Dairy Products*' prohibition on the member states' resort to self-help enforcement by reason only of the availability of the Article 169, 170 and 171 procedures, here, in Lecourt's 1965 account, it is

[87] Lecourt 1965: 21–22 [emphasis and quotations marks as in the original]. To more closely follow the wording of the official English translation of *Commission* v. *Luxembourg & Belgium* the last sentence could be translated "the States 'have renounced the ability to take the law into their own hands'", a translation which, while suggestive, may obscure the connection to states' self-help methods of enforcing international law. Lecourt's words in French are "*dès lors que les États 'ont renoncé à se faire justice eux-mêmes' (arrêt 13 Novembre 1964)*". Note that the ECJ's judgment does not contain the exact phrase that Lecourt attributes to it: the ECJ's expression is "*l'économie du traité comporte interdiction pour les états membres de se faire justice eux-mêmes*".

the principle established in the *Dairy Products* judgment that justifies the European law doctrines of direct effect and supremacy, and the role they grant to national courts and individuals in the enforcement of European law.

Lecourt's analysis strongly supports the view that one objective of the Court's judgment in *Dairy Products* was to rule out the possibility of "self-help" forms of retaliatory enforcement *between* the European member states. After all, the direct effect and supremacy of European law in the national legal order would not be particularly relevant to resolving disputes where the European institutions themselves were alleged to have failed to fulfil their duties, which was the specific topic directly under dispute in the *Dairy Products* litigation. It was certainly relevant to justifying the removal of inter-state countermeasures as possible responses to violations by the member states, however.

Compared to much subsequent scholarship on *Dairy Products*, Lecourt's 1965 paper is notable for omitting any discussion of a possible "fall back" on the use of inter-state countermeasures by the European member states. To be sure, the discussion is a brief one. Nonetheless Lecourt's focus is unmistakably on how the European legal order was being "built up", that is, moved forward, by *Dairy Products* together with *Van Gend en Loos* and *Costa* v. *ENEL*.

This 1965 article in *France-Forum* is not the only time that Lecourt connected direct effect with the Community's rejection of self-help and reciprocity behaviours by the European states. As we have seen in Chapter 2 on *Van Gend en Loos*, Lecourt's 1991 contribution to the *Festschrift* for Jean Boulouis argued that *Van Gend en Loos* and *Costa* taken together had the important impact of preventing the European states from reverting to reciprocity-type behaviours, using as justification other states' non-implementation of Court of Justice judgments prompted by the Article 169 and 170 procedures.[88] We can also see the juxtaposition of state self-help and direct effect/individual rights in the final paragraph of Lecourt's 1968 speech marking the tenth anniversary of the Treaty of Rome. There Lecourt spoke about "the reappearance, at a new level, of the unifying role of a court with jurisdiction to ensure a uniform rule of law that has so often been seen in the history of nations". Lecourt summarized the progress of European law as Europe's "peoples making substantial progress in civilization between themselves

[88] Lecourt 1991.

by renouncing self-help methods of obtaining justice through obedience to a law that is agreed in common",[89] and concluded with the declaration that "Community law . . . does not present itself merely as the 'rules of the game' for the relationships between state powers, but as an authentic law, applied judicially, to which the individual person can himself have access".[90] The possibility of falling back on reciprocity approaches to treaty enforcement in a scenario where an Article 171 finding by the Court was ineffective, and the alternative solution of relying on the direct effect of European law, was also considered in a 1963 article by Lecourt (with his *attaché* Chevallier), which will be discussed in Chapter 6 on *Van Duyn*.[91] Lecourt's 1965 discussion of the links between *Van Gend en Loos*, *Costa* v. *ENEL* and the *Dairy Products* case is however, as far as we are aware, the only occasion when Lecourt explicitly mentions the *Dairy Products* judgment when drawing these connections.[92]

The example of the NAFTA Side Agreements demonstrated that the substitutability of national court enforcement and inter-state retaliation is recognized outside the European Treaties, while the writings of Lecourt demonstrate that the substitutability of national court enforcement and inter-state retaliation was recognized by perhaps the most influential judge on the Court at the time of these judgments. Taken together, this is powerful support that *Dairy Products* should be understood as the equal, and partner, of *Van Gend en Loos* and *Costa*. Indeed, given the intense rejection of any form of self-help activities shown in Lecourt's own legal scholarship, above all in his 1931 doctoral dissertation on French property disputes – including in its concluding discussion of

[89] In the original French: "*que des peuples réalisent entre eux un substantiel progrès de civilisation en renonçant à se faire justice à eux-mêmes pour se plier à une loi arrêtée en commun*" [underline added].

[90] Lecourt 1968a: 22–23.

[91] Lecourt and Chevallier 1963.

[92] *Dairy Products* is also discussed in *L'Europe des juges*, where it is used to support claims that exceptions from fundamental European obligations must be clearly provided for and strictly interpreted, and that nothing else (e.g. failure by the Commission in its obligations) can dispense with these obligations, and that Community objectives are so fundamental that they entail a prohibition on states resorting to self-help to secure their legal rights (Lecourt 1976a: 27, 245, 247). As noted in Chapter 3 on *Costa* v. *ENEL*, Lecourt's discussion of the logic of the supremacy doctrine in *L'Europe des juges* includes a reference to its role in preventing self-help using wording similar to that in *Dairy Products*: "As elementary as it may be, the principle according to which no one may take the law into their own hands [*nul ne peut se faire justice à lui-même*] is a fundamental principle of the Community, as it is of all authentic civilization" (Lecourt 1976a: 285).

how states within international organizations should give up any form of self-help just as private individuals do within states – it seems possible that Lecourt's commitment to the principle contained in *Dairy Products* was the fundamental reason for his support for the doctrines announced in all three of the Court's most fundamental and creative judgments.[93]

Compared to previous scholarship on the *Dairy Products* judgment, this approach disagrees with those scholars who overlook the case entirely, or include it merely as one of many rejected defences to the Article 169 actions before the Court. Instead, the principle first declared in *Dairy Products* lies at the heart of the European legal order and the meaning of direct effect. It is in agreement, on the other hand, with those that argue that neither the Article 219 obligation setting out the exclusive jurisdiction of the Court of Justice nor the Article 5 obligation to ensure the fulfilment of the obligations arising from the Treaty of Rome have much direct relevance to *Dairy Products*.[94] In the case of Article 219, the Court did not rely on this principle in the *Dairy Products* case, or in the long stream of similar judgments that followed, nor would the wording of Article 219 have conflicted with any decision of the Court that had, in an alternative world, authorized the possible use of retaliatory measures

[93] Lecourt 1931, Phelan 2017. A persistent rejection of any form of self-help in resolving property disputes is the central motif of Lecourt's doctoral dissertation, which concludes with a discussion of how international law and international organizations must strive to eliminate any use of self-help in international politics in the same way that domestic law has eliminated the use of self-help by individuals within the state. As Lecourt wrote, "This is the prohibition for anyone, individuals or nations, to resort to violence and the obligation of all to present themselves before a judge instead of taking the law into their own hands. This principle has always developed in parallel with the Law. Where the Law extends to a new area, this principle appears as a foundation. Its extension is so great and so visible that although once limited to conflicts between private interests it now constantly tends to apply to disputes between peoples. This has been reflected in international law especially during the last decade through the creation of international organizations: the League of Nations, international conferences (disarmament conferences), international tribunals that play an important role in the relations between States. These organizations are called upon to prohibit violence among peoples and nations just as it has long been forbidden to individuals to take the law into their own hands [*à interdire aux nations, comme il est depuis longtemps défendu aux particuliers, de se faire justice à soi-même*]" (Lecourt 1931: 284–285). The doctrine advanced by the Court in *Dairy Products* was therefore not explicitly set out in the Treaty of Rome but was an essential element in the early legal scholarship of one of the Court's then most influential judges.

[94] E.g. Simma and Pulkowski 2006: 518, Gradoni 2008: 239–240, Gradoni and Tanzi 2008: 49, 55 ft 77, 55ff,

between the European states.[95] As for the Article 5 obligation, this provision itself did not ensure that states would fulfil their treaty obligations with enough automaticity to act as a substitute for inter-state countermeasures. In a most practical sense, above all, if a reformer wished to banish the role of inter-state retaliation from a trade-related treaty system, amending the treaty to include obligations such as those set out in Articles 5 and 219 of the Treaty of Rome would not obviously comprise sufficiently powerful ingredients to put an end to this practice.

Instead, the more direct connection of *Dairy Products* is with the Court's famous judgments in *Van Gend en Loos* and *Costa*. This can be supported by the closeness in time between these three cases; by the similarities of language between these decisions, including *Dairy Products*' reference to the Community's "new legal order", which must recall *Van Gend en Loos* and the doctrine of direct effect, rather than the Articles 169 and 170 compliance procedures;[96] by the repeated identification

[95] Note that the 1951 Treaty of Paris, which established the European Coal and Steel Community, provided in Article 87 for a prohibition on the use of alternative means of dispute settlement, similar to that contained in Article 219 of the Treaty of Rome ("The High Contracting Parties agree not to avail themselves of any treaties, conventions or agreements existing among them to submit any difference arising out of the interpretation or application of the present Treaty to a method of settlement other than those provided for herein"). That prohibition did not prevent Article 88 of the Treaty of Paris providing for the possibility of reprisals (authorized by the High Authority and subject to the control of the Court of Justice) by the other member states against a state found to be delinquent with respect to its ECSC obligations. The essential point is that reprisals or countermeasures are mechanisms to pressure a state to fulfil its treaty obligations to the benefit of its treaty partners, and so any discussion of how these have been removed from the European legal order must rest on the identification of some other mechanism for fulfilling this necessity. Article 219 of the Treaty of Rome does not fulfil that function, but the doctrine of direct effect can do so. Article 219 may at best have had a subsidiary role to play in attempting to prevent the possibility that other international tribunals, such as the International Court of Justice, might become involved in adjudicating disputes between the member states, given that these tribunals might have been more open to the use of inter-state countermeasures between the European states than was the Court of Justice in line with *Dairy Products*. We can add that judge Lecourt's brief discussion in 1963 of using classical reciprocity mechanisms to enforce the Treaty of Rome in the case of the ineffectiveness of an Article 171 finding did not raise the Article 219 issue at all, arguing instead for alternative mechanisms to ensure the effectiveness of the Treaty particularly litigation by private individuals before national courts (Lecourt and Chevallier 1963: 276).

[96] In his contemporary comment on *Dairy Products*, Kapteyn argued that the Court rejected Belgium and Luxembourg's claim of international law-style reciprocity because the rights established by the Treaty of Rome were to be enjoyed not only between the six states, but also their nationals, "according to the judgments of *Van Gend en Loos* and *Costa-ENEL*" (Kapteyn 1964–1965: 243). See also an emphasis on the similarity of wording between

by judge Lecourt of direct connections between the principles of these cases;[97] and by the recognition that domestic court enforcement can logically serve as a substitute for enforcement of treaty obligations through inter-state retaliation and reciprocity. The substitutability of inter-state retaliation and domestic court enforcement mechanisms can be demonstrated both by the design of other treaty regimes such as the NAFTA Side Agreements, as well as reformist debates about removing the harms arising from countermeasures in retaliation-based trade regimes, most prominently (as we will show in Chapter 5 on the Court's 1972 *International Fruit* judgment) debates on the possible direct effect of GATT/WTO obligations or dispute settlement outcomes within the European legal order.

This approach also differs from the leading specialist scholarship on *Dairy Products*, as outstanding and original as these contributions have been. We believe the more important focus must be on the Community legal order's historical development rather than any hypothetical future "fall back". The Community's rejection of inter-state retaliation must be connected with the Community's rejection of unilateral safeguard mechanisms, and both these distinctions embedded much more firmly in and among the collected great judgments of the Court of Justice in the 1960s and 1970s.[98] The reference, in *Dairy Products*, to the Treaty providing the "necessary procedures" for "penalising any breach" of Community law must be understood as specifically including the enforcement role of national courts in line with Court's then recently declared direct effect and supremacy doctrines.[99] Indeed, no discussion of the limits of the declaratory judgments of the Court of Justice can take place without an extensive engagement with the creation and growth of the direct effect doctrine, and the benefits it confers not just on individual litigants within their own states but on businesses and policy-makers in other member

Dairy Products and *Van Gend en Loos* in Kapteyn and VerLoren Van Themaat 1973: 26, ft 4, Rossa Phelan 1997: 71, and Louis 2013: 208.

97 Lecourt and Chevallier 1963, Lecourt 1965, Lecourt 1968a, Lecourt 1976a: 285, Lecourt 1991.

98 Note Advocate General Roemer's emphasis in *Dairy Products* on the use of the Treaty's general safeguard mechanisms as an alternative mechanism for Luxembourg and Belgium to address their difficulties. The issue is a wider one, however, as it would be impossible to effectively insist on the Community's rejection of inter-state retaliation if the Community was unable to similarly effectively prohibit the unilateral adoption of safeguards by the member states, and the effective means of control in both cases was the establishment and development of the direct-effect doctrine.

99 Lecourt 1965.

states of the Community. The Court therefore can only be said to have "wagered on the spontaneous observance of the rules" in *Dairy Products* if this is understood to mean that the Court wagered on the success of *Van Gend en Loos* and *Costa* – a bet that the Court has surely won.[100] Finally, the Court of Justice did not ban the possible use of countermeasures within the European Community before it had announced an effective substitute mechanism: *Van Gend en Loos* was decided more than a year in advance of the *Dairy Products* judgment.

By integrating in this way the decisions on the new role of individuals that the Court was creating with the decisions on old state practices the Court was rejecting, it becomes apparent how each supports the other. In 1993, some years before he became prime minister of the United Kingdom, Tony Blair propelled himself to prominence by calling for policies that were "tough on crime, tough on the causes of crime", and indeed prohibitions on unwelcome behaviours can often be most successful in combination with attempts to remedy ills at their root.[101] In *Dairy Products*, the Court of Justice had ruled out any possible use of inter-state retaliation or international law-style reciprocity. In *Van Gend en Loos* and *Costa* v. *ENEL*, however, the Court had already created doctrines which, by embedding Community law within the national legal orders, served to avoid scenarios that would most blatantly prompt the use of such mechanisms. In 1963 and 1964, therefore, the judgments of the Court of Justice were "tough on inter-state countermeasures" and "tough on the causes of inter-state countermeasures" within the newly developing European legal order.

Although the direct effect of treaty obligations can be an effective substitute for inter-state reciprocity and retaliation, it is important to recognize that not all European law obligations receive direct effect in the national legal orders, either in legal theory or in practice. The situation that has so exercised scholarly debate in the *Dairy Products* scholarship – that the infringement procedure provided by Articles 169, 170, and 171 of the Treaty could result in a finding by the Court that a state had failed to fulfil its European Treaty obligations, but that the state nonetheless might persist with the policies contrary to their European Treaty obligations – was, and indeed is, not an entirely hypothetical one. The dispute in the 1979 *Sheep Meat* case provides an excellent example of the limits

[100] Gradoni and Tanzi 2008: 59.
[101] Tony Blair, *New Statesman*, 29 January 1993.

of direct effect as a substitute for inter-state retaliation. We will postpone our discussion of this issue until our chapter on that judgment (Chapter 8).

In this chapter we have argued that the principle announced in the *Dairy Products* is closely connected with the Court's other great decisions in the early 1960s. We will now go on to show that the Community's rejection of international law-style reciprocity and retaliation, and the relationship between that principle and national court enforcement of treaty obligations, can also shed new light on many of the Court's landmark judgments in the 1970s including *International Fruit*, *Van Duyn*, *Simmenthal*, and *Sheep Meat*.

5

International Fruit, 1972

No Direct Effect for the GATT

The Case before the Court

This case came to the European Court of Justice as a request for a preliminary ruling under the Article 177 procedure by a court of the Netherlands, the College van Beroep voor het Bedrijfsleven, the Netherlands Appeals Court in economic matters, based in The Hague.[1]

Four fruit importing companies, including *International Fruit Company*, had begun a dispute with the Produktschap voor Groenten en Fruit, the Dutch competent authority for implementing rules on the import of fruit and vegetables. The dispute concerned the importation of apples from outside the Community, in circumstances where the Commission, in order to prevent serious disturbances of the Common Market, had adopted temporary measures to suspend imports of apples from outside the Community through a system of licences. The Dutch court put two questions to the Court of Justice. The first asked whether the validity of measures adopted by the institutions of the Community, a ground for a preliminary reference under the Article 177 procedure, also referred to the validity of such measures under "international law other than the law of the Community". The second asked whether, if the first question was answered affirmatively, Regulations adopted by the European Commission that restricted the importation of apples from third countries were "invalid as being contrary to Article XI of the General Agreement on Tariffs and Trade (GATT)".

The Advocate General, Henri Mayras, began his analysis with a general survey of the relationship between the Community and the GATT. He noted that the Community acted as a "block" in its commercial relations with the outside world, with the individual member states no longer entitled to independent commercial relations with third countries.

[1] Cases 21–24/72 *International Fruit Company* v. *Produktschap voor Groenten en Fruit* [1972] ECR 1219.

The Community itself "must not, however, practise autarky". On the contrary, its commercial policy was "liberal" and the member states were legally bound, in particular under the multilateral GATT. How then, asked Mayras, can conflicts between the GATT and Community law, if they arise, be resolved?

Here Mayras began by stating that

> it is undeniable that since the Community is itself subject to international law and is obliged by law to observe the agreements which bind it, the question whether measures adopted by its institution are compatible with such agreements falls within the Court's jurisdiction . . . There is no doubt that just as the Court has constantly asserted the precedence of Community law over the national laws of the Member States it cannot but recognize the superiority of the Community's international agreements over the measures adopted by its institutions.

However, that point alone did not settle both the Dutch court's questions. Mayras moved on to considering whether

> Since before these regulations may be held invalid under provisions of the law of an international agreement, . . . the applicants must, in the context of Article 177, . . . be able to rely on rights deriving from them. In other words, those provisions must have a *direct effect* within the Community.

Here Mayras referred to the Court of Justice's famous decisions in *Van Gend en Loos*, *Costa* v. *ENEL* and the 1966 *Lütticke* case, which had established the principle of direct effect of Community law within the national legal orders.

Mayras then considered whether the provisions of Article XI of the GATT were directly applicable within the Community and asserted that there were "serious reasons for thinking that this is not the case". He considered that by the GATT, the states "undertook only to adopt a particular line of conduct in commercial policy, that they did not intend to establish directly applicable rules which the national courts must protect, even when it conflicts with a domestic law" and that the GATT's dispute settlement procedures "also exclude the concept of direct effect". While GATT's general rules were "enacted in a form which is often peremptory and precise", they were subject to "so many instances of derogation" that "in the end the Agreement is characterized by a very flexible application . . . there is nothing unconditional about those rules".

Mayras added that the GATT's system of dispute settlement was also revealing, including the fact that a GATT member wishing to complain about a measure adopted by another member that conflicted with the

GATT could, at first, only make representations or proposals to which the other party "shall give sympathetic consideration". If no satisfactory adjustment is obtained, the matter may be referred to the members of the GATT who, after investigation and consultation, may authorize the affected contracting parties to "suspend their obligations towards the party responsible". Finally, the latter – the party responsible for the GATT violation – may advise the GATT's secretary-general of its intention to withdraw from the General Agreement. From this analysis, Mayras found that the provisions of the General Agreement, the machinery of which is dependent on the consensus of the contracting parties, do not concern individuals as such. More particularly, Article XI contains exceptions and derogations that in practice have been shown to leave the GATT member states, and, *mutatis mutandis*, the Community effectively as a member of the GATT "a discretion such as excludes individuals from being able to derive from the principle established by that article subjective rights capable of being profitably invoked before a court".

On 12 December 1972, the Court of Justice answered the Dutch court's questions. The Court answered first that its jurisdiction to give rulings on the validity of measures adopted by the institutions of the Community extended to all grounds capable of invalidating those measures. The Court then considered the nature of the GATT, and found that the provisions of that agreement had the effect of binding the Community:

> [I]n so far as under the EEC Treaty the Community has assumed the powers previously exercised by Member States in the area governed by the General Agreement, the provisions of that Agreement have the effect of binding the Community.

The Court then stated that

> It is also necessary to examine whether the provisions of the General Agreement [the GATT] confer rights on citizens of the Community on which they can rely before the courts in contesting the validity of a Community measure. For this purpose, the spirit, the general scheme and the terms of the general agreement must be considered. This agreement, which, according to its preamble, is based on the principle of negotiations undertaken on the basis of "reciprocal and mutually advantageous arrangements" is characterized by the great flexibility of its provisions, in particular those conferring the possibility of derogation, the measures to be taken when confronted with exceptional difficulties and the settlement of disputes between the contracting parties.

Here the Court referred to provisions of Article XXII of the GATT, which emphasized the role of consultation between GATT members in respect to all matters affecting the operation of the GATT. The Court also considered the dispute settlement procedures set out in GATT's Article XXIII, which included consultations between the GATT contracting parties, and the possibility of authorizing GATT members "to suspend the application to any others of any obligations or concessions under the General Agreement".

"Finally," explained the Court,

> where by reason of an obligation assumed by the General Agreement . . . , some producers suffer or are threatened with serious damage, Article XIX gives a contracting party power unilaterally to suspend the obligation and to withdraw or modify the concession, either after consulting the contracting parties jointly and failing agreement between the contracting parties concerned, or even, if the matter is urgent and on a temporary basis, without prior consultation.

The Court concluded: "Those factors are sufficient to show that, when examined in such a context, Article XI of the General Agreement is not capable of conferring on citizens of the Community rights which they can invoke before the courts." Accordingly, the validity of the Commission's Regulations could not be affected by Article XI of the GATT.

Related Cases

International Fruit was the first, and seminal, judgment by the Court of Justice on the relationship between the European legal order and the GATT. There have been many subsequent judgments addressing this relationship, but the Court has persisted with the logic of *International Fruit* throughout, including in its judgments relating to GATT's successor in the 1990s, the World Trade Organization.

During the GATT period, judgments of the Court repeatedly denied that provisions of the GATT should be enforceable by private parties before European courts, including in the *Schlüter* judgment in the year after *International Fruit*.[2] The Court persisted in the denial in direct effect, based on the reasoning of *International Fruit*, even when the party seeking direct effect of GATT obligations was a European member state, as in the 1994 decision *Germany* v. *Council*.

[2] For a list of judgments see e.g. Mendez 2013: 176–177 fts 3–5. The Court did however allow the European Commission to use the infringement proceedings to challenge actions by the member states that breached a GATT Agreement (Case C-61/94 *Commission* v. *Germany (IDA)* [1996] ECR I-3989).

After the coming into force of the Uruguay Round Agreements in 1995, the General Agreement on Tariffs and Trade was placed under the umbrella of the new World Trade Organization (WTO). Among the important changes introduced in the global trade regime was a new Dispute Settlement Understanding, which offered much more "automatic" progress through a sophisticated dispute settlement process than its GATT-era predecessor. After mandatory consultations between the complaining WTO member and the respondent, hearings can be held before a panel, which issues a decision about whether the "measures" of the WTO member in question are consistent or not with their WTO obligations. The decision of the panel may be appealed to the WTO's Appellate Body. Where a panel or the Appellate Body, as the case may be, concludes that the measure under dispute is inconsistent with a member's WTO obligations, it can recommend that the member concerned bring the measure into conformity with that agreement. If the WTO member in question does not change its measures to make them consistent with their WTO obligations, it may agree compensation with the complaining party. Finally, as a "last resort", if the defaulting state does not change its measures within a "reasonable period of time" and no compensation is agreed with the complaining party, the institutions provided by the Dispute Settlement Understanding may authorize the complaining party to "suspend the application to the Member concerned of concessions or other obligations under the covered agreements". In more straightforward terms, this "suspension of concessions" involves the complaining WTO member imposing retaliatory trade sanctions against the defaulting WTO member.[3]

The essentials of the WTO's dispute settlement system – except the Appellate Body – were in fact already present within the dispute settlement system included in the original postwar GATT agreements, but those original agreements required the GATT members to agree by consensus to progress various stages of the process, in effect empowering the GATT member under complaint to object to the formation of a panel or the authorization of the suspension of concessions against themselves.[4] One of the crucial changes from the GATT to the WTO's Dispute

[3] "Understanding on Rules and Procedures Governing the Settlement of Disputes", Annex 2 of WTO Agreement. The full set of procedures involved in the settlement of disputes between WTO members is of course more extensive than is set out here in brief, and the reader is referred to the Understanding for a complete account.

[4] Barton et al. 2006: 69.

Settlement Understanding, therefore, was a change to this consensus requirement, allowing for panels to be formed and for the suspension of concessions to be authorized even without the consent of the WTO member whose measures were subject to the complaint.

The WTO dispute settlement system therefore differs in several important ways from the dispute settlement system provided for under the postwar GATT. After the Uruguay Round agreement came into force, a series of disputes came before the Court of Justice questioning whether the principles underlying the relationship between the European legal order and the GATT, as first set out in *International Fruit*, would continue now that the GATT had been subsumed into the WTO. The Court of Justice, however, has adopted a similar approach to the WTO as to the postwar GATT. In the 1999 judgment *Portugal* v. *Council*, for example, the Court found that the transformation of the GATT into the WTO did not alter the relationship between WTO obligations and the European legal order: WTO obligations, just as with GATT obligations, did not enjoy direct effect.[5]

More recent cases have often involved attempts by litigants to draw a distinction, as the Court of Justice described it in the 2008 judgment *FIAMM and Fedon*,

> between the "direct effect" of the WTO rules imposing substantive obligations and the "direct effect" of a decision of the [WTO dispute settlement institutions], asserting that it should be open to individuals to have the legality of the conduct of the Community institutions reviewed by the Community courts in the light of the [WTO dispute settlement institutions'] decision itself.[6]

A number of cases have considered, and rejected, this claimed distinction, finding that the outcomes of the WTO's dispute settlement processes lacked direct effect in the same way as the obligations contained in the WTO treaties. In the 2005 case *Van Parys*, the Court refused to find that policies adopted by the European institutions following a finding of inconsistency with WTO obligations by the WTO dispute settlement institutions should be considered as intending to implement a specific WTO obligation, capable of justifying an exception to the impossibility of relying on WTO rules before the Community courts.[7] In *FIAMM and*

[5] Case C-149/96 *Portugal* v. *Council* [1999] ECR I-8395.

[6] Cases C-120 & 121/06 *FIAMM and Fedon* v. *Council and Commission* [2008] ECR I-6513.

[7] Case C-377/02 *Van Parys* v. *BIRB* [2005] ECR I-1465. Eeckhout 2011: 363–364.

Fedon, where the litigants were firms whose exports to the US had suffered as a result of WTO-authorized retaliatory tariffs by the US against the EU in the WTO 'Bananas' dispute, the Court of Justice found that the EU was not obliged to offer compensation to firms whose interests had been damaged by trade retaliation employed by WTO members following a finding by the WTO's dispute settlement institutions that the EU had failed to fulfil its WTO obligations.[8]

The Court's logic in these decisions was similar to that of *International Fruit*, emphasizing the continuing flexibility of dispute settlement processes and escape clause mechanisms within the WTO. In *Van Parys*, the Court of Justice claimed that if it were to accept that Community courts had a direct responsibility for ensuring that Community law complies with WTO rules, it would deprive the Community's legislative or executive bodies of the "discretion" enjoyed by similar bodies in other WTO members. In the *FIAMM and Fedon* dispute, Advocate General Maduro described the Court of Justice's rejection of the possibility that WTO obligations could be relied upon before the European courts as motivated by a desire to avoid restrictions on the "political freedom" that the WTO agreements allow the contracting parties.[9]

The Court has acknowledged the possibility of exception to its general policy of denying direct effect to provisions of the GATT and WTO. This exception applies where the Court of Justice has found that European legislation expressly refers to specific provisions of GATT or WTO law or the EU intends to implement an obligation assumed in the context of the GATT or WTO.[10] In *Fediol* v. *Commission*, the Court, while reiterating its emphasis on the GATT's broad flexibility, found that GATT provisions formed part of the rules to which a Regulation allowing complaints by European firms against "illicit commercial practices" referred, noting that the Regulation defined "illicit commercial practices" by reference to their incompatibility with international law, and referred expressly to the GATT in its preamble. In *Nakajima* v. *Council*, the Court held that provisions of the international Anti-Dumping Agreement could be used in a claim of incompatibility, because the EU intended to satisfy that

[8] For discussion of the US–EU WTO dispute over the EU's import arrangements for bananas, see Devereaux et al. 2006, Dani 2010: 305–306.

[9] *FIAMM and Fedon*, Opinion of Maduro AG; see also the discussion of "scope for political manoeuvre".

[10] Thies 2013: e.g. 20, 22, 25–26. Case 70/87 *Fediol* v. *Commission* [1989] ECR 1781, Case C-69/89 *Nakajima* v. *Council* [1991] ECR I-2069.

agreement by enacting its own anti-dumping legislation. The legislation had therefore been given effect in the European legal order.

Finally, we should add that the European legal order's refusal to grant direct effect to the obligations of the GATT and WTO was not matched by a similar refusal to grant direct effect to provisions of the Community's other trade agreements. From the 1970s onwards, the Court regularly found that provisions contained in the Community's preferential trade agreements with developing countries and in "association agreements" with European states could benefit from direct effect within the European legal order, and thus enforcement by private parties before European domestic courts, including the European Court of Justice.[11]

Analysis and Context

The *International Fruit* judgment, and the Court's consistent denial of direct effect to provisions of the GATT, are regularly discussed in prominent texts and surveys of the development of European law, although not always included in scholarly collections of the Court's famous judgments.[12] The decision of the Court is explained on the grounds that the provisions of the GATT were insufficiently precise and unconditional,[13] and that the GATT was too "political", with few hard and fast legal rules.[14] Many surveys place *International Fruit*, and the other GATT and WTO judgments of the Court, within the context of the Court's wider range of decisions granting or denying direct effect to international agreements.[15] The case is also used to demonstrate that the European Community assumed the powers of the member states within the GATT, using a doctrine of "functional" succession.[16]

Leading scholarship is largely in agreement on the influence and impact of the Court of Justice's judgment in *International Fruit*. There is intense disagreement, however, over the merits of the decision.

[11] E.g. Mendez 2013: 107–173.

[12] *International Fruit* is not included as a "basic community case" or a "classic of EU law" in either Rudden and Rossa Phelan 1997 or Maduro and Azoulai 2010.

[13] Craig and de Búrca 2015: 362.

[14] Schütze 2016: 112.

[15] Kuilwijk 1996.

[16] Craig and de Búrca 2011: 263, Dashwood et al. 2011: 942, Schütze 2016: 289. Also to demonstrate that the Court's jurisdiction to review the validity of Community acts extends to all grounds capable of invalidating them, including incompatibility with a rule of international law (Arnull 2006: 125 ft 185).

In fact, the Court's *International Fruit* judgment has frequently been condemned on various grounds. The result, of course, deprived private parties of the right to have the Community's GATT obligations enforced by courts, including the Court of Justice, within the Community; that is to say, it denied the direct effect of GATT provisions within the Community legal order.[17] *International Fruit* was therefore a judgment where, according to its critics, the Court put in question the meaning of binding international law.[18] As for the reasoning of *International Fruit*, many have objected to the Court of Justice's terse judgment for a variety of reasons, including for the symmetry of the way that the Court (and the Advocate General) approached the relationship between Community law and the domestic legal order, and that between Community law and international norms, by insisting that direct effect would apply only where rules of international law were capable of creating rights of which interested parties may avail themselves in a court of law;[19] for overlooking the fact that many GATT provisions were in fact clear, precise, and unconditional;[20] and for its exaggeration of the flexibility of the GATT's safeguard and derogation mechanisms, compared to those within the Community.[21]

The Court's approach to *International Fruit* can be defended, however. In a detailed study of the legal effects of the EU's international agreements Mendez has claimed that it is hard to deny the essential logic of

[17] It may help to clarify that it is widely accepted that the GATT/WTO agreements themselves do not require that their obligations be granted direct effect within the legal orders of GATT/WTO members. The question for the Court of Justice in *International Fruit* and similar cases is therefore whether European law itself required that GATT/WTO obligations be granted direct effect within the European legal order, even if the GATT/WTO agreements did not require direct effect. The Court itself did not use the language of "direct effect" in *International Fruit* but the Advocate General used the language of rights conferral and direct effect synonymously. The Court's later decisions described GATT provisions as not having direct effect for the reasons previously stated in *International Fruit* (Mendez 2013: 179 ft 11). Note that the Court later also denied that the member states themselves could require the review of European norms in the light of the Community's GATT obligations (Case C-280/93 *Germany* v. *Council* [1994] ECR I-4793).

[18] Schermers 1975: 80. Cf. Scott 1995: 149: "In the absence of direct effect, GATT has proved ineffectual as part of Community law, and its primacy largely illusory."

[19] Schermers 1975: 80–81. Schermers would have preferred the Court to apply all rules of international law binding upon the Communities.

[20] Including specifically Article XI GATT at issue in *International Fruit*, e.g. Petersmann 1983: e.g. 402, 435, Petersmann 1985: 459–460, Petersmann 1995: 1167.

[21] E.g. Petersmann 1983: 432–434, Kuilwijk 1996: 133–135, 342.

the Court's reasoning. The Community did differ from the GATT in its approach to safeguards. The best comparator within the Community for GATT's XIX safeguard mechanism was the general safeguard mechanism provided by Article 226 of the Treaty during its long transitional period, and Article 226 (unlike similar GATT safeguards)[22] did indeed prohibit the unilateral adoption of safeguard measures, requiring the member states to seek prior approval by the European Commission, as the Court had confirmed in the 1961 *Pork Products* judgment.[23] Furthermore, the GATT system as a whole has widely been recognized as characterized by considerable flexibility, of which these safeguard mechanisms are only one example. Other examples of the GATT's flexible nature include its system of waivers under Article XXV(5) and the possibility for GATT members to unilaterally withdraw previously agreed concessions under Article XXVIII.[24] This flexibility extends to the GATT's dispute settlement arrangements, which placed a premium on negotiated, diplomatic approaches to resolving trade disputes, even as they became somewhat more developed over time.[25] Thus even where the GATT contained provisions that appeared clear, precise, and unconditional, which might therefore benefit from the doctrine of direct effect, for the Court this was undermined by the spirit and general scheme of the GATT.[26] Finally, there is of course a great deal of meaning to binding rules of international

[22] The unilateral availability of safeguards and escape clauses to trading partners within the GATT has continued into the WTO era. One recent study of flexibility mechanisms in the WTO states that "Countries actually have at their disposal an arsenal of flexibility measures which, it turns out, are largely unconstrained. Member states are free to resort to these provisions at their whim" (Pelc 2016: 7).

[23] Mendez 2013: 185. The comparative study of treaty safeguard mechanisms by Paolo Gori, influential *référendaire* to judge Trabucchi at the Court of Justice, had explicitly contrasted Article XIX of the GATT with Community safeguard mechanisms (such as Article 226) that required prior authorization (Gori 1967: 36–38). Note that the Article 226 safeguard mechanism in the Treaty of Rome did not entail the compensatory or retaliatory responses envisaged in the GATT Article XIX safeguard mechanism.

[24] Mendez 2013: 186–187. The Court's short judgment did not elaborate the various potential derogation provisions in the GATT, but they were certainly there.

[25] Mendez 2013: 188–189. Here we might add that the GATT's dispute settlement system did indeed (as the Court described them) provide for the possibility of reciprocal or retaliatory responses by one GATT member vis-à-vis another, a clear distinction from the Community legal order as the Court had developed it since the 1964 *Dairy Products* judgment.

[26] Mendez 2013: 181.

law even in the absence of strict judicial enforceability by international and domestic courts.[27]

The political environment of *International Fruit* may also explain the Court's decision. After all the direct effect of Community law in the national legal orders was still relatively new, and not uncontested, so the Court would have been bold to add the direct effect of the global trade agreement as well.[28] Furthermore, the GATT's provisions on agriculture might not have been fully compatible with the Community's then developing Common Agricultural Policy, so direct enforcement of these GATT provisions within the European Community would likely have led to considerable political resistance.[29] For Mendez, therefore, while the Court's description of the GATT is curt and uninformative, the reasoning of *International Fruit* reflects both an accurate account of the essential features of GATT, including its distinctions from the Treaty of Rome, and the Court's awareness of the formidable political considerations in the background of the case.[30]

The approach of this book, of course, is to situate the great decisions of the Court of Justice within the context of problems commonly facing other trade-related treaty regimes, above all those related to the enforcement of, and escape from, demanding treaty obligations. As the leading case specifying the relationship between the global trade regime and the European legal order, a discussion of *International Fruit* is obviously compatible with that agenda. Many scholars use the doctrines that the Court of Justice applies to ensure the effective enforcement of European law within the European member states as a yardstick to measure the adequacy or otherwise of the doctrines that the Court of Justice applies to ensure the effective enforcement of GATT obligations within the EU as a member of GATT, now WTO. Such scholarship uses *Van Gend en Loos* to evaluate *International Fruit*.[31] Here, however, we will take a

[27] Mendez 2013: 180.

[28] Mendez 2013: 195.

[29] Mendez 2013: 192. For a later example, the Commission and Council strenuously contested the GATT's capacity to form a general review criterion at the time of the 1994 *Bananas* ruling (Case C-280/93 *Germany* v. *Council* [1994] ECR I-4793).

[30] Mendez 2013: 190, 191.

[31] E.g. "By making a distinction between the internationally binding character of the General Agreement and its lack of internal effects, the Court adopted a dualistic attitude which contrasts strangely with the attitude it recommends to the national courts on the question between Community law and national law" (Waelbroeck 1974: 623).

different track and instead use *International Fruit* to better understand *Van Gend en Loos*.

We will do this in two different ways. We will first demonstrate that in its persistent refusal, since *International Fruit*, to allow direct effect to the obligations of the GATT, now WTO, the Court has chosen to allow enforcement instead to take place within the context of the possibility of self-help trade retaliation, that is to say the "suspension of concessions" granted within the GATT trade regime. We will then return to *International Fruit* to discuss the text of that judgment side by side with *Van Gend en Loos* and to show that *International Fruit* provides a more compelling justification of the logic of direct effect of treaty obligations than the justification provided in *Van Gend en Loos* itself.

As we have explained above, the Court of Justice has repeatedly justified its refusal to grant direct effect to GATT and WTO obligations on the grounds of the "flexibility" of these treaty systems, and the "political discretion" and "freedom of manoeuvre" they grant to the GATT member states and, *mutatis mutandis*, the EEC, later the EU, as a participating member.[32] When examined in more detail, however, the "political discretion" and "freedom of manoeuvre" enjoyed by the EU's political bodies as a result of these Court of Justice decisions to deny direct effect to WTO obligations in the European legal order consist, fundamentally, of a freedom to maintain policies inconsistent with the EU's WTO obligations even if this provokes WTO-authorized trade retaliation from other WTO members. This is especially true in the recent cases relating to claims that decisions of the WTO dispute settlement institutions should enjoy direct effect in the European legal order.

In the *FIAMM and Fedon* case, the Court of Justice explained that:

> It should be remembered that the decisive factor here is that the resolution of disputes concerning the WTO law is based, in part, on negotiations between the contracting parties. Withdrawal of unlawful measures is admittedly the solution recommended by WTO law, but other solutions are also authorized. . . . The Court also pointed out that to accept that the Community courts have the direct responsibility for ensuring that Community law complies with the WTO rules would effectively deprive the Community's legislative or executive organs of the scope for manoeuvre enjoyed by their counterparts in the Community's trading partners. . . .

[32] The first discussion by this author of the debate over the direct effect of WTO obligations within the European legal order appeared in an article the *European Law Journal*, on which this section draws (Phelan 2015c).

> [T]he considerations linked to the nature of the WTO agreements and to the reciprocity and flexibility characterizing them continue to obtain after such [a finding by WTO dispute settlement institutions that WTO rules have not been complied with] and after the reasonable period of time allowed for its implementation has expired. The Community institutions continue in particular to have an element of discretion and scope for negotiation vis-à-vis their trading partners with a view to the adoption of measures intended to respond to the [WTO's] ruling or recommendation, and such leeway must be preserved.

The key to reading this passage is to recall that the "reasonable period of time" allowed by the WTO's Dispute Settlement Understanding is the period during which WTO members may change their policies to make them compatible with their WTO obligations, after a finding that a member's measures are inconsistent with their WTO obligations, but *before* the WTO dispute settlement institutions will authorize trade retaliation by other WTO members. By insisting that the European institutions should enjoy "leeway" *after* the reasonable period of time has expired, the Court of Justice is therefore stating that the European institutions have leeway to behave in ways that may provoke WTO-authorized retaliation by their trading partners.

Advocate General Maduro's opinion in *FIAMM and Fedon*, rejecting the claim that the decisions of WTO dispute settlement institutions should enjoy direct effect in the European legal order, sets the logic out more explicitly:

> [T]he Community remains free to make the political choice to lay itself open initially to retaliatory measures authorized by the [WTO institutions]. ... [E]ven after the authorization and adoption of retaliatory measures, an important place continues to be reserved at all events for negotiation between the parties to the dispute.[33]

The debate about these decisions in legal scholarship is also straightforward in understanding that the grant of direct effect to decisions of the WTO dispute settlement institutions in the European legal order would be a mechanism designed to remove the possibility that EU-based firms may suffer losses as a result of WTO-authorized trade retaliation by the EU's trading partners. Eeckhout's discussion provides a good example:

[33] *FIAMM and Fedon*, Opinion of Maduro AG.

> Where it comes to establishing direct effect [in favour of the outcome of WTO dispute settlement processes], it is indeed meaningful that compensation and retaliation are temporary alternatives to compliance. ... If direct effect were given, those alternatives would no longer be at the EU's disposal. Any private party could then claim the illegality of EC (or Member State) legislation, cutting off all attempts at buying time for amendment or for settlement. The Hormones Directive [an EU law that the WTO dispute settlement institutions had found to be inconsistent with the EU's WTO obligations, and that lead to WTO-authorized trade retaliation by the United States against the EU] would no longer be on the books if there were direct effect.[34]

The debate over the direct effect of WTO obligations in the European legal order makes especially clear that granting direct effect to the outcomes of treaty-based dispute settlement institutions should be understood as an alternative to enforcement through retaliatory trade sanctions. After all, scholars – like Eeckhout – and litigants often point directly to the damage inflicted by particular retaliatory trade sanctions, such as those involved in the bananas or beef-hormones disputes, in their advocacy for the direct effect of decisions of WTO dispute settlement institutions within the EU.

For the Court, therefore, and for the scholarly community discussing the Court's decisions denying European court enforcement to GATT and WTO obligations within the European legal order, the doctrine of direct effect has clearly been understood as a mechanism to remove retaliation and "suspension of concessions" processes from an international trade regime, and thus an alternative solution to one of the most pressing international collective action problems of trade politics. Indeed, it would be both rare and odd to read a discussion of whether to grant direct effect to WTO dispute settlement outcomes within the European legal order where it is not explicitly recognized that potential retaliation by another WTO member against the EU is one of the central issues being addressed.

International Fruit, and the stream of judgments on the GATT and WTO that confirmed and developed the principles first established in

[34] Eeckhout 2002: 93. For discussion of the US–EU WTO dispute over the EU's ban on the sale of beef containing certain growth hormones, see Devereaux et al. 2006. Discussion of granting direct effect to WTO obligations, or to decisions of the WTO's dispute settlement institutions, as a means to remove the effects of WTO-authorized trade retaliation is widespread in this literature (e.g. Griller 2000, Cottier 2002, Tancredi 2004, Dani 2010, Eeckhout 2011, Thies 2013).

International Fruit, therefore suggest, once again, that the direct-effect doctrine should be understood as a mechanism to remove inter-state retaliation from a trade treaty regime.[35] With that in mind, we now turn to what we can learn about *Van Gend en Loos* from a detailed comparison with *International Fruit*.

Given the usual neglect of the politics of safeguards and escape mechanisms in discussions of the direct-effect doctrine within the European legal order, we should start by noting that the issue under litigation in *International Fruit* was the Community's use of safeguard mechanisms – "temporary measures" to suspend imports of apples from outside the Community – which adversely affected firms were attempting to curtail through the invocation of the direct-effect doctrine. Rights for individuals to enforce treaty obligations before domestic courts were therefore directly connected in *International Fruit* with efforts to tame the unilateral activation of safeguard mechanisms in international trade politics, just as it was in scholarly discussion of the Court's 1961 *Pork Products* judgment.[36]

The connections between these cases go much further however. In *Van Gend en Loos*, the Court granted what came to be known as direct effect to obligations derived from the European treaties, whereby private individuals could directly enforce these obligations through litigation in the domestic courts of the European member states. In *International Fruit*, the Court denied direct effect to obligations derived from the GATT, so that private individuals could not directly enforce these obligations through litigation in the domestic courts of the European Community, including the Court of Justice. *International Fruit* can therefore be used as a mirror to *Van Gend en Loos*, providing a way to identify the Court's approach to direct effect by identifying what was entailed in the Court's understanding of the *lack* of direct effect.

This use of *International Fruit* is reinforced by the similarity of the structure and argument in these two judgments. In the essential part of *Van Gend en Loos*, the Court set out to address the question whether Article 12 of the Treaty of Rome had "direct application in national law

[35] In the case of *International Fruit* and similar disputes of course a decision by the Court to grant direct effect to the GATT obligations of the European institutions would only serve to have reduced or removed the use of GATT- or WTO-related trade retaliation against the European Community. It would not have removed all use of such enforcement mechanisms among the wider membership of the GATT or today's WTO.

[36] Cf. Wenner 1962.

in the sense that nationals of member states may on the basis of this article lay claim to rights which the national court must protect". The Court went on: "To ascertain whether the provisions of an international treaty extend so far in their effects it is necessary to consider the spirit, the general scheme and the wording of those provisions." The Court then offered its reasons for supporting the direct effect of Article 12, referring to various aspects of the Treaty and its dispute settlement systems, in particular mentioning, first, that the Preamble to the Treaty of Rome refers not only to governments but to peoples; second, that the Community had established "institutions endowed with sovereign rights" and that the nationals of the member states participated in the European institutions through the European Parliament and the Economic and Social Committee; third, that the Article 177 procedure (permitting "preliminary references") demonstrated that Community law had an authority that could be invoked by nationals before national courts; fourth, that the wording of Article 12 contained a clear and unconditional prohibition, that is to say a negative, not a positive, obligation; fifth, that the obligation in Article 12 was not conditional upon a positive legislative measure enacted under national law; and sixth, that the procedures available in Articles 169 and 170 of the Treaty did not mean that individuals cannot plead these obligations, should the occasion arise, before a national court. The Court therefore concludes, "It follows from the foregoing considerations that, according to the spirit, the general scheme and the wording of the Treaty, Article 12 must be interpreted as producing direct effects and creating individual rights which national courts must protect."

The structure of the essential part of *International Fruit* is almost identical. The Court set out to address the question, "whether the provisions [Article XI] of the General Agreement confer rights on citizens of the Community on which they can rely before the courts in contesting the validity of a Community measure". The Court went on: "For this purpose, the spirit, the general scheme and the terms of the General Agreement must be considered." The Court then offered its reasons for denying direct effect to Article XI of the GATT, referring to various aspects of the Agreement and its dispute settlement systems, in particular mentioning, first, that the Preamble to the Agreement demonstrates that the GATT is based on the principle of negotiations undertaken on the basis of "reciprocal and mutually advantageous arrangements"; second, that the GATT is "characterized by the great flexibility of its provisions" particularly in relation to safeguards and the settlement of disputes; third, that the GATT's dispute settlement measures included the authorization of contracting parties to suspend the application to any others of any obligations or concessions under the General Agreement; and fourth, that, where producers are facing serious damage from imports, the GATT allows its members unilaterally to suspend their obligations, even, if the case is urgent, without prior consultation. The Court therefore concluded, "Those factors are sufficient to show that, when examined in such a context, Article XI of the General Agreement is not capable of conferring on citizens of the Community rights which they can invoke before the courts."

The structure of the Court's arguments in the *Van Gend* and *International Fruit* judgments therefore match each other step by step, moving from a statement of the question, to a declaration that an analysis of the "spirit" of each treaty is required to answer it, an assessment of reasons relevant to understanding the "spirit" of these treaties, before finally drawing the conclusion that the treaty provisions in question created, or did not create, rights can individuals can invoke before the courts. The parallel structure of *Van Gend en Loos* and *International Fruit* is set out in Table 1.

Now if the structure of the Court's argument is obviously similar in both judgments, it is equally apparent that the particular reasons that the Court gave for its conclusions in the two judgments did not so closely parallel each other. The justifications that the Court advanced for denying direct effect to Article XI of the GATT in the European legal order are not the same-but-opposite of the justifications that the Court advanced for granting direct effect to Article 12 of the Treaty of Rome in the national legal orders. In *Van Gend en Loos*, the Court emphasized aspects of the institutional structure created by the European Treaties and the specific characteristics of Article 12 as a treaty provision, but in *International Fruit* these parallel aspects of the institutional structure of the GATT and the specific characteristics of Article XI as a treaty provision were not the focus of the judgment.

It may surprise some readers that the Court did not justify the lack of direct effect of GATT obligations within the European legal order in *International Fruit* (or, for that matter, later justify the lack of direct effect of outcomes of WTO dispute settlement institutions in decisions such as *Van Parys* in 2005) by referring to the lack of a preliminary reference procedure, similar to the Article 177 procedure of the Treaty of Rome, to offer interpretative guidance to the internal courts of GATT/WTO members in their application of treaty obligations. After all, the

Table 1 Van Gend en Loos *and* International Fruit *Compared*

	Van Gend en Loos, 1963	*International Fruit*, 1972
The Question	"The first question of the *tariefcommissie* is whether article 12 of the treaty has direct application in national law in the sense that nationals of member states may on the basis of this article lay claim to rights which the national court must protect."	"It is . . . necessary to examine whether the provisions of the General Agreement confer rights on citizens of the Community on which they can rely before the courts in contesting the validity of a Community measure."
The Process	"To ascertain whether the provisions of an international treaty extend so far in their effects it is necessary to consider the spirit, the general scheme and the wording of those provisions."	"For this purpose, the spirit, the general scheme and the terms of the General Agreement must be considered."
Reasons:	In favour of direct effect to provision of the Treaty of Rome: (1) The Preamble: "The objective of the EEC treaty, which is to establish a common market, the functioning of which is of direct concern to interested parties in the community, implies that this treaty is more than an agreement which merely creates mutual obligations between the contracting states. This view is confirmed by the preamble to the treaty which refers not only to governments but to peoples."	In favour of the denial of direct effect to provision of GATT: (1) The Preamble: This agreement which, according to its preamble, is based on the principle of negotiations undertaken on the basis of "reciprocal and mutually advantageous arrangements". (2) The GATT is "characterized by the great flexibility of its provisions, in particular those conferring the possibility of derogation, the measures to be taken when confronted with exceptional difficulties and the settlement of conflicts between the contracting parties".

Table 1 (*cont.*)

	Van Gend en Loos, 1963	*International Fruit*, 1972
	(2) Institutions: "[T]he establishment of institutions endowed with sovereign rights the exercise of which affects member states and also their citizens. The nationals of the states are brought together in . . . the European Parliament and the Economic and Social Committee." (3) The task assigned to Court of Justice under Article 177 confirms that "Community law has authority which can be invoked by nationals before courts and tribunals. The conclusion to be drawn from this is that the community constitutes a new legal order of international law for the benefit of which the states have limited their sovereign rights, albeit within limited fields, and the subjects of which comprise not only member states but also their nationals." (4) "The wording of article 12 contains a clear and unconditional prohibition which is not a positive but a negative obligation." (5) "This obligation, moreover, is not qualified by any reservation on the part of states which would	(3) Dispute settlement measures include the authorization of contracting parties to suspend the application to any others of any obligations or concessions under the General Agreement and, finally, in the event of such suspension, the power of the party concerned to withdraw from that agreement. (4) Safeguard measures: "Finally, where by reason of an obligation assumed under the General Agreement. . . , some producers suffer or are threatened with serious damage, article XIX gives a contracting party power unilaterally to suspend the obligation and to withdraw or modify the concession, . . . even, if the matter is urgent and on a temporary basis, without prior consultation."

Table 1 (*cont.*)

	Van Gend en Loos, 1963	*International Fruit*, 1972
	make its implementation conditional upon a positive legislative measure enacted under national law." (6) "The fact that articles [169 and 170] of the treaty enable the commission and the member states to bring before the court a state which has not fulfilled its obligations does not mean that individuals cannot plead these obligations, should the occasion arise, before a national court, any more than the fact that the treaty places at the disposal of the commission ways of ensuring that obligations imposed upon those subject to the treaty are observed, precludes the possibility, in actions between individuals before a national court, of pleading infringements of these obligations."	
Conclusion	"It follows from the foregoing considerations that, according to the spirit, the general scheme and the wording of the treaty, article 12 must be interpreted as producing direct effects and creating individual rights which national courts must protect."	"Those factors are sufficient to show that, when examined in such a context, Article XI of the General Agreement is not capable of conferring on citizens of the Community rights which they can invoke before the courts."

preliminary reference procedure is often correctly associated with the doctrine of direct effect in many understandings of the development of the European legal order, and appeared to be an essential part of the Court of Justice's reasoning in *Van Gend en Loos*. The question of whether a treaty provision should enjoy direct effect, however, is separate and distinct from whether a treaty system provides a communicating link connecting national courts with the interpretations of treaty obligations produced by a treaty-based dispute settlement tribunal. Many treaty provisions have been found to enjoy direct effect in the absence of any such preliminary reference procedure within the treaty in question. As we have seen, the Court itself has repeatedly found that obligations contained in the Community's preferential trade agreements with developing countries and in association agreements with European states may enjoy direct effect even in the absence of such preliminary reference procedures.[37] It is true, of course, that a preliminary reference procedure better prevents national courts in different states from adopting divergent interpretations of common treaty obligations, perhaps under the influence of national legal, economic, and political circumstances, and therefore enhances the domestic court's use of the direct-effect doctrine. However, treaty provisions are regularly however granted direct effect even without such mechanisms, so it is not surprising that the Court in *International Fruit* failed to emphasize, or even mention, the GATT's lack of a preliminary reference procedure.

As for the specific nature of Article 12 of the Treaty of Rome, the Court in *Van Gend en Loos* emphasized that this provision was a "clear

[37] Indeed, the Court of Justice has allowed the direct effect of provisions of these agreements even in the face of criticism from member states that these agreements also contained flexible or unilateral safeguard instruments and "political" dispute settlement mechanisms. In Cases 104/81 *Kupferberg* [1982] ECR 3641 and C-192/89 *Sevince* [1990] ECR I-3461, for example, the Court of Justice had declared that the presence of flexible safeguard clauses was not in itself sufficient to prevent the direct effect of provisions of EU agreements. These divergences have been the cause of scholarly discussion about how consistent, and also how wise, the Court has been in its decisions granting or denying direct effect to obligations derived from the whole universe of EU agreements. See e.g. Kuilwijk 1996 and Mendez 2013 for full-length treatments offering contrasting perspectives, with Kuilwijk questioning the Court's refusal to apply direct effect to provisions of the GATT and Mendez questioning some of the Court's decisions to grant direct effect to agreements other than the GATT. Within the narrower if vitally important scope of the Court's decisions relating to the possible direct effect of obligations derived from the GATT/WTO, however, the Court has been consistent both in its denial of direct effect and in its justification of this denial on the basis of the flexibility and negotiated nature of GATT/WTO relationships and dispute settlement.

and unconditional prohibition", a "negative obligation", and therefore "ideally adapted to produce direct effects in the legal relationship between Member States and their subjects". The Court added that its implementation was not "conditional on a positive legislative measure enacted under national law". As was discussed in Chapter 2 on *Van Gend en Loos*, the Court's emphasis on these aspects of Article 12 was not a sure guide to its decision-making in its subsequent judgments on the scope of the direct-effect doctrine, as the Court came rather quickly to grant direct effect to provisions of the European treaties that were less clear than Article 12, that contained positive, rather than negative, obligations, and that were apparently conditional on a "positive legislative measure enacted under national law".[38]

The Court's judgment in *International Fruit* further confirms the relative unimportance of the specific aspects of particular treaty provisions in the Court's jurisprudence on the scope of direct effect. Here the provision of the GATT that the Court was considering, Article XI, concerned the general elimination of quantitative restrictions and, just like Article 12 of the Treaty of Rome, contained a "clear and unconditional prohibition", a "negative obligation", and one that was "not conditional on a positive legislative measure enacted under national law", all the characteristics that the Court had used to find Article 12 of the Treaty of Rome "ideally adapted to produce direct effects in the legal relationship between Member States and their subjects".[39] Nonetheless, the Court declined to find that Article XI of the GATT was ideally adapted to produce direct effects in the same way.

From this we should draw the conclusion that the Court's reasoning about the possible direct effect of treaty provisions rested considerably on the Court's understanding of the treaty systems *as a whole*, that is, whether the Treaty of Rome, or as the case may be, the General Agreement on Tariffs and Trade, should be considered a suitable treaty for its provisions to be granted direct effect within its participating members.[40] To be sure, even if a treaty system is considered to be capable of producing direct effects, there remains the question of whether particular provisions of that treaty, or of its legislative instruments, are suitable, in terms of clarity and so on, to produce direct effects or not. The decisive

[38] E.g. Craig 1992.
[39] Petersmann 1985: 459–460.
[40] Cf. Mendez 2013: 181.

criterion however, as the Court's decisions show, is the design of the treaty system as a whole.

If the lack of a preliminary reference procedure was not a relevant criterion for the Court, and if the specific features of the treaty provision in question would have appeared to support a grant of direct effect to Article XI of the GATT just as to Article 12 of the Treaty of Rome, then the burden of justifying the direct effect of Community law in *Van Gend en Loos* must fall on the remaining elements of the judgment. Some of these are not very persuasive, however.

In *Van Gend en Loos*, the Court stated that the Treaty establishes a "Common market, the functioning of which is of direct concern to interested parties in the Community". But the same logic applies to the GATT, which established an important multilateral trading system, the functioning of which was of direct concern to interested parties within members of the GATT. The Court also referred to various institutional aspects of the European Treaties. In *Van Gend en Loos*, for example, the Court referred to the participation of the nationals of the member states in the European Parliament and the Economic and Social Committee. These institutional arrangements certainly distinguish the European Treaties from those of the GATT and, later, the WTO. It strains credulity however to believe, for example, that the existence of the Community's otherwise insignificant Economic and Social Committee was really a foundation stone of the Court's *Van Gend en Loos* judgment. The Court's reference to the Community's "establishment of institutions endowed with sovereign rights" is perhaps more compelling in the context of the European Commission but the judgment advances little specific connection between the Commission's powers and the grant of individual rights to the nationals of the member states. It is noteworthy that while much has been made of these institutional features as justification for direct effect in *Van Gend en Loos*, little or no effort was made in the *International Fruit* judgment to refer to the more limited institutions of the GATT to justify the Court's then rejection of direct effect. Neither, for that matter, does the absence in the GATT of prominent features of the Treaty of Rome, such as the Article 189 provision for direct application of Regulations relied on by the Court in *Costa* to justify the priority of directly effective Community law before domestic courts, appear to have been relevant to the Court's decision on the direct effect of the GATT.

In both *Van Gend en Loos* and *International Fruit*, the Court also discussed the text of the preambles to the international agreements at issue. In *Van Gend en Loos* the Court noted that the Preamble of the

Treaty of Rome refers "not only to governments but peoples", while in *International Fruit* the Court noted that the Preamble to the GATT referred to "reciprocal and mutually advantageous arrangements". These preambles are certainly distinct, and the Court drew an important aspect of its justification for *Van Gend en Loos* from the Treaty of Rome's address to the "peoples of Europe". Nonetheless, it is hard to see this expression in the Treaty's Preamble, standing almost alone, as a persuasive justification for the remarkable legal consequences that the Court drew from it. It is a platitude of international agreement-making that the beneficiaries of treaties include "peoples" as well as "governments". More importantly, resting our understanding of *Van Gend en Loos* largely on the Preamble's reference to the peoples of Europe is one of the reasons why that judgment is so elusive and frustrating, because it fails to connect its new role for individuals with a sufficiently detailed vision for Community law as a general system. The distinctive role for private individuals and national courts in the enforcement of the European Treaties would have important consequences for actors other than litigating individuals and national courts, above all for firms and state policymakers, but the Court did not set those out with any clarity or specificity. It is hardly surprising that scholars continue to criticize the inadequacy of the judgment or are tempted to rewrite it more convincingly.[41]

In short, particularly when viewed in comparison with *International Fruit*, the reasoning presented in the Court's *Van Gend en Loos* judgment is less than compelling. The text of *Van Gend en Loos* may have been well suited to influencing national governments, courts, scholars, lawyers, and litigants over the subsequent decades. Its success in those terms cannot be denied. As a clear justification for the Court's decision to make direct effect the driving doctrine of the European legal order, however, the text of *Van Gend en Loos* must be considered a failure. That failure is derived from the decision's focus on specific features of Article 12, and a phrase in the Treaty's Preamble, when the Court appears in fact to have had a conception of the European legal order that went far beyond these specific features, and from the decision's focus on sometimes trivial aspects of the European institutional arrangements, rather than the more profound ways in which the European legal order, as the Court would develop it, would come to differentiate itself from other forms of treaty-based dispute settlement. The Court's failure to elaborate the essential

[41] For criticisms of *Van Gend en Loos* and *Costa*, see e.g. Malenovský 2013: esp. 43, Somek 2017. An extensive rewrite is set out in Weiler 2003.

logic of direct effect in *Van Gend en Loos* has contributed to widespread and persistent confusion about possible justifications for the essential doctrines of the European legal order that has lasted to this day.

The reasons provided by the Court in *Van Gend en Loos* are not, of course, the only way of justifying the Court's decision to grant direct effect to Article 12 and eventually many other provisions of the Treaty of Rome and other obligations derived from the European treaties. *International Fruit* allows us to see that there could be others.

In *International Fruit*, the Court wrote:

> It is necessary to examine whether the provisions of the General Agreement confer rights on citizens of the Community on which they can rely before the courts in contesting the validity of a Community measure.
>
> For this purpose, the spirit, the general scheme and the terms of the General Agreement must be considered.
>
> This agreement ... is characterized by the great flexibility of its provisions, in particular those conferring the possibility of derogation, the measures to be taken when confronted with exceptional difficulties and the settlement of conflicts between the contracting parties. ...
>
> If any contracting party should consider "that any benefit accruing to it ... is being impeded as a result of", inter alia, "the failure of another contracting party to carry out its obligations under this agreement", Article XXIII lays down in detail the measures which the parties concerned, or the contracting parties acting jointly, may or must take in regard to such a situation.
>
> Those measures include, for the settlement of conflicts, ... authorizing certain contracting parties to suspend the application to any others of any obligations or concessions under the General Agreement and, finally, in the event of such suspension, the power of the party concerned to withdraw from that agreement.
>
> Finally, where by reason of an obligation assumed under the General Agreement... , some producers suffer or are threatened with serious damage, Article XIX gives a contracting party power unilaterally to suspend the obligation and to withdraw or modify the concession, ... even, if the matter is urgent and on a temporary basis, without prior consultation.
>
> Those factors are sufficient to show that, when examined in such a context, Article XI of the General Agreement is not capable of conferring on citizens of the Community rights which they can invoke before the courts.

Now this discussion of the logic of flexibility in the GATT regime is admirably clear and frank – much clearer and franker, in fact, than the Court ever was about the equivalently essential features of its own, Community, legal order. If we take the Court's characterization of a treaty system that does not enjoy direct effect in *International Fruit* and use that wording, suitably reversed, to characterize a treaty system such as the Treaty of Rome that *does* enjoy direct effect we could get something like this – amendments to the text are signalled by underlining or strikethrough text.

> It is necessary to examine whether the provisions of the Treaty of Rome confer rights on nationals of the member states on which they can rely before the national courts . . .
>
> For this purpose, the spirit, the general scheme and the terms of the Treaty of Rome must be considered.
>
> This agreement . . . is characterized by the great rigidity of its provisions, in particular those conferring the possibility of derogation, the measures to be taken when confronted with exceptional difficulties and the settlement of conflicts between the contracting parties.
>
> If any contracting party should consider "that any benefit accruing to it . . . is being impeded as a result of", inter alia, "the failure of another contracting party to carry out its obligations under this agreement", the Treaty lays down in detail the measures which the parties concerned, or the contracting parties acting jointly, may or must take in regard to such a situation.
>
> Those measures do not include, for the settlement of conflicts, . . . authorizing . . . contracting parties to suspend the application to any others of any obligations under the Treaty . . .
>
> Finally, where by reason of an obligation assumed under the Treaty. . . , some producers suffer or are threatened with serious damage, the Treaty provides a contracting party with no power unilaterally to suspend the obligation and to withdraw or modify the concession, . . . even if the matter is urgent . . .
>
> Those factors are sufficient to show that, when examined in such a context, the Treaty of Rome is ~~not~~ capable of conferring on nationals of the member states rights which national courts must protect.[42]

[42] This rewriting of *Van Gend en Loos* can be compared to that set out in Weiler 2003. We agree with Weiler's emphasis on explaining direct effect as part of "the bargain the Member-States have made" but believe this bargain can be advanced with much more specificity by drawing out the connection with the Community legal order's rejection of

This text – which we will call "*International Fruit* in reverse" – conveys the logic of direct effect in structuring the trade relationships between the member states in the European Economic Community rather better than the text of *Van Gend en Loos* itself. It focuses on Treaty of Rome as a whole, without a potentially misleading emphasis on aspects of Article 12. It is clear of trivia and platitudes. It connects the new litigation role for individuals, inspired in part perhaps by the Preamble's reference to the peoples of Europe, with a detailed vision for Community law as a whole, setting out the consequences for actors other than litigating individuals and national courts. Those consequences are, of course, a much more rigid and inflexible system of treaty enforcement, with considerable restrictions on mechanisms by which state policy-makers could derogate from their Treaty obligations, and a comprehensive rejection of any inter-state reciprocity or retaliation mechanisms.[43]

In *International Fruit*, it is fundamentally because the GATT allows unilateral use of safeguard and derogations mechanisms, and retaliatory suspension of obligations, that the GATT should not receive direct effect. Logically therefore if the GATT had rejected both unilateral use of

inter-state retaliation and unilateral safeguards. Weiler's rewriting of *Van Gend en Loos* also maintains the original judgment's emphasis on the fact that Article 12 was "clear and unconditional", "not a positive but a negative obligation", and so on, but these aspects of the judgment are more apt to confuse than clarify the essence of the direct-effect doctrine as it came to be developed by the Court. They are perhaps better removed in any revision exercise of this sort. Adapting the text of *International Fruit* also has the advantage of more closely using the Court's own words, albeit originally employed in another context. Note that on the approach to direct effect advanced here, with its emphasis on the Community's distinctive approach to safeguards, the Court's reference in *Van Gend en Loos* to "institutions endowed with sovereign rights" should be understood to include a reference to the European Commission's ability to authorize, or refuse to authorize, safeguard measures and derogations by the member states under Article 226 and similar provisions of the Treaty (cf. Gori 1967: 37–38, 71–72 connecting the European institutions' prior control of safeguards mechanisms with the Community's "new legal order" and its role for individuals). The reference to the powers and rights of the Community institutions in the text of *Van Gend en Loos* therefore should be understood to have similarities to the reference to the powers and rights of the Community institutions in the text of *Costa* v. *ENEL*, where the Court justified the supremacy doctrine by explaining that "applications by member states for authority to derogate from the treaty are subject to a special authorization procedure [such as set out in Article 226] which would lose their purpose if the Member States could renounce their obligations by means of an ordinary law".

43 This way of understanding direct effect matches judge Lecourt's 1965 explanation that Community law must be integrated into the judicial system of the member states because the Treaty of Rome "imposes its obligations on all without exception" (Lecourt 1965: 21). By contrast, the ready availability of exceptions, as in the GATT, stands contrary to the logic of direct effect.

safeguard and derogation mechanisms and retaliatory suspension of obligations, the Court's reasoning would have allowed direct effect.[44] With this in mind, the logic of *International Fruit* again indicates a connection between the Court's 1963 declaration of direct effect in *Van Gend en Loos* and the Court's 1964 rejection of self-help retaliation within the European legal order in *Dairy Products.* Indeed, the logic of direct effect as set out in *International Fruit* is much more intimately connected to the principles established in the Court's *Dairy Products* and *Pork Products* judgments *considered as a linked pair* than to, for example, the inspiration drawn from provisions in Articles 177 and 189 for the preliminary reference procedure and the direct applicability of Regulations, or for that matter the Court's understandings of the autonomy and uniformity of Community law. In *International Fruit*, the logic of the relationship between self-help, safeguards, and direct effect is on open display, all these other aspects to one side.[45]

[44] As has been discussed in Chapter 1 on *Pork Products* and Chapter 4 on *Dairy Products*, a comprehensive rejection of inter-state retaliation and unilateral safeguard mechanisms is in fact one of the great distinctions of the European legal order in comparison with other trade treaty systems.

[45] *International Fruit* links the doctrine of *direct effect* to questions of inter-state retaliation and unilateral safeguard mechanisms, and so do many subsequent scholarly discussions of the possibility of direct effect for GATT or WTO obligations within the European legal order. In *Costa*, however, the reader will remember that it is the *supremacy* doctrine that the Court of Justice links with the Treaty of Rome's rejection of unilateral safeguard mechanisms, and in *L'Europe des juges* Lecourt associates the *supremacy* doctrine with both the Treaty's rejection of unilateral safeguard mechanisms and the European legal order's rejection of self-help (Lecourt 1976a: 285). As we have explained, however, the complete mechanism for removing inter-state retaliation and unilateral safeguards from a trade treaty involves both granting the direct effect of treaty provisions and protecting that direct effect from contrary national law, even though this is not necessarily clearly stated in any single Court decision. *International Fruit* therefore discusses the potential direct effect of GATT obligations as if a related supremacy question does not arise, while the famous decisions of the Court of Justice in 1963 and 1964 discuss the direct effect and supremacy doctrines in somewhat artificial distinction from each other, partly because the *Van Gend en Loos* reference from the Dutch court did not require the Court of Justice to address the supremacy question, which was settled in any event in favour of directly effective treaty obligations by the Dutch Constitution, and partly it seems because of the "softly, softly" approach to addressing the supremacy question advocated by judge Trabucchi in the Court's internal deliberations during *Van Gend en Loos* (De Witte 1999: 181–182, Azzalini and Sandei 2008: 223). Note that publications by judge Lecourt and legal *attaché* Gori connect the EU's rejection of inter-state retaliation, and the EU's rejection of unilateral safeguard mechanisms, to the direct effect and supremacy doctrines in combination with each other (on inter-state retaliation: Lecourt 1965, Lecourt 1991, on safeguards: Gori 1967). Later scholarship on the possibility of requiring direct effect of WTO obligations does at times acknowledge that this would be "near-indissociable" from requiring supremacy (Eeckhout 2002: 94).

"*International Fruit* in reverse" therefore provides a clearer, more compelling *Van Gend en Loos*. It demonstrates that the Court could describe the doctrine of direct effect, and its impact on actors other than litigating individuals and national courts, with much greater specificity than it did in February 1963, and it highlights the frankly rigid nature of the Court's "new legal order" by comparison with enforcement and escape mechanisms in many other trade treaties. All those interested in Community law should therefore read the Court's 1972 *International Fruit* judgment, because, reflected in a mirror, it shows how *Van Gend en Loos* was connected to the construction of a new and distinctive relationship between the European member states.

6

Van Duyn, 1974

Direct Effect of Directives

The Case before the Court

This case came to the European Court of Justice as a request for a preliminary ruling, under the Article 177 procedure, by a court of the United Kingdom, the High Court of England and Wales in London, in a dispute over the limits imposed on the free movement of workers by considerations of public policy and public security.[1]

A Dutch national, Yvonne van Duyn, had been prevented from entering the United Kingdom in May 1973 to take up employment with the Church of Scientology, a decision taken in accordance with United Kingdom policy that considered the activities of the Church of Scientology to be socially harmful. Van Duyn took an action in the High Court claiming that the United Kingdom's policy was contrary to Article 48 of the Treaty of Rome as well as Article 3 of Directive 64/221, which coordinated special measures concerning the movement of foreign nationals that were necessary for public policy, public security, and public health. The High Court in turn referred three preliminary questions to the Court of Justice. The first concerned whether Article 48 of the Treaty enjoyed direct effect. The second concerned whether Directive 64/221 was also directly applicable, so as to confer on individuals rights enforceable by them in the courts of the member states. The third concerned whether when the authorities of a member state decided to refuse a Community national leave to enter that state on the basis of personal conduct, those authorities were entitled to take into account, first, the fact that the individual was associated with an organization the activities of which the member state government considers are contrary to the public good but which are not unlawful, and second, the fact that the individual intends to take up employment with such an organization,

[1] Case 41/74 *Van Duyn* v. *Home Office* [1974] ECR 1337.

it being the case however that no restrictions are placed upon nations of the member state who take up similar employment.

In its observations before the Court, the United Kingdom maintained that

> since Article 189 of the Treaty distinguishes between the effects ascribed to Regulations, Directives, and Decisions, it must therefore be presumed that the Council, in issuing a Directive rather than making a Regulation, must have intended that the Directive should have an effect other than that of a Regulation and accordingly that the former should not be directly applicable.

The opinion of Advocate General, Henri Mayras, noted that as regards the first question, Article 48 of the Treaty of Rome had already been recognized as enjoying direct effect in a decision of the Court of Justice taken after the High Court had made its reference in the *Van Duyn* case.[2] As regards the second question, the Advocate General's analysis was more extensive. Mayras began by noting that Article 189 of the Treaty distinguishes between Regulations, which are directly applicable in the member states, and Directives, which are also binding on the states but which have, in principle, no direct effect inasmuch as they leave to the states the choice of methods for their implementation. Mayras noted, however, that decisions of the Court of Justice had included statements indicating that, apart from Regulations, other Community acts may have direct effect. In *S.A.C.E.* v. *Italian Ministry of Finance* for example, the Court stated

> a Directive, the purpose of which is to set a final date for the implementation by a member state of a Community obligation, concerns not only the relations between the Commission and that state, but also entails legal consequences on which individuals in particular may rely whenever, by its very nature, the provision enacting that obligation is directly applicable.[3]

The Advocate General then examined the Directive 64/221, finding that the provision in question imposed a clear and precise obligation, not subject to the adoption of subsequent acts by the member states or the Community, and imposed a specific limitation on the competence of the member states. As for the third question, Mayras considered whether the United Kingdom had violated the principle of non-discrimination, in that Community nationals, such as Van Duyn, were prevented from

[2] Case 167/73 *Commission* v. *France* [1974] ECR 359.

[3] Case 33/70 *S.A.C.E.* v. *Finance Minister of the Italian Republic* [1970] ECR 1213.

moving to the United Kingdom to work for the Church of Scientology, while United Kingdom nationals were free to work for the Church of Scientology. He considered, however, that this discrimination was not in fact contrary to the Treaty, in that the Treaty's proviso in relation to public policy and public security had the effect of maintaining the competence of the member states in that area, retaining both the assessment to threats of their security and the choice of measures to counteract such a threat.

On 4 December 1974, the Court of Justice's decision stated that the limitations on freedom of movement provided by Article 48(3) did not prevent Article 48 from conferring on individuals rights that must be protected by national courts. As regards the direct effect of Directives, the Court explained that

> It would be incompatible with the binding effect attributed to a directive by Article 189 to exclude, in principle, the possibility that the obligation which it imposes may be invoked by those concerned. In particular, where the Community authorities have, by directives, imposed on member states the obligation to pursue a particular course of conduct, the useful effect (*effet utile*) of such an act would be weakened if individuals were prevented from relying on it before the national courts.

As regards Directive 64/221 in particular, the Court found that Article 3(1) conferred "on individuals rights which are enforceable by them in national courts of a member state and which the latter must protect". The use of public policy as a justification for derogating from a fundamental principle of Community law "must be interpreted strictly . . . subject to control by the institutions of the Community". Finally, the Court found that a member state was, in the circumstances under discussion, entitled to take into account "the fact that the individual is associated with some body or organization the activities of which the member state considers socially harmful but which are not unlawful in that state, despite the fact that no restriction is placed upon nationals of the said member state who wish to take similar employment with the same bodies or organizations".

Related Cases

The central element of the Court's *Van Duyn* decision was its finding that a provision of a Directive should enjoy direct effect in the national legal order. This feature of the *Van Duyn* decision had similarities to several other then-recent decisions of the Court, where provisions contained in other instruments of European law had been found to produce "direct effect". In *Franz Grad*, in a case "concern[ing] the combined effect of provisions contained in a Decision and a Directive", the Court found that

> it would be incompatible with the binding effect attributed to Decisions by Article 189 to exclude in principle the possibility that persons affected may invoke the obligation imposed by a Decision. Particularly in cases where, for example, the Community authorities have by means of a Decision imposed an obligation in a Member State or all the Member States to act in a certain way, the effectiveness (*l'Effet utile*) of such a measure would be weakened if the nationals of that state could not invoke it in the courts and the national courts could not take it into consideration as part of Community law.[4]

The Court went on to find that Article 4 of a Council Decision "prohibiting the Member States from applying the common system of turnover tax concurrently with specific taxes levied instead of turnover tax, is capable, in conjunction with provisions of Council Directives . . . of producing direct effects . . . [and] of creating . . . the right to invoke these provisions before the courts". The Court reached this decision despite observations by the German government that "by distinguishing between the effects of Regulations on the one hand and of Decisions and Directives on the other, Article 189 precludes the possibility of Decisions and Directives producing the effects mentioned in the question [rights for individuals which national courts must protect], which are reserved to Regulations".

In *S.A.C.E.*, the Court was asked to consider the effect of a Directive implementing a directly effective treaty provision. The Court found that a Directive imposing a final date for the implementation of a provision of the Treaty (Article 13) requiring states, by the end of the transitional period, to abolish charges having an effect equivalent to a customs duty on imports before "entails legal consequences of which . . . individuals may avail themselves when, by its very nature, the provision establishing this obligation is directly applicable".[5] The provision of the Treaty itself would have had conferred rights on individuals from the end of the transitional period, and the provision therefore conferred the same

[4] Case 9/70 *Franz Grad* v. *Finanzamt Traustein* [1970] ECR 825.

[5] Case 33/70 *S.A.C.E.* v. *Finance Minister of the Italian Republic* [1970] ECR 1213.

rights on individuals when the date of its implementation was brought forward by the Commission Directive to a date prior to the end of the transitional period.[6]

After *Van Duyn*, the Court continued to find that provisions of Directives could be granted direct effect. As Prechal explains in her influential monograph *Directives in EC Law*, ever since *Van Duyn* the question has been no longer whether Directives *can* have direct effect but rather *under what circumstances* this may be the case.[7] The Court continued to develop its reasoning however, and in the 1979 case *Ratti* the direct effect of Directives was for the first time justified by the argument that a member state may not rely on its own failure to fulfil its obligations (an argument sometimes referred to as the 'estoppel theory' of the direct effect of Directives).[8] For this reason, a member state should not be able to rely on its own recalcitrance in order to escape its obligations – either to the other member states under the agreement or to the individuals to whom the right has been extended. The Court's approach in *Ratti* seems to some observers to suggest the Court's caution in the face of criticism of previous judgments on the direct effect of Directives in several member states.[9] This caution has had consequences, because the "estoppel" theory's emphasis on the *member state*'s failure to fulfil its obligations under the Directive as the basis for direct effect constitutes an obstacle to recognition of the so-called "horizontal" direct effect of Directives, that is to say whether rights conferred by Directives can be enforced against private parties.[10]

[6] Prechal draws out the distinctions between *Grad* and *S.A.C.E.* and *Van Duyn* as follows: "With respect to directives, however, neither *Grad* nor *S.A.C.E.* clarified the problem entirely. Both cases related to the combined effect of directives and other provisions… Moreover, the judgments concerned direct effect of a provision of a directive fixing a deadline. For these reasons they could be considered special cases. However, from the *Van Duyn* judgment it was deduced that both substantive provisions of directives and directives standing alone may also have direct effect" (Prechal 2005: 217).

[7] Prechal 2005: 218.

[8] Case 148/78 *Pubblico Ministero* v. *Ratti* [1979] ECR 1629. Prechal 2005: 220. This aspect has been emphasized in later cases, including *Faccini Dori* where the Court explained "That case-law [on the possibility of relying on directives against State entities] seeks to prevent 'the State from taking advantage of its own failure to comply with Community law'," Case C-91/92 *Faccini Dori* [1994] ECR I-3325.

[9] Prechal 2005: 223–224. For a detailed history of the direct effect of Directives, with an emphasis on the positive role of European Commission and negative responses in various of the member states, see Rasmussen 2017.

[10] Prechal 2005: esp. 223, 257–258.

Disputes over the possibility of such "horizontal" direct effect for Directives have come to the Court in subsequent cases. In *Marshall*, the Court stated that, "according to Article 189 of the EEC treaty, the binding nature of a Directive, which constitutes the basis for the possibility of relying on the Directive before a national court, exists only in relation to 'each member state to which it is addressed'" and therefore that "a Directive may not of itself impose obligations on an individual and that a provision of a Directive may not be relied upon as against such a person".[11] The Court has therefore rejected the possibility of horizontal direct effect of Directives. However, as Craig has pointed out, the Court's use "of itself" in *Marshall*'s formulation was later used by the Court to justify the imposition of such obligations in various cases where the Court found that there was "something 'in addition'" to the Directive, in cases such as *Viamex* and *Mangold*.[12]

Analysis and Context

Van Duyn is regularly included in prominent texts and surveys of the development of European law, as well as in many scholarly collections of the Court's famous judgments.[13] It is accepted as the landmark judgment justifying the "direct effect of Directives". Scholars are nonetheless frequently sceptical of both the outcome and the reasoning of the Court's decision, as going beyond what the Treaty provided for.

As Wyatt and Dashwood put it, for some time it was widely assumed that Directives gave rise exclusively to rights and obligations as between the member states and European institutions, but *Van Duyn* signalled a different approach.[14] Weatherill states baldly that the Treaty suggested that a Directive, in contrast to a Regulation, would not be directly effective, yet the Court decided otherwise in *Van Duyn*.[15] Chalmers, Davies and Monti even declare forthrightly that *Van Duyn*'s reasoning is "remarkably weak", pointing out that the Court starts from an *a contrario* position

[11] Case 152/84 *Marshall* v. *Southhampton and South-West Hampshire Health Authority* [1986] ECR 723.

[12] Craig 2009: 352 and throughout. Cases C-37 & 58/06 *Viamex* v. *Hauptzollamt Hamburg-Jonas* [2008] ECR I-69, Case C-144/04 *Mangold* v. *Helm* [2005] ECR I-9981.

[13] Craig and de Búrca 2011: 363, Craig and de Búrca 2015: 189–190, 201–203, Schütze 2016: 96–98. *Van Duyn* is included as a "basic community case" in Rudden and Rossa Phelan 1997 but not as a "classic of EU law" in Maduro and Azoulai 2010.

[14] Dashwood et al. 2011: 259.

[15] Weatherill 2014: 112.

as to whether there is any good reason why Directives should not have direct effect. The Court of Justice's argument that their binding nature and their effectiveness require that they can be invoked in national courts are "simply *non sequiturs*", they say, adding that "neither of these qualities prescribes the types of effects Directives should have in a domestic legal system".[16]

It appears clear to many, therefore, that the Court in *Van Duyn* was really motivated on the "policy grounds" or even by the "political argument" that Directives should be made more effective than would be possible if their binding nature could only be enforced by use of the Article 169, 170 and 171 procedures, and not before national courts.[17] That policy goal justifies the direct effect of Directives; that is to say, these individual rights were instrumentally created in order to serve the public-policy purpose of the increased effectiveness of Community obligations. It is sometimes suggested that this policy may have been a response to the limited number of Article 169 actions that the European Commission is capable of pursuing each year, given the Commission's scarce resources.[18]

Van Duyn therefore continues to be a controversial case even now. As the British government's lawyers pointed out before the Court, the provisions of the Treaty of Rome that set out the rule-making instruments available to the European institutions drew a distinction between Regulations, on the one hand, which were to be "binding in [their] entirety and directly applicable in all Member States", and Directives, on the other, which were to be "binding, as to the result to be achieved, upon each Member State to which it [was] addressed, but shall leave to national authorities the choice of form and methods".[19] The distinction and contrast between these instruments as set out in the Treaty appeared to many to indicate that while provisions of Regulations should benefit from direct effect in the national legal orders, in much the same way that the Court had found that articles of the Treaty itself could enjoy direct effect, direct effect should not be granted to provisions of Directives. Indeed, the Court's own reasoning on direct effect, where it used similar language to describe the rights conferred on individuals by provisions

[16] Chalmers et al. 2014: 309–310, also Schütze 2016: 97 on *Van Duyn*'s "lack of a convincing *legal* argument", cf. Rasmussen 1986: 12.

[17] Hartley 2014: 220, Schütze 2016: 97.

[18] Craig 1992: 472, Hartley 2014: 221.

[19] E.g. Wyatt 1975: 672.

of the Treaty, and the rights conferred on individuals by Regulations, appeared to imply that provisions of Directives would not be found directly effective.[20]

The *Van Duyn* decision therefore, as perhaps the clearest example of the series of Court decisions finding that Community instruments other than Regulations could be enforced by individuals before national courts, raised the question of whether the Court could be criticized for "blurring", or "eroding", the distinctions between the legislative instruments that the Treaty had provided for in Article 189.[21] Critical views of the Court of Justice's reasoning in *Van Duyn* appear to have been shared by some national courts, with the French Conseil d'État denying in 1978 that Directives could be referred to by a national of one of the member states against an individual administrative act, on the basis (contrary to *Van Duyn*) that the text of Article 189 of the Treaty specified that Directives bind the addressed states.[22]

For a readily available illustration of how natural the denial of direct effect to Directives might appear to leading Community lawyers, one need look no further than Advocate General Lagrange's opinion in *Costa* v. *ENEL* in 1964, which describes this distinction between Regulations and Directives in a straightforward manner.[23] As Lagrange there explained, the Treaty provides two classes of provisions that are directly applicable: "the provisions of the Treaty which are considered as 'self-executing'" and "those which have been the subject of implementing Regulations", and the protection of the "individual rights" derived from "the Treaty

[20] For the Court's occasional lack of clarity in distinguishing direct effect and direct applicability, see Easson 1979. See also Lecourt's discussion of *Van Gend en Loos* in *L'Europe des juges*, where he says that the Court's judgment could have included a reference to the direct effect of Regulations in Article 189 of the Treaty, as it did in *Costa* v. *ENEL*. "If a simple Regulation" was directly applicable, "then for even stronger reasons so should be the provisions of the Treaty itself" (Lecourt 1976a: 252, similarly 285).

[21] Blurring: Simmonds 1975: 434. Erosion: Wyatt 1975: 672. Rasmussen's fascinating history of the direct effect of Directives using government sources within the member states gives another contemporary example: "In a debate in the House of Lords on 15 April 1975, Lord Diplock, the chair of the [European Communities] Committee, argued in favour of such a solution [for the Council to make it routine practice to explicitly state if a Directive could produce direct effect or not] because it 'would restore the position to what it was before. Regulations directly applicable, yes; Directives directly applicable, no – then we know where we are'" (Rasmussen 2017: 298).

[22] Plötner 1997: 48–49. Belgian courts however arguably appear to have allowed the direct effect of Directives even in advance of *Van Duyn* (Bribosia 1997: 9–10, as noticed by Lecourt 1970: 24, again in advance of *Van Duyn*).

[23] See Chapter 3 on *Costa* v. *ENEL*.

or Community regulations ... falls upon the national courts" while by contrast, in the case of Recommendations or Directives or Treaty provisions that are not directly effective, "the Treaty only becomes part of the domestic legal system as a consequence of national measures adopted by the competent organs of the State in question", with the implication that they could only be enforced before the Court of Justice by the European Commission or the member states, not by individuals in national courts.[24]

The criticisms of *Van Duyn* did not go unanswered, of course. To the charge that the Court had blurred the distinction between Regulations and Directives came the reply that the instruments remained distinct, in that the "direct effect" granted to Directives was not as extensive as the "direct effect" granted to Regulations, particularly in that it could not directly impose obligations on individuals.[25] However, even commentators who are sanguine about the expansion of direct effect over time use the *Van Duyn* judgment as a marker of how far the Court had come from *Van Gend en Loos*.[26] All can agree that *Van Duyn* provides an excellent example of the ambitious way that the Court has developed the Treaty.[27]

What was not always clear in commentary at the time of *Van Duyn* was that a debate about the possibility of direct effect for provisions of Directives had been ongoing for many years prior to the 1974 judgment. The issue had been considered at length in a conference held in Paris in November 1965, where many of the main lines of later debate were already aired.[28] The British government's position in *Van Duyn* – that the Treaty had distinguished "clearly and consciously" between two forms of expressing the Community will – was put forward in 1965 by German scholar Everling and others, while Waelbroeck, Ophuls and

[24] Similarly, Rasmussen's history of the direct effect of Directives describes Rolf Wägenbaur, presenting the Commission's position before the Court of Justice in *Franz Grad*, as "quite open about the fact that neither decisions nor Directives had originally been considered to produce direct effect" (Rasmussen 2017: 296). Note that Rasmussen's account indicates that the Legal Service of the Commission discussed the direct effect of Directives "for the first time in March 1968" (Rasmussen 2017: 295). As we will see, judge Lecourt had already indicated a clear view on this issue in 1963 and again in 1964.

[25] Easson, writing soon after *Van Duyn*, emphasized possible continuing limits to the direct effect of Directives (Easson 1979: 342ff). Waelbroeck had earlier argued that preventing national acts contrary to Directives being imposed on individuals would not obscure the distinctions between Regulations and Directives (Louis 1966: 93).

[26] Craig 1992: 470.

[27] Schütze 2016: 86–87.

[28] Louis 1966.

others argued against such a "rigid distinction", allowing at least some domestic legal effects for certain provisions contained in Directives.[29] Those who know Pierre Pescatore from his later role as an ECJ judge between 1967 and 1985, as well as a scholarly advocate of ambitious European law doctrines, may be interested to note that his intervention in 1965 was against any application of the Court's direct effect doctrine to Directives which, he argued, should be considered to apply at the intergovernmental level and only enforceable by the European Commission.[30] That such a view could be advanced by Pescatore (albeit then still an employee of the government of Luxembourg as well as a university professor) only reinforces the view that the Court of Justice's later decisions in this area should not be considered the only way in which the Treaty or the direct effect doctrine first announced in *Van Gend en Loos* could have been developed but represented further and distinguishable decisions by the Court.[31]

Judge Lecourt himself had indicated his outlook on this topic at a very early stage. In a talk entitled "Le rôle du droit dans l'unification européenne" delivered at the conference of the Association des Juristes Européens on 22 February 1964, Lecourt had distinguished Regulations, which enjoyed direct applicability without transmission by any internal act, from Directives, which by contrast only have their effect by the intermediary [*truchement*] of a domestic legal text.[32] This, went on Lecourt, raised a variety of interesting questions about how these texts should be embedded in the internal legal orders:

> What, for example, could be the legal effect of a text adopted by a member state in execution of a Directive which set out a regulation contrary to the provisions of that Directive? Would such a text impose itself on private individuals in this state? We know that the Directive is obligatory for the

[29] Louis 1966: 92–93.

[30] Louis 1966: 92.

[31] E.g. Wyatt 1975: 672.

[32] Lecourt 1964b: 9. The talk was also published in the *Gazette du Palais* (Lecourt 1964a). Vauchez has described this speech of Lecourt as "arguably the first systematic conceptualization of the Court's contribution to the dynamics of what would today be referred to as 'integration-through-law'" (Vauchez 2015: 142; see discussion in the recent history of the "Integration through Law project" in European legal scholarship in Byberg 2017). As we will see, Lecourt and Chevallier's article characterizing the Court as the Community's emergency engine [*moteur de secours*] appeared even earlier, in late 1963 (Lecourt and Chevallier 1963). Indeed, the general thrust towards the expansion of the direct- effect doctrine over the early decades of European law, later ably described by Craig, appears to have been signalled in advance by Lecourt's writings in 1963 and 1964 (Craig 1992).

> state addressed as far as the result to be obtained and that, on the other hand, the Treaties have an authority superior to national laws. Well then? [*Alors?*][33]

Lecourt declined to offer an answer to this "simple question" but referred the reader to a pertinent observation by Savatier (a scholar at Poitiers University) that the legislation derived from the Treaty "'engages either their government... *or their courts, bound by decisions of the Community, or their nationals and residents, as far as internal contracts among themselves*'".[34] Despite Lecourt's refusal to directly answer the question posed, his discussion demonstrates a clear inclination towards requiring a legal effect for Directives before the member states' domestic courts even in the absence of satisfactory national implementing norms.[35] Later in his talk Lecourt indicated that, given the difficulties in interpreting a new system of law, research into the *effet utile* of the Treaties could sometimes provide a solution to problems where the Treaty texts did not speak for themselves.[36] In many ways, therefore, important aspects of the Court's judgements on the direct effect of Directives had been prefigured in Robert Lecourt's talk ten years before *Van Duyn*.

Lecourt had even touched on this issue a little earlier, with an argument more closely related to the general themes of this book. In December

[33] Lecourt 1964b: 9.

[34] Lecourt 1964b: 10, emphasis added by Lecourt, cf. Savatier 1960: 56, also Lecourt 1964a: 51. The words of Savatier that Lecourt includes read in French: "*Au depart, la législation qu'il (le Traité) promulgue est une loi-cadre, une loi-programme, plus souvent qu'une loi immédiatement exécutoire de la Communauté. Elle y engage soit leur gouvernement... soit leurs tribunaux, liés par les décisions de la Communauté, soit leurs nationaux et habitants, jusque dans les contrats internes de ceux-ci.*" In light of the breadth of issues touched on by this last sentence, it is worth mentioning that the Court has so far found that so-called "horizontal direct effect", i.e. direct effect of EU law obligations between private persons (natural or legal) is not permitted in the case of Directives. The Court's refusal to extend "horizontal direct effect" to Directives may have been part of an effort to accommodate criticism of the *Van Duyn* and similar decisions in scholarship and by national judges and politicians. See discussion in Prechal 2005.

[35] Lecourt also raises the possibility of reducing member state autonomy in areas where the Community has legislated through Directives in another passage of this 1964 speech (Lecourt 1964b: 10). Describing the various Community obligations, he refers to norms that are inserted directly into the national legal orders, whose entry is therefore final and whose modification can only be accomplished through the Community procedures. If Community obligations enter the national legal orders through the intervention of a domestic legal text, Lecourt goes on, one could ask oneself the question whether these texts, once adopted, remain subject to the reach of national authorities [*on peut se demander si ces textes, une fois pris, restent à portée de la main des autorités nationales*].

[36] Lecourt 1964b: 11.

1963, Lecourt and his legal *attaché* (we would now say, *référendaire*) Chevallier published a paper in *Recueil Dalloz* entitled "Chances et malchances de l'harmonisation des législations européennes" [Opportunities and difficulties facing the harmonization of European legislation] focusing on the challenges of harmonizing legislation through the use of Directives.[37] Elaborating various problems in this area, including conservative attitudes and the Commission's budgetary difficulties, Lecourt and Chevallier indicated that these problems could result in violations of the harmonization provisions of the Treaty, and asked whether such violations could become the object of judicial sanctions. If so, the Court of Justice would become the emergency engine [*moteur de secours*] of a harmonization in difficulty. However, this subject raised so many questions that it was only possible to touch on them.[38] After considering violations by the Commission or the Council, the authors went on:

> If it is a Member State which appears to be failing in its obligations, refraining from satisfying the obligations of the Treaty in the matter, the Commission, following the terms of Article 169, may produce a reasoned opinion, after having given the Member State the opportunity to submit its observations. If the latter does not conform with this opinion, the Commission can take action before the Court. The same facility is available to the other Member States in virtue of Article 170.
>
> Is it necessary to be specific about the next steps in the Community procedures? According to the terms of Articles 171 and 176, the institution or the Member State, which has been found in non-compliance, is obliged to take measures to execute the judgment of the Court. Should we imagine the worst and suppose – gratuitously, since experience indicates otherwise – that a State could refuse to do so and thus aggravate its original non-compliance? The EEC Treaty – differing from the ECSC Treaty, whose Article 88 provides for the measures of reprisals [*mesures de rétorsion*] – did not envisage this pessimistic scenario. No doubt it was not convenient to do so. If things were to come to that point, the Treaty itself could experience a critical situation. To avoid an extreme situation, perhaps we would be resigned to fall back on the classical methods which organize respect for Treaties through the reciprocity of commitments. [*Pour éviter une issue extrême, peut-être se resignerait-on à recourir aux méthodes classiques qui règlent le respect des Traités dans la réciprocité des engagements.*]

[37] Lecourt and Chevallier 1963.
[38] Lecourt and Chevallier 1963: 275.

> Without attaching to this scenario more importance than the authors of the Treaty have done, we can instead ask ourselves if the institutions, the States, and – who knows? private individuals themselves [*qui sait? les particuliers eux-mêmes*] – could find alternative means of effectiveness in the Treaty.[39] Thus the Member State which had the right to expect the punctual respect of all the deadlines fixed by common agreement in a Treaty which constitutes the law of the parties, can it obtain the cessation of a distortion or discrimination which is causing them injury? Could it argue, to obtain this outcome, from the fact that this distortion or discrimination should not have been tolerated after the date fixed by the Treaty for the entry into force of the harmonization? Beyond this period of tolerance, do States which are victims of an inequality maintained in violation of the Treaty have the right to act?
>
> But non-compliance with a harmonization clause [of the Treaty] could be only partial. A Directive could have given rise to an incomplete execution on the part of one or more States, or could have allowed to persist the inequalities or distortions which it was set out to put to an end. What would be the attitude of a national legal system where action has been taken by an individual from this State against the irregularity of a domestic legal text, established or maintained in infraction with the Directive or the Treaty? The Treaties having, in virtue of Article 55 of the French Constitution, "an authority superior to those of the laws, subject to the proviso, for each agreement or treaty, of its application by the other party to the Treaty", the question thus raised would be susceptible to lead either directly, or by the possible use of Article 177 of the Treaty, to decisions of great interest to the application of judicial harmonization clauses of the latter [Treaty].[40]

Thus in this passage from 1963 – posed just as in Lecourt's February 1964 speech as the authors touching on interesting "questions" – Lecourt and Chevallier raised the possibility of using litigation by private parties before national courts and use of the Article 177 procedure as an enforcement mechanism in the context of missed deadlines or "domestic

[39] Note that "alternative means of effectiveness" here is in contrast with classical reciprocity methods of enforcing treaties.

[40] Lecourt and Chevallier 1963: 275–276. Lecourt and Chevallier's article appeared after *Van Gend en Loos* in February 1963 but before *Costa* v. *ENEL* in July 1964, so that the supremacy question had not yet been addressed from the perspective of European law by the Court of Justice. Lecourt and Chevallier address the supremacy question instead by referring to Article 55 of the French Constitution, which appeared to offer a French legal foundation for the supremacy of treaty obligations in the French legal order, even though Article 55 was in practice a "dead letter" in the face of subsequently enacted national legislation since French judges were unwilling to control national legislation even to ensure the application of international law (e.g. De Witte 1986: 274).

legal texts" that involved "incomplete execution" of Directives. Essential elements of *Van Duyn*, and the direct effect of Directives, were therefore floated as possibilities by judge Lecourt more than once even before the Court of Justice had decided *Costa* v. *ENEL*.

This passage is notable for other reasons too. Lecourt and Chevallier explicitly discuss the possibility of falling back on the reciprocal mechanisms of international law in the context of a Member State failing to comply with an Article 171 finding by the Court, showing that this option was readily conceivable at the time. It also demonstrates the authors' preference *not* to pursue that route but instead to find other means of making the Treaty effective, above all litigation before national courts by private parties (*qui sait? les particuliers eux-mêmes*, in the authors' perhaps coy expression). Thus litigation of European law rights by private individuals before national courts was recognized by judge Lecourt and *référendaire* Chevallier as an alternative to inter-state reciprocity and retaliation, including within the context of Directives.[41]

The approach of this book, of course, is to situate the great judgments of the Court of Justice within the context of treaty provisions and state practices in other trade-related treaty regimes, above all those related to the enforcement of, and escape from, demanding treaty obligations. When this approach is extended to *Van Duyn*, it reveals a further and more fundamental policy argument underlying the Court's judgment. Just as *Van Gend en Loos* must be understood as an element in the creation of a specific relationship between the European states, distinct from that of ordinary trade treaty systems, so must *Van Duyn*. The reader is invited

[41] Note that Lecourt and Chevallier's discussion of the suppression of inter-state reciprocity mechanisms makes no reference to Article 219's prohibition of the member states submitting a dispute "to any method of settlement other than those provided for" in the Treaty of Rome, and that Lecourt and Chevallier's discussion of the possible enforcement of European obligations before national courts is straightforwardly derived from the need to suppress inter-state retaliation rather than, for example, the Treaty's Preamble or the particular details of Article 12 that had been emphasized in the then recent *Van Gend en Loos* judgment. Interestingly, the following paragraph of Lecourt and Chevallier's article connects the issue of non-fulfilment of the harmonization clauses of the Treaty with the question of derogations, arguing that failing to harmonize would prompt hard-to-resist requests for derogations (such as provided by Article 226) by states that were victims of inequalities resulting from the failure to apply the harmonization provisions of the Treaty. Thus again, discussions of weaknesses in the effectiveness of the Treaty's 169 and 170 Article procedures and the possibility of remedying them through an enhanced role for individuals and national courts took place against a background of wishing to maintain the robustness of the distinctive safeguard and derogation mechanisms set out in the Treaty.

to step back from too close a focus on debates about the appropriate similarities and differences between the various legislative instruments – Regulations and Directives, above all – set out in Article 189 of the Treaty of Rome. These debates can obscure as well as enlighten, because the logic of *Van Duyn* may not rest solely on the details of that particular contrast.

Consider for a moment the hypothetical case that the Treaty of Rome had provided only one legislative instrument, a "Directive", in the terms that are now familiar to us: "A directive shall be binding, as to the result to be achieved, upon each Member State to which it is addressed, but shall leave to the national authorities the choice of form and methods." By such a Treaty provision, the European institutions would have been empowered to issue such Directives creating obligations for the member states to, notably, lower barriers to trade and facilitating economic and policy integration between themselves.

Now consider the scenario where one of the member states is alleged by another member state (perhaps at the urging of affected firms) to have failed to fulfil the obligations required of it by a Directive designed to lower barriers to trade. How can such a dispute be resolved? Well, the dispute resolution mechanisms explicitly provided for in the Treaty set out a mechanism by which a member state, or the European Commission prompted by such a state, could bring a member state before the Court of Justice. The Court, in turn, could make a finding as to whether the member state's actions in relation to the Directive had failed to fulfil its obligations under the Treaty. As Article 171 of the Treaty provides, the State would then be "required to take the necessary measures to comply" with the judgment of the Court of Justice.

What, however, if the member state persisted in its failure even after a finding by the Court? The Treaty provided no formal sanction against such a member state. In general international law and in the practice of many international trade agreements, however, where a state persists in its failure to fulfil its treaty obligations even after the completion of any specified dispute settlement procedures, then at that moment its trading partners may proceed to threaten or even impose countermeasures in the form of reciprocal trade restrictions. The declaratory judgments of international tribunals are therefore frequently vitally reinforced by the possibility of self-help retaliatory action by a state's trading partners.

Within the European Economic Community, however, the Court had declared, above all in its *Dairy Products* decision of November 1964, that any use of such self-help behaviours was comprehensively ruled out.

That rejection of any form of inter-state retaliatory action by the Court was, we know now, justified by judge Robert Lecourt on the basis that, instead, Community obligations would be enforced by national courts as required by the doctrines of direct effect and supremacy. As discussed in Chapter 4 on *Dairy Products*, Lecourt wrote as follows in his article in *France-Forum* in 1965:

> [T]he Court was led to conduct a sort of x-ray analysis of the Treaties . . . the Court finally observed that in instituting certain obligations in relation to individuals the Common Market should also inevitably confer on them "rights that enter into their judicial patrimony" (decision of 5 February 1963) and which should be protected by national courts. But a delicate problem emerged . . . : what is then the authority of the community law in the face of national law? . . . To decide such a finding in respect of the Treaty, it was necessary to analyse its terms and spirit. That is what the Court did. . . No unilateral legal act of a state "can prevail against the Treaties" (decision of 15 July 1964) because the States "have renounced the ability to take self-help action to enforce their legal rights" (decision of 13 November 1964).[42]

Lecourt's simple argument applies just as much to a treaty system that legislates only through Directive-style instruments as to a treaty system – as was actually the case for the Treaty of Rome – where Directives are only one among several legislative instruments. If a treaty is to require states to renounce their general international law rights to make use of self-help mechanisms to enforce Community obligations, then an effective alternative mechanism for enforcing such obligations must be provided. The alternative mechanism could not be direct enforcement actions before the Court by other states, or by a treaty-based secretariat such as the Commission. These would not sufficiently address the situation in which states persist in their behaviour despite a contrary declaration by the Court, perhaps justifying their infractions by the ever-present infractions of their trading partners.[43] If demanding Community obligations had been created through means of Directives that were only enforceable before the Court by the Commission or other member states, then the failures of some member states to fulfil their obligations would likely have prompted others to reciprocally withhold their own

[42] Lecourt 1965: 22. The "decision of 5 February 1963" is *Van Gend en Loos*, the "decision of 15 July 1964" is *Costa* v. *ENEL*, and the "decision of 13 November 1964" is the *Dairy Products* judgment.

[43] Lecourt 1991.

fulfilment. This would result in disruptions to the inter-state market, and indeed to inter-state diplomatic relations.[44] (This situation applies, of course, even if the Commission faces no resource constraints at all when pursuing Article 169 actions, which is why the limited resources of the Commission can be considered an issue of secondary importance.) Instead, of course, the true substitute for such inter-state retaliatory mechanisms is the direct-effect doctrine, which allows private parties to litigate before national courts, which are obliged to vindicate European law rights in the national legal orders. Thus a treaty system that legislated *only* through means of Directive-style instruments would require the application of a direct-effect doctrine to provisions contained in Directives if it were effectively to rule out the use of self-help actions by the member states to enforce their treaty rights.

The Treaty of Rome, of course, provided for several diverse legislative instruments, including Regulations and Directives. The logic of the above argument continues to apply, however. If many demanding Community obligations had been created through legislative instruments that relied entirely on such a potentially ineffective enforcement mechanism, as Directives appeared to do even after the *Van Gend en Loos* judgment, the failures of some member states to fulfil obligations contained in Directives even after a finding by the Court of Justice would have opened up the possibility that others might reciprocally withhold their own compliance in retaliation. The extension of the direct-effect doctrine to provisions contained in Directives therefore protected one of the European legal orders most fundamental commitments: if the Community was to comprehensively rule out any possible use of self-help by its member states, a broad range of important Community obligations – including Directives as one of the main legislative instruments of the Community – must become enforceable by private parties before national courts. Just as with *Van Gend en Loos*, the meaning of *Van Duyn* can best be understood in the light of *Dairy Products*, that is to say, in light of the Court's use of the direct-effect doctrine to address important international collective action problems.

Because of the relationship between direct effect and the principle first declared in the *Dairy Products* case, the Court's direct-effect doctrine was

[44] Indeed, states and litigants did advance justifications of failures to comply with Directives on the basis of inter-state reciprocity, i.e. delays or unsatisfactory compliance in the other member states, e.g. Case 52/75 *Commission* v. *Italy* [1976] ECR 277, Case C-38/89 *Ministère Public* v. *Guy Blanguernon* [1990] ECR I-83.

necessarily an expansionary one. Any issue that might prompt self-help enforcement or reciprocity behaviours by the member states would need to be potentially addressed by the direct involvement of national courts and private parties. Whereas aspects of the text of *Van Gend en Loos*, such as its emphasis on the negative nature of the Article 12 obligation at issue, perhaps suggested that the scope of the new direct-effect doctrine might be relatively limited, Lecourt's article in *France-Forum* implied by contrast the potentially limitless ambitions of the direct-effect doctrine. The wording of Lecourt's 1965 article was, in fact, fully compatible with Lecourt's expansive later definition, in *L'Europe des juges* (1976), of direct effect as "the right of every person to demand from their judge the application of Community treaties, Regulations, Directives or Decisions" [*le droit pour toute personne de demander à son juge de lui appliquer traités, règlements, directives ou décisions communautaires*].[45]

It is no surprise, therefore, that *Van Duyn* was decided the way it was in 1974. The relationship between the European states that the Court had established through the combination of the direct-effect doctrine and the principle announced in the *Dairy Products* judgment points remorselessly towards the outcome of *Van Duyn*. So while Prechal's discussion of possible justifications for the direct effect of Directives in *Directives in EC Law* is extensive, it omits perhaps the most fundamental reason of all.[46] It omits the possibility that the direct effect of Directives could be justified by European law's rejection of inter-state countermeasures and reciprocity. This is the explanation most obviously prompted by the comparison between the European legal order and the enforcement and escape mechanisms of other trade treaty systems, and this is also the explanation for the direct effect of Directives first intimated by judge Lecourt and his *attaché* Chevallier in 1963.[47]

Van Duyn is also relevant to one of our other themes, the Community's distinctive approach to the management of safeguards and derogations within the Community legal order. After all, Article 48(3) of the

45 Lecourt 1976a: 248. *Van Duyn* is discussed elsewhere in *L'Europe des juges* as an example of "social law" in the first court case relating to the United Kingdom, as demonstrating that a state could refuse entry for reasons of "*ordre public*", even if no similar restriction is applied to nationals of that state, and as part of an assessment of the "much discussed" direct effect of Directives, where Lecourt stresses the first part of Article 189's discussion of Directives, that a "result must be achieved", emphasizing the "*effet utile*" of allowing national judges to apply Directives (Lecourt 1976a: 158, 165, 255–257).

46 Prechal 2005.

47 Lecourt and Chevallier 1963.

Treaty of Rome had provided that the member states could limit the freedom of movement for workers on various policy grounds. Since the *Pork Products* judgment, however, the Court has insisted that such exceptions be strictly controlled, and contemporary commentary on *Pork Products* insisted that such control could only be effective if Community law benefited from direct effect in the national legal orders.[48] In *Costa v. ENEL*, as we have explained, the Community's distinctive approach to safeguards and derogations is one of the Court's major justifications for its decision to require the supremacy of directly effective Community law in the national legal orders. And here in *Van Duyn*, the Court's decision to require the direct effect of Directives subjected the use by the member states of the derogations permitted in these Directives to judicial control which, by embedding this litigation within the national legal orders, is subject neither to the delays of the Article 169 procedure nor to the weaknesses of the declaratory judgments of the Court of Justice under Article 171 of the Treaty. As Craig explains, in *Van Duyn* the Court sought to utilize the doctrine of direct effect to ensure that general obligations contained in the Treaty were not compromised by more particular discretionary provisions.

So the expansion of direct effect in *Van Duyn* can also be understood as related to the principle that the Court had so often emphasized, namely, the need to ensure Community control of state use of derogations from their Treaty obligations. Indeed, the explanation, advanced above, of why a hypothetical Community legislating entirely through the use of Directives would nonetheless require a direct-effect doctrine can be repeated, *mutatis mutandis*, from the imperative of effectively requiring the participating states to refrain from unilateral adoption of safeguards or derogations. As the Court stated in *Van Duyn*, in words that recall the *Pork Products* judgment, justifications for derogations from the Treaty "must be interpreted strictly", and "subject to control by the institutions of the Community".

[48] Wenner 1962.

7

Simmenthal, 1978

Obligations of "Lower" National Courts

The Case before the Court

This case came to the Court of Justice as a request for a preliminary ruling, under the Article 177 procedure, by an Italian court, the Pretore di Susa, in a dispute over imports of beef into Italy from France.[1]

At the frontier, the beef underwent a veterinary and public health inspection as defined by an Italian law dating from 1934, with associated fees at a scale laid down under a law of 30 December 1970. Simmenthal, the importing firm, claimed that this procedure was incompatible with Community provisions on the free movement of goods and brought an action before the Pretore di Susa for repayment of the fees. During these proceedings, an application was made for a preliminary ruling from the Court of Justice. The Court of Justice's ruling found that pecuniary charges imposed by reason of veterinary or public health inspections of products on occasion of their crossing the frontier are to be regarded as charges having an effect equivalent to customs duties. Accordingly, on 24 January 1977, the Pretore di Susa made an order for the repayment of fees together with interest, giving as his reason that the levying of the fees was unlawful.

The Italian fiscal authorities objected to this order, pointing out that the prohibition on charging fees under Community law was found in Community Regulations made in 1964 and 1968,[2] while the basis under Italian law for charging the fees was to be found in the law of 30 December 1970. In relation to the Community provisions, that Italian law was therefore a *lex posterior*, a subsequently enacted law. For that reason,

[1] Case 106/77 *Amministrazione delle Finanze* v. *Simmenthal SpA* [1978] ECR 629.

[2] Regulation 14/64/EEC of the Council of 5 February 1964 on the progressive establishment of a common organization of the market in beef and veal [1964] JO 562 and Regulation (EEC) 805/68 of the Council of 27 June 1968 on the common organization of the market in beef and veal [1968] OJ L148/24.

having regard to the principle of the separation of powers, the national court could not simply fail to apply a national law that ostensibly conflicted with Community law. So long as the legislature does not affect an amendment, the Italian court was required to bring the matter before the Constitutional Court, which might then in pursuance of Article 11 of the Italian Constitution declare that the national law is unconstitutional, in line with decisions of the Italian Constitutional Court.[3]

Simmenthal objected, first, that the requirement for inspections derived from the 1934 law, while the 1970 law only fixed new scales of fees. More fundamentally, however, the company claimed that, if the Italian finance administration's argument was followed, the fact that under Italian constitutional law the Constitutional Court alone could declare a subsequent national law to be incompatible with Community law would not be in conformity with the leading decisions of the Court of Justice on the effectiveness of Community law in the legal systems of the member states and on the direct applicability of Community provisions that national courts must protect. The Italian legal system led to an unacceptable result because its courts were unable to avoid applying national law conflicting with Community law until the Italian Constitutional Court made its decision. Furthermore, the decisions of the Constitutional Court in this field only took effect *ex nunc*, so that such a finding of unconstitutionality was not a remedy possessing retroactive effect.

In view of this difference of opinion, the Pretore di Susa decided to stay its proceedings again and referred two questions to the Court of Justice. The first question asked whether Community law required that subsequent national measures conflicting with directly applicable Community provisions must be forthwith disregarded without waiting until those measures have been eliminated by action on the part of the national legislature concerned (repeal) or of other constitutional authorities (declaration that they are unconstitutional). The second question asked whether, in circumstances where Community provisions may be suspended until any conflicting national measures are actually repealed by the competent national authorities, was such repeal in all cases to have a wholly retroactive effect, so as to avoid any adverse effects on individual rights arising from directly applicable Community provisions.

[3] For example, Italian Constitutional Court Decision No. 232 of 1975.

In its observations before the Court, the Italian government pointed out that an Italian law of 1977 provided that fees may no longer be charged in pursuance of the 1970 law for veterinary and public health inspections, and that in judgment No. 163 of 1977, the Constitutional Court held that the charging of fees for veterinary and public health inspections of goods covered by the Community Regulations was unconstitutional. The Italian government therefore claimed that the question raised by the Pretore di Susa no longer had any purpose, in that the Italian court could determine the case before it without requiring an answer to the question whether it could of its own motion decline to apply the Italian law of 1970 or whether it can only do so after the Italian Constitutional Court has declared it to be unconstitutional.

The Advocate General, Gerhard Reischl, began by noting that the case concerned the effectiveness of directly applicable provisions of Community law

> as against *subsequently* enacted national laws and specifically the question whether the latter are to ceased to be applied forthwith or whether on the other hand it is necessary to await the decision of the [Italian] Constitutional Court. There is no unequivocal case-law on this point and for this reason we ought not to miss the opportunity of throwing light upon this fundamental question of Community law [emphasis in the original].

And as regards the contention of the Italian government that a response to the question raised by the Pretore di Susa was no longer necessary, the Advocate General stated that "the questions raised are of such fundamental importance and are so very likely to be raised again in other proceedings that for these reasons alone there is no justification for not determining them now once and for all".

Reischl then began a comprehensive account of the Court of Justice's decisions "on the nature of Community law and on its effectiveness for citizens of the Common Market as well as on the relationship between Community and national law", because, he contended, "the cases hitherto decided give a definite indication of the solution of the problem before us". The Advocate General then elaborated on the Court's case law, including its most famous decisions in *Van Gend en Loos*, *Costa* v. *ENEL*, *Internationale Handelsgesellschaft*, and others. He reminded the Court that the Community constitutes a "new legal order of international law", that "Community law is independent of the legislation of Member States", that the "member states have limited their sovereign rights", that "the subjects of this law include the nationals of the Member States", that "a whole host of provisions of Community law . . . have direct effect in the national law of all Member States, that is to say they confer upon individuals rights which they may invoke before their national courts and which national courts are bound to apply". As regards the relationship between Community law and national law, the Advocate General went on, the Court had found "that Community law takes precedence over national provisions", that "this precedence applies as against national provisions of every kind", that "later national measures. . . as well as constitutional law are expressly mentioned", and accordingly "all contrary provisions of internal law are rendered inapplicable".[4] The Court had also claimed that the "executive force of Community law cannot vary from one State to another in deference to subsequent domestic law",[5] and that the treaty cannot have different legal consequences varying with the member state concerned. The Advocate General also drew attention to the Court's statement that "the argument that [the infringement of a directly applicable Community rule] can be terminated only by the adoption of measures constitutionally appropriate to repeal the provision establishing the tax would amount to saying that the application of the Community rule is subject to the law of each Member State and more precisely that this application is impossible where it is contrary to a national law".[6]

Against this background, Reischl declared, the only possible answer to the first question is that, in the case of directly applicable Community provisions, conflicting national provisions that were adopted subsequently may no longer be applied, and that this position applies with immediate effect and it is not necessary to await repeal by the legislature or a declaration by a constitutional court that they are unconstitutional. He pointed out the requirement to approach the Constitutional Court involved complicated and expensive proceedings, which frequently took up to three years, and that during such proceedings national law continued to be applied, especially by national authorities, and the validity of Community law was thereby suspended. The Italian procedures therefore disregarded the precedence of Community law and imperilled the uniformity of the Community legal order. Reischl therefore rejected the argument that, in the case of a conflict between national and Community law, it was for the national legal system to confer upon the Constitutional

[4] Last fragment from Case 167/73 *Commission* v. *France* [1974] ECR 359.

[5] Case 6/64, *Costa* v. *ENEL* [1964] ECR 585.

[6] Case 48/71 *Commission* v. *Italy* [1972] ECR 527.

Court the exclusive jurisdiction to find the necessary solution. Reischl refused to allow that the potentially beneficial effects for Community law of the Italian procedure, involving a mandatory approach to the Constitutional Court, such as the reinforcement of Community law for future Italian cases through the *erga omnes* decisions of the Constitutional Court, justified the fact that the "Constitutional Court *alone* is to have jurisdiction to bar the application of national law conflicting with Community law". There could not be "a kind of counterbalancing" of the disadvantages to individuals in Italy and in the other member states as a result of Community law remaining unapplied, or the disadvantages such as the need to carry on proceedings before several courts, with the advantages that may be derived from the decisions of the Constitutional Court "by reason of the fact that it is then established with binding force that certain national provisions can in no circumstances be applied any longer".

Reischl finished by stating that there was no need for further consideration to be given to the second question, noting however that if an Italian court actually had to await a decision of the Constitutional Court with a view to avoiding the application of national law conflicting with Community law, it was essential that the Constitutional Court's judgment should have retroactive effect as from the date of entry into force of the relevant provision of Community law, including for the necessary compensation for its temporary non-application.

Reischl therefore proposed to answer the question raised by the Pretore di Susa by stating that the effectiveness of directly effective Community law

> cannot be impaired by incompatible national provisions whether they were adopted earlier or later. The fact that a constitutional law may declare such a national law to be unconstitutional cannot be allowed to prevent the national court from applying directly applicable provisions of Community law, even if the conflicting national provisions have not yet been declared unconstitutional.

On 9 March 1978, the Court of Justice answered the Italian court's questions. The Court emphasized that the direct applicability of Community law "means that the rules of Community law must be fully and uniformly applied in all the member states from the date of their entry into force and for so long as they continue in force", that such provisions of Community law "are an integral part of, and take precedence in, the legal order applicable in the territory of each of the Member States" and that "any recognition of that national legislative measures which ... are incompatible with the provisions of Community law had any legal effect would ... imperil the very foundations of the Community". For this reason, "*every* national court must, in a case within its jurisdiction, apply Community law in its entirety and protect rights which the latter confers on individuals and must accordingly set aside any provision of national law which may conflict with it" [emphasis added].

> Accordingly, any provision of a national legal system and any legislative, administrative or judicial practice which might impair the effectiveness of Community law by withholding from the national court having jurisdiction to apply such law the power to do everything necessary at the moment of its application to set aside national legislative provisions which might prevent Community rules from having full force and effect are incompatible with those requirements which are the very essence of Community law. This would be the case in the event of a conflict between Community law and a subsequent national law if the solution of the conflict were to be reserved for an authority with a discretion of its own, other than the Court called upon to apply Community law, even if such an impediment to the full effectiveness of Community law were only temporary.

The Court concluded therefore that a national court was under a duty to give full effect to provisions of Community law, "if necessary refusing of its own motion to apply any provision of national legislation, even if adopted subsequently, and it is not necessary for the court to request or await the prior setting aside of such provision by legislative or other constitutional means". In light of this answer to the first preliminary question, the Court considered that the second question – concerning whether, in circumstances where the Community obligations were suspended until their repeal by competent national authorities, such a repeal was required to have a wholly retroactive effect – appeared "to have no purpose".

Related Cases

The central element of the Court's *Simmenthal* decision was its finding that all national courts were obliged to give immediate effect to directly applicable European law obligations even if these conflicted with subsequently enacted national legislation and – more specifically – even if national constitutional rules did not provide every national court with such a power. Although, as Advocate General Reischl allowed, the Court of Justice's prior decisions did not provide unequivocal authority on this precise scenario, the Court's answer to the questions raised in *Simmenthal* was certainly consistent with many of its earlier decisions, as is demonstrated by Reischl's references to the *Costa* v. *ENEL* judgment among others.

Perhaps the most relevant case after *Costa* is the 1972 judgment *Commission* v. *Italy*, where the court held that national courts and national authorities of a member state in default are required to disapply any law deemed incompatible with directly effective Community law following a declaratory judgment under Article 171, without the necessity of any parliamentary procedure:[7]

> Since it is a question of a directly applicable Community rule, the argument that the infringement can be terminated only by the adoption of measures constitutionally appropriate to repeal the provision establishing the tax would amount to saying that the application of the Community rule is subject to the law of each Member State and more precisely that this application is impossible where it is contrary to a national law. In the present case the effect of Community law ... is a prohibition having the full force of law on the competent national authorities against applying a national rule recognized as incompatible with the treaty and, if the circumstances so require, an obligation on them to take all appropriate measures to enable Community law to be fully applied ... The grant made by member states to the community of rights and powers in accordance with the provisions of the Treaty involves a definitive limitation on their sovereign rights and no provisions whatsoever of national law may be invoked to override this limitation.

Even though *Commission* v. *Italy* referred to the constitutional role of the Italian legislature, the Court's firm condemnation there of restrictions on the applicability of Community law derived from "constitutionally appropriate" procedures prefigures the Court's condemnation of Italy's "constitutionally appropriate" procedures to ensure the application of directly effective Community law by the Italian courts.

Subsequently to *Simmenthal*, one of the more prominent related cases must be the 1990 *Factortame* judgment.[8] *Factortame* concerned the right of English judges to grant interim relief against national law where European law rights were at issue, even though no such power for

[7] Case 48/71 *Commission* v. *Italy* [1972] ECR 527.

[8] Case C-213/89 *The Queen* v. *Secretary of State for Transport, ex parte Factortame* [1990] ECR I-2433.

English judges to suspend Acts of Parliament existed at national level. The Court of Justice held that

> the full effectiveness of Community law would be just as much impaired if a rule of national law could prevent a court seized of a dispute governed by Community law from granting interim relief in order to ensure the full effectiveness of the judgment to be given on the existence of the rights claimed under Community law. It follows that a court in which those circumstances would grant interim relief, if it were not for a rule of national law, is obliged to set aside that rule.

Accordingly, the court held that "Community law must be interpreted as meaning that a national court which, in a case before it concerning Community law, considers that the sole obstacle which precludes it from granting interim relief is a rule of national law must set aside that rule."

Analysis and Context

Simmenthal is regularly included in prominent texts and surveys of the development of European law, as well as in scholarly collections of the Court's famous judgments.[9] Analysis of the case draws attention above all to *Simmenthal*'s intervention in the roles of different types of judges within the national legal orders, emphasizing that it is not open to national law to determine which national courts can hear conflicts between national and Community law.[10] Rather the obligation to apply Community law falls on *all* national judges.[11] Commentators also stress that the obligation placed by the Court of Justice on the national courts is to disapply contrary national law, without however rendering the national law void or invalid.[12] Scholarship on *Simmenthal* therefore concentrates on the way in which this decision brought out the role that the European legal order imposed on national courts in the member states – their obligation to apply European law obligations in place of conflicting national law obligations even if the national law obligations were subsequently enacted, and even if national constitutional rules

[9] E.g. Craig and de Búrca 2011: 442. *Simmenthal* is included as a "basic community case" and as a "classic of EU law" in both Rudden and Rossa Phelan 1997 and Maduro and Azoulai 2010.

[10] Chalmers et al. 2014: 208.

[11] Dashwood et al. 2011: 271, 296, Craig and de Búrca 2015: 271.

[12] Dashwood et al. 2011: 271, Craig and de Búrca 2015: 273, Schütze 2016: 125.

denied to particular national courts the power to set national law obligations aside in such circumstances.

The logic of *Simmenthal* had been heavily foreshadowed by previous judgments of the Court of Justice. Nonetheless, *Simmenthal* addressed a specific situation that had only latently been implied by the Court's *Van Gend en Loos* and *Costa* decisions. The role of national supreme or constitutional courts that the Court addressed in *Simmenthal* related to any special competence of such courts to control decisions within their national legal orders relating to conflicts between European law and subsequently enacted national legislation. The *Simmenthal* decision therefore addressed a "who decides?" question within national court systems.[13] This topic had come up obliquely in the earlier *Costa* litigation, also a case involving Italy of course, where Advocate General Lagrange had at the time stated cautiously that "this is a matter relating to the division of internal jurisdiction between the courts of a member state, a question with which you do not have to concern yourselves".[14]

To be sure, the question posed and answered in the context of the *Simmenthal* litigation related to a scenario where the national constitutional court was reliably resolving conflicts between European legal obligations and subsequently enacted national legal obligations in favour of the application of the European obligations – in *Simmenthal* itself, the Italian Constitutional Court had in fact already made such a decision. The Court of Justice may however also have been aware of the possibility of the alternative scenario – where such a national supreme or constitutional court might decide, in whatever circumstances, to resolve such a conflict in favour of the continued application of the subsequently enacted national legislation. Certainly the latter case would have struck even more seriously at the effectiveness of the European legal order than the mere delays associated with national procedures leading eventually

[13] Rudden and Rossa Phelan 1997: 53.

[14] The full passage of Lagrange's text reads as follows: "The only problem which could possibly arise is whether, in the case of a law, a court might be justified in refusing to apply it in those cases where, pursuant to the interpretation given by the Court of Justice, it would be bound to reach the conclusion that such a law was contrary to the Treaty. In other words, do Italian courts, other than the Constitutional Court, have the right to decide on the plea of unconstitutionality or are they bound, in any event, to refer the matter to the Constitutional Court? Otherwise, there is no doubt that the court should have referred the matter to the Constitutional Court leaving it to such court to call upon you to interpret the Treaty. But that is a matter relating to the division of internal jurisdiction between the Courts of a member state, a question with which you do not have to concern yourselves."

nonetheless to a reliable solution of conflicts in favour of European law. Attempting to restrict the supervisory role of national supreme or constitutional courts over the application of European law by other courts within their national legal orders therefore also served towards attempting to disarm such national high courts in scenarios beyond those explicitly discussed in *Simmenthal*.

The Court of Justice's decision in *Simmenthal* emphasized the independence of national courts, of whatever sort, from the rules of their national constitutions, and from the roles assigned to them by those national constitutional courts, when it came to the application of European law, even in the case of conflicts between European law and subsequently enacted national law. *Simmenthal* therefore instructed "lower" national courts to ignore national constitutional rules restricting such a power to higher courts.[15] That aspect of the decision is perhaps the most striking and the one most emphasized by scholarship. Carreau, for example, wrote that *Simmenthal* attempts to "untie the inferior judge from their hierarchical subordination" within their national legal orders, as far as concerns their application of European law, and added, more colourfully, that in *Simmenthal* the Court offered advance justification for "rebellion" by such inferior judges against their national superiors.[16]

The application of European law by such ordinary judges throughout the member states does of course serve to help ensure the uniformity of application of European law across and within the European member states. It therefore serves an important purpose in securing and promoting the effectiveness of the European legal order for private parties throughout the Community. At the same time, from the perspective of what might be called the "politics of courts", *Simmenthal* provides a clear example of the way in which the essential doctrines of the European legal order can appear to strengthen both the Court of Justice and "lower" national courts within the member states at the cost of a partial sidelining of the role of national supreme or constitutional courts. There is certainly evidence that judges on the Court itself noted the relatively greater enthusiasm for European law among the "lower" national courts. Judge Robert Lecourt, for example, speaking at Gray's Inn in London in 1973, explained that in practice judicial cooperation had developed more intensely with national courts of first instance and appeal courts, rather than national supreme courts, and it was often at the prompting of those

[15] Rudden and Rossa Phelan 1997: 53.
[16] Carreau 1978: 416–417.

jurisdictions that the most important principles of Community law had been established.[17] It is for good reason, therefore, that *Simmenthal* is widely understood as both the banal result of long-standing legal principles that had been germinating within the Community since 1963 and a stark novelty in its explicit attempt to marginalize a national constitutional court.

The approach of this book, however, is to situate the great judgments of the Court of Justice in the context of treaty provisions and state practices in other trade-related treaty regimes, above all those related to the enforcement of, and escape from, demanding treaty obligations. Just as *Van Gend en Loos* must be understood in the context of its relationship with the *Dairy Products* case, so too can the specific features of the Court's *Simmenthal* decision be understood within the context of the European legal order's use of national courts as enforcement mechanisms in combination with a firm rejection of any role for self-help or retaliatory behaviour by the member states vis-à-vis each other.

For a trade-related treaty system that seeks to remove the threat or use of inter-state countermeasures as potential mechanisms to enforce treaty obligations, then, when speaking in broad terms, it may be sufficient to state that an adequate substitute for such retaliatory mechanisms may be found by providing a direct and automatic enforcement role to the national court systems of the participating states. Beyond such a broad-brush characterization, however, such a system may benefit from a variety of more detailed and specific features. Most obviously perhaps, a mechanism may be included to help ensure that the application of the treaty obligations by such domestic courts incorporates the interpretation of those obligations by treaty-based dispute settlement institutions. Within the European legal order that role has been fulfilled by the preliminary reference procedure, which allows the national courts to communicate questions concerning the interpretation of European law to the Court of Justice.

Another aspect of such a system, most relevant to *Simmenthal*, is the need to reinforce the degree to which individual domestic courts within the treaty states can be reliable executors of the treaty-based obligations. After all, states within such a treaty system would be foregoing what is often understood to be a vital right to adopt retaliatory measures against other states that fail to fulfil their treaty obligations. To stabilize such a

[17] Lecourt 1973b: 172.

bargain, the enforcement role to be taken on by such domestic court systems needs to be as unequivocal as possible. Measures to ensure that outcome may also include the partial isolation of such domestic courts from potentially competing and distracting aspects of their domestic legal structures, even those that are normally considered hierarchically superior within their national legal order.

Here again we can benefit from looking at other treaty systems that use domestic court enforcement as a substitute for inter-state retaliation mechanisms. As discussed in Chapter 4 on *Dairy Products*, the NAFTA Side Agreements between the United States and Canada allow retaliatory enforcement of dispute settlement panel outcomes for complaints by Canada against the United States, as is common in trade-related treaty systems. Complaints by the United States against Canada, however, forbid any use of inter-state retaliation and require instead the enforcement of dispute settlement panel outcomes within the Canadian legal order by Canada's Federal Court. These Side Agreements therefore illustrate the issues that were addressed by a treaty system explicitly designed by states to remove inter-state retaliation as an enforcement mechanism. This system includes direct links between treaty-based dispute settlement institutions and domestic court enforcement, which serve a similar function to the preliminary reference procedure within the European legal order. Relevant to our discussion of *Simmenthal*, the NAFTA Side Agreement enforcement arrangements also include obligations on Canada to restrict the Federal Court's normal relationship with other Canadian courts.

Annex 36A of the North American Agreement on Environmental Cooperation provides that in the case of complaints by the United States against Canada, the retaliation-authorization mechanism set out in the main body of the treaty "shall not apply".[18] Instead, any remedial "action plan" or "monetary penalty" specified by the treaty-based dispute settlement panel is instead to be enforceable by the Federal Court in Canada, with that court being required to "promptly refer any question of fact or any question of interpretation of the panel determination to the panel that made the panel determination, and the decision of the panel shall be binding on the court".[19]

[18] North American Agreement on Environmental Cooperation, Sept. 14 1993, Can.–Mex.–U.S., 32 I.L.M. 1480 (1993).

[19] E.g. Grayson 1995: 143, Cameron and Tomlin 2000: 198, Hockin 2003: 245–246.

Annex 36A goes on to limit the possibility of review or appeal of the Federal Court's order, stating that:

> (g) a panel determination that has been made an order of the court shall not be subject to domestic review or appeal; and
> (h) an order made by the court in proceedings to enforce a panel determination that has been made an order of the court shall not be subject to review or appeal.

These provisions mirror the purpose of *Simmenthal* within the European legal order. They must be understood as an attempt to loosen the ties of the specified "lower court" Canadian judge, charged with the direct enforcement of the NAFTA Side Agreement panel's action plan, from their ordinary "hierarchical subordination" to mechanisms of appeal and review against their decision within the Canadian legal system.[20] The US interest in these provisions appears to have been to ensure that the enforcement role of the Canadian Federal Court in the NAFTA Side Agreement would be as straightforward and automatic as possible, without mischief-making.[21]

Provisions of the NAFTA Side Agreements, once again therefore, demonstrate that aspects of the great judgments of the Court of Justice in the building of Community law can be matched with provisions of a treaty regime explicitly designed to replace enforcement through the use of inter-state retaliation mechanisms with enforcement by domestic courts. *Simmenthal* has been widely and correctly understood as a landmark case in the development of European law's supremacy doctrine and as a vital case in any discussion of the "politics of judges" within the European legal order. Here we add that the provisions of Annex 36A of the Environmental Side Agreement to NAFTA suggest that the logic of *Simmenthal*, in its emphasis on straightforward enforcement by "ordinary" national courts and marginalization of the national judicial hierarchy, also follows from attempts to make reliable use of domestic court systems to substitute for self-help retaliation as enforcement mechanisms within demanding treaty regimes.

In this chapter we have argued that the principle announced in *Simmenthal* is a logical consequence of the role that the Community

[20] Cf. Carreau 1978: 416–417.

[21] Interview in 2014 with an official directly involved in the NAFTA Side Agreement dispute settlement negotiations.

legal order sought to create for national courts, that is to say, to replace the role of inter-state retaliation. We will now turn to our final case on the interaction of direct effect and the prohibition on inter-state retaliation within the European legal order, the *Sheep Meat* case, which demonstrates both the strengths and the limits of the enforcement system of Community law as the Court of Justice developed it.

8

Sheep Meat, 1979

No Inter-State Retaliation Revisited

The Case before the Court

The *Sheep Meat* case came to the Court of Justice as a consequence of the Article 169 procedure, which provided that if the Commission considered that a member state had failed to fulfil an obligation under this Treaty, then the Commission could bring the matter before the Court.[1]

The case concerned the compatibility of the French organization of the market for mutton and lamb with provisions of Community law. The National Cattle and Meat Trades Board [Office National Interprofessionel du Bétail et des Viandes] organized the marketing of such products in France. The Board's import regulations were in practice only then relevant in relation to the United Kingdom. Imports of frozen mutton and lamb were, for example, in principle forbidden, while imports of live animals, and fresh and refrigerated meat, were permitted only when French market prices exceeded national threshold prices, and an import licence was required. The British government protested to the Commission, and the Commission in turn initiated proceedings under the Article 169 procedure, alleging that France, by continuing to apply its national system for the importation of mutton and lamb from the United Kingdom, had failed to fulfil its obligations under Articles 12 and 30 of the EEC Treaty.

The French government, in brief, claimed that its national marketing system for sheep products was permitted by transitional arrangements provided for in the Treaty of Accession by which the United Kingdom adhered to the European Community, that such mechanisms were necessary – and indeed permitted – until the establishment of a common, European-level, market organization for these products, and that the effect of abolishing the French measures would be fierce competition

[1] Case 232/78 *Commission* v. *France (Sheep Meat)* [1979] ECR 2729.

from cheap British mutton and lamb, which would constitute a threat to the economy in certain less-favoured areas of France. The French government also pointed out that the United Kingdom continued to maintain an unmodified national market organization for mutton and lamb.

Advocate General Reischl's assessment was critical of French policy and the arguments put forward by the French government. He argued that the Act of Accession did not permit arrangements such as those under discussion that violated important provisions of the Treaty of Rome, and that, even if effects claimed by France of any abolition of the French measures were to materialize, Community law precluded "only *unilateral* national measures" to address such concerns. It did not in any way preclude measures, including aids, *adopted by the Community*, if warranted by the circumstances.

On 25 September 1979, the Court of Justice rejected the arguments put forward by France. Rejecting an attempt by the Commission to amend its arguments to include allegations against French policy during the transitional period provided by the Act of Accession, the Court confined its judgment to the period *after* the ending of the transitional period permitted by the Act of Accession, that is 1 January 1978, stating therefore that the dispute must be resolved on the basis of EEC Treaty alone, that is, Articles 12 and 20.

Declaring that it, the Court, was aware of the "genuine problems" that the French authorities had to solve in the sheep meat sector, the Court of Justice insisted nonetheless that, after the expiration of the transitional period, a national market organization may no longer operate in such a way as to prevent the treaty provisions relating to the elimination of restrictions on intra-community trade from having full force and effect. Where it is still necessary to take special measures, a decision to adopt them could no longer be made unilaterally by the member state concerned, but rather adopted within the Community system. It similarly rejected the claims that either the continuing failure to agree on the establishment of a Community market organization for sheep meat products or the maintenance of a national market organization for sheep meat by the United Kingdom could justify the French system. If France was of the opinion, so the Court declared, that features of the British system were incompatible with Community law, it had the opportunity to take action, "either within the Council, or through the Commission, or finally by recourse to judicial remedies". "A member state", the Court continued, "cannot under any circumstances unilaterally adopt, on its own authority, corrective measures or measures to protect trade designed to prevent any failure on the part of another Member State to comply with the rules laid down with the Treaty."

The Court concluded that the French system of organizing the market in sheep meat was incompatible with the Treaty of Rome in as much as it includes the fixing of a threshold price protected by a system of import bans and the levying of duty on imports from another member state. The French Republic therefore had failed to fulfil its obligations under Articles 12 and 30 of the Treaty.

Related Cases

The central element of *Sheep Meat* was the Court's firm rejection of any possibility that member states were entitled to respond to injuries to sensitive sectors of their own economies, or to failures by other states to fulfil their Community obligations, by unilateral restrictions on trade with other member states. *Sheep Meat* thus demonstrates the Court's continued adherence to the principles that it had first defended in *Pork Products* and *Dairy Products.*

After *Dairy Products*, but before *Sheep Meat*, the Court had repeated and developed its rejection of inter-state reciprocity and retaliation between the member states in various judgments. In *Commission* v. *Italy*, for example, the Court had stated:[2]

> In permitting Member States to profit from the advantages of the Community, the Treaty imposes on them also the obligation to respect its rules. For a state unilaterally to break, according to its own conception of national interest, the equilibrium between advantages and obligations flowing from its adherence to the Community brings into question the equality of Member States before Community law and creates discriminations at the expense of their nationals, and above all of the nationals of the state itself which places itself outside the Community rules. This failure in the duty of solidarity accepted by Member States by the fact of their adherence to the Community strikes at the fundamental basis of the Community legal order.

Other related judgments included *Charmasson*, where the Court had emphasized that after the expiry of any transitional period ordinary Community rules of free exchange would apply.[3] Judge Pescatore wrote

[2] Case 39/72 *Commission* v. *Italy* [1973] ECR 101.

[3] Case 48/74 *Charmasson* v. *Ministre de l'économie et des finances* [1974] ECR 1383.

that *Sheep Meat* was expressly linked to both *Dairy Products* and *Charmasson*, and illustrated the continuity of the jurisprudence.[4]

Analysis and Context

Sheep Meat is rarely included in prominent texts and surveys of the development of European law, or in scholarly collections of the Court's famous judgments.[5] Where *Sheep Meat* is included, it may be as an explicit example of the Court ruling out the ability of a member state to rely on failure by another member state as a defence for violating Community law, or even as an example of the Court's insistence that the Commission's submission to the Court must be substantially the same as its previous reasoned opinion.[6] The *Sheep Meat* judgment does however play a prominent role in Hjalte Rasmussen's well-known monograph, *On Law and Policy in the European Court of Justice*, where Rasmussen is critical of the Court's limited awareness of the "socio-economic" facts of the dispute, which underlay France's unwillingness to comply with its Community law obligations even after the Court's finding.[7] France's "flat refusal" to comply with the judgment is indeed one of the striking aspects of this case.[8]

The Court's rejection in *Sheep Meat* of any unilateral adoption of safeguard measures by individual member states is entirely consistent with the earlier decisions discussed in this book. As in *Pork Products*, and again in *Dairy Products*, the Court allowed that serious hardships resulting from the liberalization of agricultural trade might merit the adoption of safeguard measures protecting production in a particular member state, but that any such safeguards must only be adopted through the procedures provided by the Treaties, that is, by a formal application by a member state for the authorization of such mechanisms by the European institutions. As in *Dairy Products*, the Court rejected any argument that the failure of the Community to establish an envisaged common market organization for the agricultural products authorized any unilateral action by a member state in response. As in *Dairy*

[4] Pescatore 1981: 628.

[5] It is omitted in e.g. Craig and de Búrca 2011, Chalmers et al. 2014, Weatherill 2014, Schütze 2016. *Sheep Meat* is not included as a "basic community case" or a "classic of EU law" in either Rudden and Rossa Phelan 1997 or Maduro and Azoulai 2010.

[6] Dashwood et al. 2011: 144, Craig and de Búrca 2015: 441.

[7] Rasmussen 1986.

[8] Rasmussen 1986: 454.

Products, the Court rejected any argument that the behaviour of other parties to the European treaties could justify any form of unilateral behaviour by a member state in response. Indeed, because the concrete dispute in the *Sheep Meat* case concerned the relationship between one member state and another – France and the United Kingdom – while the concrete dispute in the *Dairy Products* case concerned the relationship between the member states and the European institutions, the *Sheep Meat* case is a clearer example of the Court's rejection of a common scenario in international trade politics – the use of retaliatory measures by one state within a trade treaty regime in response to alleged violations by one of their treaty partner states. As Kovar's analysis of *Sheep Meat* explained, the French government's argument advanced a sort of "exception on the basis of reciprocity" of the sort that the Court had always refused to accept as being radically incompatible with the very essence of the Community legal order.[9]

The *Sheep Meat* judgment therefore fits straightforwardly into the approach of situating the great decisions of the Court of Justice within the context of the challenges of enforcement and escape facing many other trade-related treaty regimes. It provides a high-profile example of the Court of Justice insisting on its own particular approach to both inter-state reciprocity and escape mechanisms within the Community legal order.

The facts and the law of the *Sheep Meat* case can, however, also be used to prompt a useful discussion of some of the tensions and limitations that lie at the heart of the European legal order. What *Sheep Meat* illustrates is that the European legal order's rejection of any use of inter-state retaliation mechanisms required, as a consequence, that the European member states had to accept that their European partners could at times persist in Treaty violations even after a finding of the Court under the Article 169 and 170 non-compliance procedures.[10] As we have discussed, the most serious weakness of the Article 169 and 170 procedures was that they could lead only to a declaratory judgment by the Court that a member state had failed to fulfil its obligation. Nowhere, perhaps, is this

[9] Kovar 1981: 109.

[10] It is of course when another state is failing to fulfil its obligations that a state's obligation to forgo any use of inter-state sanctions becomes most challenging and most important. Weiler is clear on this point, emphasizing that Community law prohibits any use of inter-state reciprocity and countermeasures "even in the face of actual or potential failure" (Weiler 1991: 2422).

weakness more prominently displayed than in the *Sheep Meat* case, where – and this is the essential point – the French government made clear, both before and again after the Court's judgment, that it would not be lifting the ban on importing sheep meat from Britain into France.[11] So, for a matter of several years, the French persisted in that policy after it had been comprehensively condemned by the European Court.

Of course, within many other international trade regimes, and certainly within the GATT or WTO, a scenario where an authoritative finding by an authorized dispute settlement tribunal that a participating state had failed to fulfil its treaty obligations was combined with a confirmation by that state's government that it intended to persist nonetheless with that policy, would be easily recognizable as leading to the possible authorization of retaliatory trade restrictions. Within the European legal order, however, as the Court had developed it in *Dairy Products* and other cases, no such action could under any circumstances be permitted. The European member state whose interests are damaged by such treaty non-compliant behaviour by another member state appears to have no effective remedy to address this issue. No wonder that this very scenario is so often emphasized in discussions of the possibility that the member states might "fall back" on the use of inter-state countermeasures against their Community partners.[12]

Sheep Meat shows that there are two related responses to such claims about the ineffectiveness of the Article 169 and 170 procedures. The first is that the essential substitute for the potential ineffectiveness of the declaratory judgment produced at the end of the process by the Article 169 and 170 procedures is the national court application of European obligations to the benefit of private individuals in line with the doctrines of direct effect and supremacy. The second is that the member states must accept *both* the limitations of the Article 169 and 170 procedures *and* the limitations of the direct-effect doctrine, if they are to obtain the many benefits to be derived from the Community legal order.

As for the first, contemporary discussion of *Sheep Meat* recognized the likely ineffectiveness of the Court's declaratory judgment and, at

[11] Hall 1979: "[T]he French Minister of Agriculture indicated that, despite the ruling, France would not lift its curbs on British sheepmeat imports until the EEC had adopted a common policy for sheepmeat: this stipulation was subsequently linked with a demand that the importation of New Zealand lamb into the United Kingdom be restricted." See also Rasmussen 1986: e.g. 340.

[12] E.g. Simma 1985, Dero 2006, Gradoni 2008.

the same time, emphasized that a viable alternative mechanism might involve the attempt to use the French domestic courts to further pursue the dispute. Hall, writing in the (UK-based) *Law Society's Gazette*, noted that neither the Court nor the Commission were empowered by the Treaty to enforce the judgment, and asked whether those attempting to import sheep meat from the United Kingdom should perhaps try to seek assistance from the French courts in their battle with the French government, using if necessary of the Article 177 procedure.[13] Domestic court enforcement was therefore envisaged as a reinforcement to the Article 169 and 170 procedures, in this case explicitly in the context of the potential for persistent ineffectiveness of the declaratory judgment of the Court.

National court application of European obligations is therefore a potentially powerful reinforcement of the declaratory judgments of the Court. Relying on national court application of European obligations involves, however, limitations of its own. After all, not all European obligations enjoy direct effect, and even where they do, the effectiveness of enforcement by domestic courts requires litigation by affected private interests as well as domestic courts who are willing to vindicate European law rights. None of these conditions is guaranteed to hold in any particular case, and so domestic court enforcement does not always remedy the failure of a particular member state to fulfil their European treaty obligations, even where they have been identified by the Court through the use of the Article 169 and 170 procedures.

The lesson of *Sheep Meat* is therefore that, while pervasive national court enforcement of European obligations is essential to permitting the European states to give up any possible use of inter-state retaliation, those states must accept the many failures and disappointments of national court enforcement as well.

Communicating the distinctive and interrelated advantages and disadvantages of the enforcement mechanisms offered by the Community legal order, as they are highlighted by the *Sheep Meat* case, is not straightforward. Perhaps the best way to convey this complex relationship is through a series of paired comparisons between differing enforcement systems from the perspective of a state seeking to have trade-related treaty obligations enforced in one of its treaty partner states. We will start close to the enforcement mechanisms offered in more common

[13] Hall 1979.

forms of retaliation-based trade treaty systems and then move step-by-step from there towards the essential features of treaty enforcement in the European legal order as the Court developed them over the 1960s and 1970s.

Our first comparison will be between an inter-state enforcement mechanism where states themselves make allegations about the non-compliance of other states and dispute settlement outcomes are merely declaratory together with an absolute prohibition on any inter-state retaliation, with the alternative where such declaratory dispute settlement outcomes may be followed by the authorization of inter-state retaliation or "reciprocal measures". It is straightforward to see that, of these two alternatives, state policy-makers may prefer the second one. An absolute prohibition on any inter-state retaliation would appear to remove an important incentive for the target state to make its policies compatible with its treaty obligations, likely an intolerable outcome for state policy-makers whose constituents depend for their livelihoods on the treaty-compliant policies of other states. Indeed, it is quite possible that various reciprocity and retaliation behaviours would emerge of their own accord in the first scenario, any prohibitions on such behaviours notwithstanding.[14] The second scenario however comes with substantial disadvantages of its own, because the threat or imposition of retaliatory measures themselves disrupt economic exchange as well as diplomatic relationships, without any certain guarantee of effectiveness.[15] This tends to encourage considerable hesitation and caution by state policy-makers in activating retaliation-based dispute settlement mechanisms against their trading partners, even when violations are clear.

Let us then compare this second system – a state-to-state enforcement mechanism where declaratory dispute settlement outcomes may be followed by the authorization of inter-state retaliation – with a third

[14] Axelrod 1984, and see Gradoni 2008: 70 for retaliation emerging in the GATT system, despite GATT rules that appeared to some to require that GATT members needed to consent to retaliation against themselves.

[15] Note that the text of the Treaty of Rome was silent as to whether any reprisals or countermeasures could be a consequence of a state's refusal to take the necessary measures to comply with an Article 171 finding by the Court of Justice. The Treaty neither explicitly provided for the possibility of reciprocal countermeasures nor ruled them out, so both options might have been possible depending on how the Court of Justice chose to develop the Treaty, accepting or rejecting the role that such countermeasures play in many other treaty systems (e.g. Lecourt and Chevallier 1963).

option – a state-to-state enforcement mechanism where dispute settlement outcomes are then effectively enforced by domestic courts within the participating states. It should again be straightforward to see that highly interdependent state policy-makers might prefer this third system to the second one, which provides a way for valid claims about the non-compliance by trading partners to lead to legal and policy change in those other states but at the same time removes the uncertainties to international economics and diplomacy associated with threats of inter-state retaliation and countermeasure in trade politics. The third system therefore provides two distinct benefits: the benefits of an effective form of treaty enforcement and the benefit of avoiding all the disadvantages of retaliation-based enforcement mechanisms. To be sure, such a system relies for its effectiveness on the domestic courts of the trading partner state enjoying a sufficiently independent and authoritative role within their own political system, and no doubt other facilitating factors, but the logic of exchange between state policy-makers is readily apparent.[16]

Now compare this third option – a state-to-state enforcement mechanism where dispute settlement outcomes are effectively enforced by domestic courts – with a fourth and final alternative, close to that developed by the Court of Justice over the 1960s and 1970s – an enforcement mechanism where on the one hand, states themselves can make allegations about the non-compliance of other states, but dispute settlement outcomes from such a process are merely declaratory, without any possibility of authorized inter-state retaliation, while on the other hand private parties within the participating states can seek to have treaty obligations effectively enforced by domestic courts within their own legal orders. Again, it should be straightforward to see that state policy-makers, in circumstances of considerable interdependence, might prefer this fourth and last system, which not only has the benefit of removing all the uncertainties to international economics and diplomacy associated with threats of inter-state retaliation, but also – where economic interests are

[16] Note that the text of the Treaty of Rome had not provided that the obligation on the member states to take the necessary measures to comply with an Article 171 finding by the Court of Justice entailed a direct obligation on the national courts to apply such measures in their own legal orders, and that by the time of *Van Gend en Loos* in 1963, the Court of Justice had, in the *Humblet* judgment, already rejected the argument that the Article 171 procedure involved the power to annul or repeal legislative or administrative measure of the member states, so this third option was not obviously readily available to the Court of Justice in the 1960s.

suitably aware of their treaty rights and where domestic courts sufficiently effectively take on the role granted to them – is likely to be much controlling of the domestic law and policies of their trading partners than where enforcement mechanisms can be activated only by state policy-makers.[17]

The overall benefits of this fourth and last system could be very significant even if they come at a cost, namely that inter-state complaints instigated by state policy-makers themselves can neither lead to authorized retaliation nor necessarily to direct domestic court enforcement within a participating state, and may therefore allow states to persist in violations so identified by this inter-state mechanism. These benefits could also be significant even if the effectiveness of private party enforcement through domestic courts in a trading partner varies significantly in its reliability and activity from issue to issue and over time. In the European context, for example, the number of "national court decisions relevant to EEC law" counted by the administrative services of the Court of Justice totalled almost 400 in France and over 700 in Germany between 1958 and 1979, and has of course continued to grow rapidly thereafter.[18] These figures demonstrate the unparalleled intrusiveness of the European legal order within the legal systems of the member states, a benefit obtained without the disruptions and stresses that would have been involved in an expansive use of potentially retaliatory enforcement mechanisms.

The sheer quantum of European law disputes heard by the national courts must be an essential part of any understanding of the political and legal context surrounding the possibility of "fall back" scenarios that so occupy scholarly debates on European law's rejection of inter-state retaliation. As the reader will recall, this debate concerns whether and under what circumstances a member state might revert to the threat or use

[17] Of course it may be that the merely declaratory inter-state enforcement system itself also gains indirectly in its practical effectiveness from its association with an enforcement system that provides rights that national parties can enforce through national courts. (Indeed, the effectiveness of the Article 169 procedure within the European legal order has no doubt benefited from the growth of the direct-effect doctrine.) But the benefits to policy-makers and business within the participating trading states from this fourth system of enforcement would primarily be the direct result of enforcement by private parties before their own national courts.

[18] I thank Carolin Hübner for providing these data. For Hübner's research on national court decisions on European law, see e.g. Hübner 2016.

of inter-state countermeasures against another member state for failing to fulfil its European obligations, particularly in the case of persisting to do so after the behaviour has been authoritatively condemned by the Court of Justice.[19] For a treaty with a single important obligation, the definitive failure of a system of direct enforcement by national courts to enforce that obligation would indeed likely prompt the possibility of a fall back on inter-state countermeasures.[20] For a treaty such as the Treaty of Rome, however, with the extensive participation by national courts in the enforcement of a huge variety of obligations, the situation is quite otherwise. To fall back on the use of inter-state countermeasures within such a treaty system in response to failure by a state to fulfil one prominent obligation would be to reintroduce all the risks and costs associated with enforcement through threats of inter-state retaliation even though an extraordinarily extensive and intrusive alternative mechanism has been founded and continues to thrive in many and growing areas of European law – a system, for all its many faults and limits, widely considered much more effective and practically useful than any retaliation-based system of treaty enforcement has ever been.

It would be easy to understand, for example, why a trading state like Japan might be willing to accept comprehensively forgoing the right to retaliate against the United States for failures to fulfil its WTO obligations if in return domestic courts within the United States were to be put under an obligation to directly enforce WTO obligations in litigation open to private parties. Such an arrangement would likely considerably advance the interests of Japanese business trading with the United States, and thus Japan's gain from this inter-state relationship, even though this bargain would explicitly weaken the inter-state enforcement mechanism available to the Japanese government itself. Of course, the American political system is not willing to offer such an arrangement, and in any event Japan and the United States are not as commercially interdependent as are the European states, so there is less pressure than in Europe for a more effective and intrusive trade treaty enforcement mechanism. This hypothetical comparison serves nonetheless to illustrate how the political and legal advantages of an expansionary doctrine of direct effect can serve to overwhelm the disadvantages of forgoing the right to impose countermeasures against a persistently defaulting treaty partner.

19 E.g. Simma 1985, Dero 2006, Gradoni 2008.

20 Cf. Gradoni 2008: 259 ft 90.

The essential value of *Sheep Meat* is therefore that it demonstrates that states benefiting from the Community legal order must be prepared to accept both the lack of direct consequences arising from the Article 169 and 170 procedures and the intermittent ineffectiveness of enforcement through direct effect. This case therefore makes for a fitting close to our discussion of how the early landmark judgments of the Court of Justice can be understood within the context of international collective action problems of trade-related treaty regimes. We will now turn to the topic of the protection of fundamental rights in Community law with a discussion of the Court's famous 1970 judgment, *Internationale Handelsgesellschaft*.

9

Internationale Handelsgesellschaft, 1970

Protection of Fundamental Rights

The Case before the Court

This case came to the European Court of Justice as a request for a preliminary ruling, under the Article 177 procedure, by a German court, the Verwaltungsgericht in Frankfurt am Main, in a dispute over the system of export licences and deposits attached to them in the Community organization for the market for cereals.[1]

A German cereals trader had claimed that the burdens imposed by this system of deposits, which would be forfeited if the envisaged trades did not take place except strictly in cases of *force majeure*, were excessive. Such requirements contradicted the principle of "proportionality" by which obligations should not be imposed on citizens other than those strictly necessary for the public policy purpose. The source of this proportionality requirement for Community policies was, so the Frankfurt court claimed, Articles 2 and 12 of the German Basic Law (the *Grundgesetz*, as the German Constitution is known). Those provisions state that "Every person shall have the right to free development of his personality insofar as he does not violate the rights of others or offend against the constitutional order or the moral law" and that "All Germans shall have the right freely to choose their occupation or profession, their place of work and their place of training. The practice of an occupation or profession may be regulated by or pursuant to a law."[2]

The Advocate General, Alain Dutheillet de Lamonthe, discussed four cases before the Court that related to preliminary references arising from disputes before various German courts complaining about aspects of this system of deposits, including whether the forfeits of such deposits were

[1] Case 11/70 *Internationale Handelsgesellschaft* v. *Einfuhr- und Vorratsstelle für Getreide und Futtermittel* [1970] ECR 1125.

[2] We use the translation of the German Basic Law by Professor Tomuschat et al., available at www.gesetze-im-internet.de/englisch_gg/englisch_gg.html, downloaded 22 August 2017.

equivalent to a system of fines or financial penalties, and whether the Community authorities had employed the correct procedures for the issuing of the Regulations in question. Here we will focus on what Dutheillet de Lamonthe described as the questions relating to the "*internal legality* of the provisions in respect of which the essence of the complaint is the violation of a so-called principle of proportionality which is alleged to bind the Community authorities".

The Advocate General discussed this issue at length. He defined the principle of proportionality as the principle "under which citizens may only have imposed on them, for the purposes of the public interest, obligations which are strictly necessary for those purposes to be attained". Before proceeding to discuss whether the system of deposits at issue might violate such a principle, the Advocate General raised the prior question, "what *legal source* this principle must be taken from in order to be applied against a measure issued by the Community authorities" [emphasis in original]. Three arguments were considered: the first, put forward by the Frankfurt court, that the principle of proportionality "results from the combined effect of Articles 2 and 12 of the Basic Law of the Federal Republic of Germany, Community measures may not infringe those constitutional provisions, an argument [so Dutheillet de Lamonthe went on] from which the court has drawn all the consequences since, before referring this question to the Court of Justice, it has held invalid as contrary to the Basic Law, the provisions disputed today before the Court"; the second, put forward in a related dispute concerning the system of deposits by a court in Hesse, found the legal source of this principle of proportionality in "the unwritten law of the Community, the general principles of Community law"; and finally that which the Advocate General himself suggested, "which would in this case find the source of this principle in an express and very clear provision of the Treaty".

Dutheillet de Lamonthe was clear that the Court must address the issue of the sources of the proportionality principle in Community law, and offered his own views. He began by stating: "One first point seems certain. The argument which seduced the Frankfurt court must be rejected categorically." As the Advocate General continued, "the legality of a Community measure can be judged only in the light of the common law,[3] whether written or unwritten, but never in the light of the national law, even if that is a constitutional law". He emphasized the passage of

[3] The English text uses "ordinary law" but the French text uses "*loi commune*", meaning the law that is common to all the member states, or even "Community law".

the Court's *Costa* v. *ENEL* judgment, which stated that Community measures cannot be overridden by domestic legal provisions "however framed", and referred to two early decisions where the Court had held that the validity of a Community decision could not be judged in the light of the Basic German law, including in relation to the very Articles 2 and 12 that were the foundation of the dispute in *Internationale Handelsgesellschaft*.[4] The Advocate General then carefully proceeded to deny that this implied that the fundamental principles of national legal systems had no function in Community law, asserting that they "contribute to the forming that philosophical, political and legal sub-stratum common to the Member States from which through the case-law an unwritten Community law emerges, one of the essential aims of which is precisely to ensure the respect for the fundamental rights of the individual". As Dutheillet de Lamonthe pointed out, the Court itself, in its recent 1969 decision *Stauder*, had affirmed that Community law itself would ensure the protection of fundamental human rights.[5]

The Advocate General then argued that the fundamental right invoked before the Court in this case – proportionality – was already guaranteed both by the general principles of Community law, as affirmed by the Court in two early judgments,[6] and by an express provision of the Treaty of Rome, which in Article 40 specified that the measures adopted for the Community organization of agricultural markets "may include only those measures *required* to attain the objectives set out" [emphasis in Advocate General's opinion]. Of these competing foundations for the proportionality principle that were embedded solely in Community law, Dutheillet de Lamonthe preferred to recommend Article 40 of the Treaty, largely on the ground that "it is good judicial technique to apply unwritten law only in cases of obscurity, insufficiency or gaps in the written law".

After that important opening, the Advocate General turned to a consideration of whether the Community system of export licences and associated deposits for trade in cereals did in fact violate the principle of proportionality, whether in principle or in practice.

[4] Case 1/58 *Stork* v. *High Authority* [1959] ECR 17, and Cases 36–38, 40/59 *Präsident Ruhrkohlen-Verkaufsgesellschaft and others* v. *High Authority (Comptoirs de Vente)* [1960] ECR 423.

[5] Case 29/69 *Stauder* v. *City of Ulm* [1969] ECR 419.

[6] Case 8/55 *Fédération Charbonnière de Belgique* v. *High Authority* [1954–1956] ECR 245, and Case 15/57 *Compagnie des Hauts Fourneaux de Chasse* v. *High Authority* [1957–1958] ECR 211.

Here Dutheillet de Lamonthe went on to argue that the licence and deposit system adopted by the European institutions was "probably the least restraining measure that could be imagined to guarantee a correct functioning of that market", certainly compared to alternatives such as reserving to Community agencies a monopoly of external trade, or periodic fixing of import and export quotas for external trade. Those alternatives might have imposed "too great restrictions on traders, restrictions which in the eyes of many did not appear absolutely necessary for the attainment of the aims in view". Instead, the traders retain their freedom of action subject to a system of licences together with associated deposits. "The obligations imposed by this system on importers and exporters are", the Advocate General asserted, "the minimum ransom, the indispensable ransom for the freedom of action that has been conceded to them." The Advocate General ended his discussion of this issue as follows:

> To conclude on these questions on the internal legality of the disputed provisions, I think that the system of deposits which they institute is both in its principle and in its detailed application necessary and even indispensable for the proper functioning of the common market in cereals as it has been organized and that the Community authorities, in adopting these provisions, have perfectly respected the obligations resting upon them under Article 40(3) of the Treaty.

On 17 December 1970, the Court of Justice replied to the questions put by the Frankfurt court. It found no factor capable of affecting the validity of the Community regulations making the issue of import and export licences conditional on the lodging of a deposit, or the regulations limiting the release of the deposit to circumstances to cases of *force majeure*. It is of course the logic of the Court's decision, rather than this finding, that has had the long-term impact on the European legal order, as the Court took the opportunity to consider the issues of principle in some detail.

As the European Court described it, the Verwaltungsgericht's claim was that the system of deposits was "contrary to certain structural principles of national constitutional law which must be protected within the framework of Community law, with the result that the primacy of Community law must yield before the principles of German Basic Law, in particular Article 2(1) and Article 14".[7] The system of licences and

[7] Article 14 of the Basic Law guarantees a right to property and inheritance. It reads in part: "Property and the right of inheritance shall be guaranteed. Their content and limits shall be defined by the laws."

deposits required by the Community regulations was an excessive intervention in the freedom of disposition in trade, "as the objective of the Regulations could have been attained by methods of intervention having less serious consequences".

Here the European Court set out its objections in detail:

> Recourse to legal rules or concepts of national law in order to judge the validity of measures adopted by the institutions of the Community would have an adverse effect on the uniformity and efficacy of Community law. The validity of such measures can only be judged in the light of Community law. . . . [T]he validity of a Community measure or its effect within a member state cannot be affected by allegations that it runs counter to either fundamental rights as formulated by the constitution of that state or the principles of a national constitutional structure.

Having claimed therefore that measures of European law could not be subjected to national constitutional rights protections, the European Court went on to state that it itself would take on the role of assessing whether measures of European law violated citizens' fundamental rights:

> However, an examination should be made as to whether or not any analogous guarantee inherent in Community law has been disregarded. In fact, respect for fundamental rights forms an integral part of the general principles of law protected by the Court of Justice. The protection of such rights, whilst inspired by the constitutional traditions common to the member states, must be ensured within the framework of the structure and objectives of the Community. It must therefore be ascertained, in the light of the doubts expressed by the *Verwaltungsgericht*, whether the system of deposits has infringed rights of a fundamental nature, respect for which must be ensured in the Community legal system.

The Court therefore relied on the "general principles of law" as the source of fundamental rights within the Community, rather than taking up the Advocate General's suggestion of finding such a protection in this case in Article 40 of the Treaty. It may be that the Court wished to make a statement about the protection of fundamental rights within the Community legal order of more general applicability than a decision whose logic rested the wording of Article 40 in relation to the common organization of agricultural markets.

The Court then proceeded to find that the system of licences and deposits required by the Community had the dual advantage over other systems "of simplicity and efficacy", compared to both mere declaration of exports effected, and to a system of fines imposed *a posteriori*. The Court then went on to reject the claim that "certain detailed rules of the system of deposits" supported the allegation that the "burden of the deposit is excessive for trade to the extent of violating fundamental rights". As for the question of whether the definition of *force majeure* – under which deposits might not be forfeit even if the envisaged trades had not been completed – was too narrow, the Court insisted on the one hand that *force majeure* did not refer only to cases of "absolute impossibility" but also in the sense of "unusual circumstances, outside the control of the importer or exporter". The Court also criticized the cases cited by the Verwaltungsgericht as imposing an unjustified burden as appearing to "concern situations in which exportation has not taken place either through the fault of the exporter himself or as a result of an error on his part or for purely commercial considerations". Such a view would lead to the substitution of considerations "based solely on the interest and behavior of certain traders for a system laid down in the public interest of the Community". The Court therefore concluded that:

> It therefore appears that by limiting the cancellation of the undertaking to export and the release of the deposit to cases of *force majeure* the Community legislature adopted a provision which, without imposing an undue burden on importers or exporters, is appropriate for ensuring the normal functioning of the organization of the market in cereals, in the general interest as defined in article 39 of the Treaty. It follows that no argument against the validity of the system of deposits can be based on the provisions limiting release of the deposit to cases of *force majeure.*

Related Cases

Among related cases before *Internationale Handselsgesellschaft* are two judgments of the Court of Justice (then of the European Coal and Steel Community) in 1959 and 1960, where the Court tersely rejected claims that the Court should consider conflicts with Community law and fundamental rights protected by national constitutions. In the 1959 judgment *Stork*, the Court of Justice stated:

> Under Article 8 of the [European Coal and Steel] Treaty the High Authority is only required to apply Community law. It is not competent to apply the national law of the member states. Under Article 33 of the Treaty, the Court is only required to ensure that in interpretation and application of the Treaty, and of rules laid down for implementation thereof, the law is observed. It is not normally required to rule on provisions of national law. Consequently, the High Authority is not empowered to examine a ground of complaint which maintains that,

> when it adopted its decision, it infringed principles of German Constitutional law (in particular Articles 2 and 12 of the Basic Law).[8]

In the 1960 judgment *Comptoirs de Vente*, the Court of Justice stated:

> The applicant supports its arguments with German case-law on the interpretation of Article 14 of the Basic Law of the Federal Republic, which guarantees private property. It is not for the Court, whose function is to judge the legality of decisions adopted by the High Authority . . . to ensure that rules of internal law, even constitutional rules, enforced in one or other of the Member States are respected. Therefore the Court may neither interpret nor apply Article 14 of the German Basic Law in examining the legality of a decision of the High Authority.[9]

There was also the 1965 case *Sgarlata* where the judgment explained:

> The applicants object that, if recourse to Article 173 were to be refused by reason of a restrictive interpretation of its wording, individuals would thus be deprived of all protection by the Courts both under Community law and national law, which would be contrary to the fundamental principles governing all the member states. However these considerations, which will not be discussed here, cannot be allowed to override the clearly restrictive wording of Article 173, which it is the Court's task to apply.[10]

Internationale Handelsgesellschaft shows a marked change in the Court's approach from these early judgments.

Internationale Handelsgesellschaft itself was only one of several judgments in the late 1960s and 1970s in which the Court of Justice combined a rejection of the relevance of national constitutional rights to Community law with the claim that the Court itself would take on a role in the protection of fundamental rights on a Community basis. The first of these decisions was *Stauder*, a case concerning whether revealing the names of beneficiaries of sales of butter at a reduced price under certain welfare schemes was compatible with the general principles of Community law. In its judgment of 12 November 1969, the Court of Justice explained that, in light of inconsistencies in the various language versions of the texts of the Community Decision, the provision in question must be interpreted as not requiring the identification of beneficiaries by name, and therefore that "interpreted in this way the

[8] Case 1/58 *Stork* v. *High Authority* [1959] ECR 17.

[9] Cases 36–38, 40/59 *Präsident Ruhrkohlen-Verkaufsgesellschaft and others* v. *High Authority (Comptoirs de Vente)* [1960] ECR 423.

[10] Case 40/64, *Sgarlata* v. *Commission* [1965] ECR 215.

provision at issue contains nothing capable of prejudicing the fundamental human rights enshrined in the general principles of Community law and protected by the Court". In *Stauder*, however, the Court did not set out a full elaboration of the relationship between national constitutional and Community law protections for fundamental rights.

Then, after *Internationale Handelsgesellschaft* in 1970, judgments of the Court of Justice continued to elaborate its new role. The *Nold* case concerned restrictions on trading activities, which an adversely affected business claimed were in violation of its proprietary rights, as well as its right to the free pursuit of business activities, as protected by the German Basic law, as well as the constitutions of other member states and treaties including the European Convention on Human Rights.[11] In its judgment of 14 May 1974, the Court of Justice explained that, as the Court had already stated, fundamental rights formed an integral part of the general principles of law, the observance of which it ensures:

> In safeguarding these rights, the Court is bound to draw inspiration from constitutional traditions common to the Member States, and it cannot therefore uphold measures which are incompatible with fundamental rights recognized and protected by the constitutions of those states. Similarly, international treaties for the protection of human rights on which the Member States have collaborated ... can supply guidelines which should be followed within the framework of Community law.

The Court found however that rights of ownership must be viewed in light of the social function of the property, and subject to limitations laid down in accordance with the public interest, and accordingly dismissed the complaint. The *Hauer* case concerned a Community prohibition on the planting of new vines, which an adversely affected landowner claimed were in violation of the right to property protected by the German Basic Law. The German court making the preliminary reference had explained that the provision of the Community Regulation in question "might have to be considered inapplicable in the Federal Republic owing to doubts existing with regard to its compatibility with the fundamental rights" in the German Basic Law protecting the right to property and freedom to pursue trade and business activities. In its judgment of 13 December 1979, the Court of Justice first explained that, as it had stated in *Internationale Handelsgesellschaft*, "the question of a possible infringement of

[11] Case 4/73 *Nold* v. *Commission* [1974] ECR 491.

fundamental rights by a measure of Community law can only be judged in the light of Community law itself". The Court then went on to consider the provisions relating to property in the European Convention on Human Rights and various constitutions of the member states, each of which permitted controls on the use of private property in accordance with the general interest, and further to assess in some detail whether the contents of the Regulation in question were disproportionate to the objectives of general interest pursued by the Community. The Court finally concluded that the Regulation's restrictions on the use of private property were justified by the objectives of general interest pursued by the Community.

After the 1970s, disputes concerning possible violations of fundamental rights by Community law have repeatedly come before the Court of Justice, and controversies over clashes between the protections for fundamental rights granted by national constitutions and the projections granted by European law continue to this day. In the 2013 case *Melloni*, for example, a case concerning the use of a European Arrest Warrant, the Court of Justice found that a Spanish constitutional provision ensuring a right to a fair trial could not prevent an extradition where there had been a prior conviction *in absentia*, citing *Internationale Handelsgesellschaft* for the assertion that "[i]t is settled case law that . . . rules of national law, even of a constitutional order, cannot be allowed to undermine the effectiveness of EU law on the territory of that State".[12] The individual in question was therefore subject to the arguably "lower" standard of fundamental rights protection offered by European law, rather than the "higher" standard offered by Spanish constitutional law.

Analysis and Context

The *Internationale Handelsgesellschaft* judgment is discussed in many leading texts on European law and regularly included in scholarly collections of the Court's famous judgments.[13] Leading texts use this case to demonstrate Community law's claim to supremacy vis-à-vis the most fundamental provisions of member states' written constitutions, even as a

[12] Case C-399/11 *Melloni* v. *Ministerio Fiscal* [2013] 2 CMLR 43.

[13] *Internationale Handelsgesellschaft* is included as a "basic community case" and as a "classic of EU law" in both Rudden and Rossa Phelan 1997 and Maduro and Azoulai 2010.

classic assertion of the full supremacy of Community law.[14] As Rudden and Rossa Phelan describe it, in *Internationale Handelsgesellschaft* the Court declared in forthright terms "that Community law must not be tested by national courts against their own Bill of Rights, else it would lose its character as law common to the Community".[15] Scholars sometimes emphasize that the Court of Justice's decision itself to take on a role in protecting fundamental rights was connected with its aim of securing the supremacy of Community law at the national level, particularly to overcome the reservations of the German and Italian constitutional courts.[16] Indeed, discussion of *Internationale Handelsgesellschaft* is often connected with lengthy assessments of the "uneasy and complex" relationship between the Court of Justice and the German Constitutional Court.[17] The judgment is also used to demonstrate the Court's use of the "general principles" of Community law to advance the development of the Community legal order, and for its discussion of proportionality as a general principle of Community law.[18]

Scholarship on *International Handelsgesellschaft* has concentrated on the way that this judgment demonstrated the new role of the Court of Justice in the protection of fundamental rights, and defined a change in the Court of Justice's evolving relationship with national constitutional courts charged with the protection of nationally defined constitutional rights, particularly in Germany and Italy.

Before the Court of Justice's landmark decisions at the end of the 1960s and the early 1970s, of which *Internationale Handelsgesellschaft* is perhaps the most famous, the European legal order appeared to offer no recourse to individuals who sought to claim that European obligations violated their fundamental, or human, rights. The Treaty of Rome made no explicit reference to the protection of fundamental rights, unlike the treaties of the failed European Defence Community and European Political Community earlier in the 1950s.[19] To be sure, the European Economic Community itself largely addressed economic and social matters,

[14] Craig and de Búrca 2011: 342, Dashwood et al. 2011: 271, Weatherill 2014: 71, Craig and de Búrca 2015: 268–269, Schütze 2016: 121–122.

[15] Rudden and Rossa Phelan 1997: 60.

[16] Dashwood et al. 2011: 338–339, Kaczorowska 2013: 216, Chalmers et al. 2014: 251ff.

[17] Kaczorowska 2013: 217. At more length, see the excellent study by Davies 2012.

[18] Chalmers et al. 2014: 254, 400, Craig and de Búrca 2015: 383.

[19] Pescatore 1968: 631 ft 2. Writing in *L'Europe des juges*, Judge Lecourt recognized that the Treaty of Rome did not mention fundamental rights (Lecourt 1976a: 209).

far perhaps from the most obvious sources of human rights violations, but even in these areas violations of fundamental rights to legal due process, to property ownership, to the free choice of profession, to free speech and so on, were quite conceivable. As early as the Coal and Steel Community cases *Stork* and *Comptoirs de Vente* of 1959 and 1960, litigants before the Court had complained that European obligations violated their fundamental rights as defined in their national constitutions. In these cases, the Court of Justice had refused to allow that these national constitutions provided fundamental rights standards against which the validity of Community law could be assessed, without however proposing any alternative standard or institutional arrangement by which fundamental rights review might take place.

After *Internationale Handelsgesellschaft*, however, the Court had clearly provided a mechanism by which complaints that European obligations violated the fundamental rights of individuals could be assessed. That mechanism was review by the Court of Justice itself, where fundamental rights became part of the Court's "general principles of law", inspired by the Treaty of Rome's authorization of the Court to make use of "general principles common to the laws of the Member States" when assessing the possibility of damages in the case of non-contractual liability (Article 215). The essential standard of review appeared to be a protection of human rights "inspired" by constitutional principles common to the various member states as well as by the provisions of international treaties for the protection of human rights, particularly the European Convention on Human Rights. This formulation allowed the Court to declare its openness to the influence of national constitutions and international human rights treaties while retaining for itself considerable discretion in how these principles would be applied in the particular circumstances of the Community. Certainly, the Court did not say that it would be strictly bound by the definition of such rights by national constitutions or international treaties, or by the interpretation of such rights in the decisions of national or international tribunals.

If we ask why the Court of Justice was willing itself to take on a role protecting against the violation of fundamental rights by European obligations in the late 1960s, but not in the late 1950s, we are lead to an interesting aspect of the judicial politics of the European legal order. To be sure, the Court had indeed, over the 1960s, come to find that European law was obliged to respect various important principles of legality and the protection of individuals, such as *non bis in idem*, so that the Court had, by the late 1960s, a greater engagement with aspects of the law more directly relevant to the protection of fundamental rights.[20] The crucial difference between the late 1950s and the late 1960s, however, appears to have been the appearance of decisions by the German and Italian constitutional courts that called into doubt whether European obligations could be applied in the German and Italian legal orders if they were in conflict with fundamental rights as defined by the national constitutional law of those states.

Both the German and Italian constitutional courts were postwar creations, charged with offering a process to assess claims that the fundamental rights of individuals had been violated by laws or administrative action. These courts were among the most significant constitutional innovations of post-1945 Germany and Italy, and part of the reaction against fascism and authoritarianism in both of those two new democracies. The ability of these courts to give a hearing to German and Italian citizens who alleged that their fundamental rights had been violated was potentially threatened by the growth of Community law, however.

As the 1960s went on European law norms increasingly claimed both direct effect and supremacy within the national legal orders. These European legal obligations appeared to fall outside the scope of review against constitutional law fundamental rights offered by national courts, without falling inside the scope of review against fundamental rights standards by any other body or tribunal. The growth of Community law would therefore lead to a growing range of legal obligations being applied in the national legal orders, which no court was empowered to review in the light of fundamental rights protections.

This scenario clearly disquieted some national lawyers and constitutional court judges, and one apparent solution was for the national constitutional courts to insist on reviewing Community law in the light of national constitutional rights, even if this put the supremacy and uniformity of Community law in jeopardy. It is in view of this possibility that Weiler, for example, sees national constitutional protections of fundamental rights as a profound problem facing the development of the European legal order. Weiler has claimed that the *status quo* position when the EEC was founded in 1957 was that Community measures coming into conflict with national guarantees of human rights "would be subordinated to them"; that it was "virtually impossible" that national courts would accept Community law supremacy without a guarantee of human rights protection; that national constitutional courts, particularly

[20] E.g. Cases 32/62 *Alvis* v. *Council* [1963] ECR 49 and 18&35/65 *Gutmann* v. *Commission* [1966] ECR 103 (Lecourt 1979: 95 ft 38).

in Germany and Italy, would find it difficult to accept that European obligations could lead their citizens to lose "any" of their protections under national constitutions; and that German courts would expect the Court of Justice's scrutiny of legislation for violations of human rights to match the "German standard".[21] On this basis, the Court of Justice faced the vital challenge of "detaching" the Italian and German constitutional courts from their national standards of fundamental rights protections in the interest of European legal integration.

It is hard to know how widespread, and how urgently felt, was the appreciation of this 'gap' among national lawyers and judges in the early 1960s. What we do know is that by the mid and late 1960s litigants had raised the question of whether national constitutional law fundamental rights could prevent the application of contrary European law obligations before both the Italian and German constitutional courts. The Italian Constitutional Court, in its *San Michele* decision of 16 December 1965, emphasized that the internal effects within Italy of the European institutions must be compatible with the "inviolable rights of man" that formed part of the fundamental principles of the Italian Constitution.[22] The German Constitutional Court, in its decision of 18 October 1967, expressly left open for a future judgment the question whether, and to what extent, it would review Community law against the fundamental rights set out in the German Constitution.[23] This aspect of these decisions was highlighted by contemporary scholarly commentary on the cases.[24]

[21] Weiler 1986: 1104, 1106, 1113; Weiler 1991: 2417–2418; Weiler 1996, Part II.

[22] No. 98 of 1965. From the Italian Constitutional Court's judgment: "It is not denied that these effects [the internal effects of international cooperation] take place without prejudice to protection under the law; this right is one of the inviolable rights of man which the Constitution guarantees under Article 2 [and which is also provided for by Italy's participation in the ECHR.]" 4 CMLRev, 1966, 81 at 83. For a commentary on the case in English, see Berri 1966.

[23] 22 BVerfGE 293. From the final section of the German Constitutional Court's judgment: "No ruling is given here regarding the question of whether the Federal Constitutional Court, within the framework of proceedings properly initiated before it, could examine the compatibility of Community law with the provisions of the Basic Law setting out fundamental rights. Neither is any decision taken here with regard to the question of to what extent such a function could be undertaken by the Court . . . This would depend on whether and to what extent the institutions of the European Communities might be subject to a system of basic rights in the Federal Republic of Germany or to what extent the Federal Republic could exempt Community institutions from being subject to a system of basic rights, where it has transferred sovereign powers to the Community pursuant to Article 24(1) of the Basic Law" (Oppenheimer 1994: 414).

[24] E.g. Berri who described the Italian Constitutional Court as affirming that, while the Community system may be extraneous to the Italian internal one, that did "not exclude the fact that the Community system has to fulfil itself in respect of the inviolable rights of

ECJ judges appear to have been aware of these German and Italian constitutional court decisions, and the Court of Justice's judgments seem to have been motivated by the threat to the supremacy of European law latent within this national jurisprudence, at least as much by any concern for the protection of fundamental rights in itself.[25] Writing at length on the relationship between human rights and European integration in 1968, and thus before *Stauder* and *Internationale Handelsgesellschaft*, judge Pescatore saw the whole problem through the lens of the possibility that notions drawn from this or that national constitution might compromise the unity of Community law, that is to say, barely as a human rights problem at all.[26] The solution Pescatore proposed in 1968, that the Court itself could protect fundamental rights within the context of the "general principles of law", drawing on the European Convention on Human Rights for inspiration only, while drawing more concretely on convergent principles of constitutional law among the various member states, in light of the needs of the Community, is close to that adopted by the Court itself in *Internationale Handelsegesellschaft*.[27] Pescatore noted that Advocate General Lagrange had earlier proposed a similar source for

man mentioned in the first place in the fundamental principles of our Constitution" (Berri 1966: 242), and Torrelli who described the German Constitutional Court's discussion of reviewing Community law against German constitutional law fundamental rights as a "threat" [*menace*], particularly given that the protection of individuals was far from assured within Community law (Torrelli 1968: 723).

25 Pescatore's 1968 article discusses the German Constitutional Court's judgment of 18 October 1967, noting that the German Court had left the 'final word' on the relationship of European law to the German Constitution to be decided in a future case (Pescatore 1968: 635), as well as various decisions of the Italian Courts including the Italian Constitution Court's decision of 16 December 1965 (Pescatore 1968: 636). Pescatore was also aware of the scholarly debate on this topic, particularly in German academia (Pescatore 1968: 632–634). Because the Court of Justice's judgments first setting out the Court's own role in the protection of fundamental rights in the national application of European law (*Stauder* in 1969, *Internationale Handelsgesellschaft* in 1970) pre-dated the best-known judgments of the German and Italian Constitutional Courts on the possibility of conflicts between national constitutional rights and European law (*Frontini* in 1973, *Solange I* in 1974), it is sometimes doubted that the Court of Justice could have been responding to the fundamental rights concerns of these national courts (and associated legal communities). Both Pescatore's and Lecourt's direct discussion of the earlier (if less well-known) judgments of the Italian and German Constitutional Courts in 1965 and 1967, however, suggest that this was indeed an important part of the Court of Justice's motivation (Pescatore 1968: 635–636, Lecourt 1979: 96–97).

26 Pescatore 1968: 638.

27 Pescatore 1968: 642 (general principles), 651 (inspiration from the ECHR), 652–655 (convergences among national constitutions).

a Community guarantee of fundamental rights in his opinion in the 1960 case, *Comptoirs de Vente*, which the Court had not at that time taken up.[28]

Writing after his retirement from the Court of Justice, judge Lecourt himself explained the Court's earlier, "timid and reserved" jurisprudence as part of its struggle against arguments that used reasons of national law to prevent the application of Community law, arguments that if accepted would have ruined the very basis of the Community legal order.[29] In light however of the Italian and German constitutional court decisions of 1965 and 1967, so Lecourt explained, where the courts had both been careful not to discard all control where a Community act was claimed to be in violation of the freedoms guaranteed by their national constitutions, it made sense for the Court of Justice to take precautions [*se prémunir*] against the risk either that Community law might breach fundamental rights protected by national constitutions or that the unity of Community law might be ruptured.[30] Again, Lecourt's account offers little emphasis on the Community protection of fundamental rights as a goal in its own right, indicating the Court of Justice's major objective was the protection of the unity and effectiveness of Community law.[31]

[28] Pescatore 1968: 638, similarly Lecourt 1979: 91–92. As Lagrange's opinion in *Comptoirs de Vente* stated, "[I]t is not for the Court, whose function is to judge the legality of the authorizations, to apply, *or at least to do so directly*, rule of national law, even constitutional rules, in force in one or other of the Member States (judgment of 4 February 1959 in *Stork* v. *High Authority*). It may only allow itself to be influenced by such rule in so far as, where appropriate, it may see in them the expression of a general principle of law which may be taken into consideration in applying the Treaty" [emphasis in original].

[29] Lecourt 1979: 91.

[30] Lecourt 1979: 96–97.

[31] A similar upfront emphasis on maintaining the foundations of the Community against possible breaches by national constitutional jurisdictions reviewing Community rules vis-à-vis national conceptions of fundamental rights is demonstrated in *L'Europe des juges*, where Lecourt notes that some ("fortunately rare") national court decisions had advocated such review (Lecourt 1976a: 209–210). *Internationale Handelsgesellschaft* is also discussed in *L'Europe des juges*, to demonstrate that "force majeure" in case of deposits was not limited to situations of absolute impossibility, and that the system of deposits was required by the heavy financial responsibilities of the Common Agricultural Policy (Lecourt 1976a: 134–135). Lecourt refers to *Internationale Handelsgesellschaft* when arguing that recourse to national concepts in assessing the validity of Community acts would have damaged the unity of Community law – their validity could only be assessed by Community law itself. The "conducting wire" [*le fil directeur*] of the judge in this matter is therefore once again the uniform application of Community law (Lecourt 1976a: 211–212). *Internationale Handelsgesellschaft* and the problem of national constitutional rights is also discussed by Lecourt in a chapter in *Mélanges offerts à Pierre-Henri Teitgen*, where he explains that the constitutional courts in Germany and Italy made reciprocal efforts to reduce the scope of the problem. When the former observed that in

Of course, for the risk to the unity of Community law to be eliminated or even reduced, national constitutional courts would have to accept the new role of the Court of Justice as an adequate substitute for the process of fundamental rights review that they themselves would otherwise be conducting. In landmark decisions in the 1970s that set out the relationship between Community law and national law, the German and Italian constitutional courts gave somewhat equivocal responses. In its *Frontini* decision (no. 183 of 1973), the Italian Constitutional Court declared that

> It is hardly necessary to add that by Article 11 of the Constitution limitations of sovereignty are allowed solely for the purpose of the ends indicated therein, and it should therefore be excluded that such limitations of sovereignty, concretely set out in the Rome Treaty, signed by countries whose systems are based on the principle of the rule of law and guarantee the essential liberties of citizens, can nevertheless give the organs of the EEC an unacceptable power to violate the fundamental principles of our constitutional order or the inalienable rights of man. And it is obvious that if ever Article 189 [of the Treaty of Rome] had to be given such an aberrant interpretation, in such a case the guarantee would always be assured that this Court would control the continuing compatibility of the Treaty with the above-mentioned fundamental principles.[32]

And the "*Solange I*" decision of the German Constitutional Court in 1974:

> The part of the Constitution dealing with fundamental rights is an inalienable essential feature of the valid Constitution of the Federal Republic of Germany and one which forms part of the constitutional structure of

the actual state of Community law, they could not refrain from imposing a national constitutional control, the Court of Justice, for its part, indicated its willingness to exercise a similar vigilence on Community Regulations, which would allow one to expect that the last resort power of the German and Italian constitutional courts would not have to be exercised (Lecourt 1984: 234). Again, this topic is introduced with an emphasis on the uniform application of Community law, with Lecourt stressing the risk posed to the common value of the rules of the Treaties. For a brief discussion of this topic by Lecourt when still serving as a member of the Court, see e.g. Lecourt's 1973 speech welcoming Advocate General Reischl, where Lecourt explains: "One knows then in what peril this law would be placed if national imperatives, even of the most elevated sort, required it to yield its Community nature. Thus can be explained the concern always possessed by the Advocates General, like the Court itself, to assure that the law derived from the Community protects those rights of the person [*les droits de la personne*] that are protected in every member State, in such a manner as to maintain intact the Community goal of the treaties" (Lecourt 1973a: 16). Again, the Court of Justice's protection of the "rights of the person" is justified by reference to the objective of protecting the application of Community law in the national legal orders.

32 Oppenheimer 1994: 640.

the Constitution. Article 24 of the Constitution does not without reservation allow it to be subjected to qualifications. In this, the present state of integration of the Community is of crucial importance. The Community still lacks a democratically legitimated parliament directly elected by general suffrage which possesses legislative powers and to which the Community organs empowered to legislate are fully responsible on a political level; it still lacks in particular a codified catalogue of fundamental rules, the substance of which is reliably and unambiguously fixed for the future in the same way as the substance of the Constitution and therefore allows a comparison and a decision as to whether, at the time in question, the Community law standard with regard to fundamental rights generally binding in the Community is adequate in the long term measured by the standard of the Constitution with regard to fundamental rights ... What is involved is, therefore, a legal difficulty arising exclusively from the Community's continuing integration process, which is still in flux ...

Provisionally, therefore, in the hypothetical case of a conflict between Community law and a part of national constitutional law or, more precisely, of the guarantees of fundamental rights in the Constitution, there arises the question of which system of law takes precedence, that is, ousts the other. In this conflict of norms, the guarantee of fundamental rights in the Constitution prevails ...[33]

As can be seen, both the Italian and German constitutional courts insisted that they retained the power to review European Community law obligations in light of the fundamental rights protections set out in their national constitutions, and more generally the fundamental principles of their national constitutional orders. Both indicated a potential willingness to rupture the unity of Community law on these grounds if necessary. These courts' responses to the possibility of conflicts between Community law and national constitutional rights were more ambiguous and conciliatory than their fundamental position on point of principle would suggest, however. As the extracts above show, this issue was discussed by these courts in somewhat distancing terms – "if ever...", "in the hypothetical case..." – and suggested that any such review would take place against a more limited set of fundamental constitutional principles, rather than every provision of the national constitution. Crucially, in both these decisions and in the series of decisions by the constitutional courts of Italy and Germany that developed (and at times modified) these principles over the following decades, these

[33] 37 BVerfGE 271, Oppenheimer 1994: 447, 448.

constitutional courts never declared that any directly effective Community obligation was inapplicable in their national legal orders because of its violation of national constitutional rights.

It is not surprising that the question of the protection of human rights within the European legal order plays a prominent part in many accounts of the interactions between the Court of Justice and the national constitutional courts. This is a fascinating story, as well as a continuing one, as the German Constitutional Court, in particular, has taken a variety of different stances towards its own role in the protection of fundamental rights within the Community legal order over the decades that followed, all however within a context of restraint in actually exercising the option of finding that a directly effective Community law obligation should be found inapplicable on national fundamental rights grounds.

So far, this discussion has followed the common approach of considering this question only within the context of Community law itself, where the determinants of the eventual equilibrium were set by the interactions of the Court of Justice, determined to head off a possible breach in the uniform application of Community law across the member states, and the national constitutional courts, apparently determined to ensure that Community law did not violate any of the fundamental rights protections set out in their national constitutions. As such, this topic appears to address a challenge particular to Community law, and deserving of attention as a topic that engages the most difficult aspects of the development of the European legal order.

The approach of this book, however, is to examine the content and impact of the Court of Justice's great judgments in a comparative context. For the other judgments under consideration here, the comparative context we have been using is the enforcement and escape mechanisms common to other international trade regimes, above all the self-help retaliation systems and unilateral safeguards provided for in the GATT and many other trade treaty systems. However, the question of how individuals are to be protected from violations of fundamental rights arising from treaty obligations is not very directly connected with the challenges of enforcement and escape in international trade politics. Indeed, it is hard to think of any scholarly discussion of enforcement and escape in international trade politics where this is topic is given any prominence. This itself is a noteworthy observation on the Court of Justice's judgments on the protection of fundamental rights within the Community legal order, and one we will return to at the close of this chapter. For the moment, however, it is sufficient to say that an alternative comparative context may shed more light on the Court's *Internationale Handelsgesellschaft* judgment.

A more appropriate context to understand the challenge faced by the Court of Justice in *Internationale Handelsgesellschaft* is the wider group of cases where national constitutional courts, particularly in Germany and Italy, were called upon to review whether treaty obligations violated fundamental rights protected by their national constitutions. This wider group of cases involves, above all, treaties *other* than the European treaties. After all, both postwar Italy and postwar Germany were parties to a great many international agreements, these international agreements imposed a great variety of rules and obligations affecting private individuals, and these private individuals in turn could litigate in the national courts to seek the protection of their constitutional rights against possible violation by treaty obligations. The decisions of the German and Italian constitutional courts addressing the question of possible conflicts between the European Treaties and national constitutional law fundamental rights can therefore be considered a subset of a wider group of decisions where the German and Italian constitutional courts addressed the question of possible conflicts between a great many treaties and national constitutional law fundamental rights.

Now, once this perspective is adopted, it turns out that these national constitutional courts adopted a consistent approach in such scenarios. This can be characterized as a combination of declarations of high principle, of the necessity of the possibility of review of treaty obligations in light of nationally defined fundamental rights, with very cautious specific decisions. These decisions rarely found that treaty obligations did in fact conflict with fundamental rights, and recognized that the standard of review for treaty obligations must be more flexible, more sensitive to international political realities, and, often, in relation only to a more limited set of fundamental constitutional principles, than the approach ordinarily applied to purely national legislation.

The landmark decision for the German Constitutional Court's approach to reviewing treaty obligations against the German Constitution, including fundamental rights review, was the Court's 1957 *Saar Agreement* judgment, concerning the agreement that settled the territorial status of that disputed territory after the Second World War. The German Constitutional Court rejected arguments that the Saar Agreement was unconstitutional, and as the reader will observe, quite explicitly acknowledged that constitutional review of treaty obligations must be conducted differently from constitutional review of ordinary German legislation:

> Above all, the German Constitutional Court, when it evaluates an international treaty, which regulates the political relations of the Federation (Art 59.2 GG [of the German Constitution, "*Grundgesetz*" or "GG"]), against the Constitution, should not leave out of its consideration the political situation from which the treaty has arisen or the political realities which it undertakes to arrange or alter. This is particularly important if, as in the Saar agreement, the political situation has been created in a part of Germany by the other party by virtue of their occupation authority . . .
>
> The undoubted constitutional principle that any exercise of state power in the Federal Republic of Germany is bound by the Basic Law (Art 20.3 GG) compels the question, in relation to international treaties of this type, whether only such agreements which fully correspond to the Basic Law are to be recognised by the Constitution, or whether we will allow voluntary undertaken Treaty measures which have a tendency to get closer to the achievement of the fully constitutional state, as far as is politically practicable. The German Constitutional Court finds it necessary to answer this question in the latter sense. . . . In treaty-making, a broad range of political discretion must be preserved because the respective parties limit the treaty solutions that are politically achievable in practice . . .
>
> These principles, taken together, may have the practical result that political agreements that gradually reduce the occupation regime, without also at the same time setting up a satisfactory new system in its place, retreat into an area of non-justiciability for the constitutional court. The constitutional boundaries drawn in this case, which if the law implementing the treaty transgressed would result in its constitutional invalidity, approximate those designated in Art 79.3 and 19.2 GG. Limitations of other constitutional principles are acceptable for a transitional period when they are directly related to the treaty's objective which is in its overall tendency directed to becoming closer to the fully constitutional situation. Up to the indicated limits, the contracting authorities of the Federal Republic are only politically responsible for the obligations entered into by them. The legal finding of unconstitutionality is generally excluded by the fact that the contract created by the state is "closer to the Basic Law" than the previously existing ones. If one only wanted to allow the validity of a treaty regulation fully corresponding to the German Constitution, that would mean following a constitutional law rigour ["*Rigorismus*"], which can be expressed in the sentence: the bad should not yield to the better because the best (or from this point of view: the only good outcome) is not obtainable. That result cannot be the will of the German Constitution. . . .

The principles developed by the German Constitutional Court in the *Saar Agreement* decision were later applied and extended to a wider range of scenarios (including those outside the ambit of agreements that reduced the occupation regime), where again and again the Constitutional Court insisted that treaty obligations must be potentially subject to review in light of German constitutional rights, but repeatedly found that such treaty obligations did not in fact violate those rights, particularly in the context of the flexible interpretation of such rights appropriate to international agreements.[34] In the whole postwar period up to the mid-1990s, in fact, there appear to have been only two instances of the German Constitutional Court finding that a clause contained in an international treaty could not be applied in Germany on grounds of a conflict with the fundamental rights protected by the German Constitution – both arising from dual taxation agreements between Germany and Switzerland.[35]

In Italy too, the Constitutional Court had regularly been called upon to consider whether Italy's treaty obligations should found contrary to Italian constitutional rights. And in Italy too, the Constitutional Court had consistently approached these questions with a combination of, on the one hand, an insistence that such constitutional review must be possible, and, on the other, an understanding that the standard of such review must be flexible, and only in relation to the most essential principles of the Italian Constitution. The Italian Court has only rarely found that treaty obligations could be considered unconstitutional on fundamental rights grounds.[36] Of the five cases where the Italian Constitutional Court found treaty obligations unconstitutional on such grounds from the start of the postwar period into the mid-1990s, two concerned extradition agreements that could have subjected individuals to the potential risk of the death penalty, one concerned extradition of a minor, and the last two concerned the Warsaw Convention on liability for carriage by aircraft, and an International Labour Organization (ILO) convention restricting night work by women.[37] Scholarship on the role

[34] Zeitler 1973: 262, Kischel 2000: 12–14, and by this author Phelan 2014.

[35] Frowein and Oellers-Frahm 1996: 87. The first decision was 30 BVerfGE 272, the second 72 BVerfGE 200. On the first decision, see Rupp 1977: 295. On the second, see Frowein and Hahn 1991: 384–385.

[36] Examples of cases where the Italian Constitutional Court rejected claims that laws implementing treaty obligations had violated fundamental human rights include cases no 20. of 1966, no. 109 of 1971, and no. 446 of 1990.

[37] These are Italian Constitutional Court cases no. 54 of 1979 (extradition agreement with France) [NB listed as 1976 in Treves], no. 132 of 1985 (Warsaw Convention), no. 210 of 1986 (ILO convention), no. 128 of 1987 (extradition agreement with the United States), and 223 of 1996 (extradition agreement with the United States).

of the Italian Constitutional Court in reviewing international treaties regularly acknowledges its willingness to allow the constitutionality of otherwise unconstitutional international agreements. As Barile has explained, while in theory treaty norms cannot be applied in the Italian legal order if they come into conflict with any norm of the Italian Constitution, in practice only the Italian Constitution's "fundamental principles" – its hard core (*nucleo forte*) – has had such an effect.[38]

In short, therefore, the equilibrium achieved by the national constitutional courts and the Court of Justice in the context of the European treaties has a great deal in common with the equilibrium achieved by these national constitutional courts in the context of other international treaties.[39] In both cases German and Italian courts continued to insist that treaty obligations could be potentially subject to national constitutional review on fundamental rights grounds, but in fact conducted such review with great flexibility and political sensitivity, favouring the constitutionality of such treaty obligations even if they might be unconstitutional if enacted as national law. The way that these courts came to accommodate European law was therefore not really a distinctive achievement of European law, and should not be seen as primarily the result of the Court of Justice's interactions with national constitutional courts in decisions such as *Internationale Handelsgesellschaft*.[40] Rather, it was in many ways the banal result of German and Italian judicial relationships with postwar treaty politics, adapted to the particular circumstances of the stream of obligations derived from the European treaties. So while Davies, in his admirable history of European law in Germany, is correct to write that the development of the European legal order required West Germany to consent that its citizens would be subject to treaty obligations contrary to their guaranteed basic rights, that essential point of principle had already been conceded by the German Constitutional Court in its *Saar Agreement* judgment in 1957.[41]

[38] Barile 1987: 84, 85–86, 91, also Cannizzaro 1991: e.g. 185.

[39] The reader interested in a more detailed analysis of the judgments of the German and Italian constitutional courts on conflicts between treaty obligations and constitutionally protected fundamental rights in the early decades of European legal integration (as well as briefer discussions of similar issues in the Irish and Danish legal orders) is referred to the fuller treatment of this question in the 2014 edition of the *Irish Journal of European Law*, on which this chapter draws (Phelan 2014).

[40] This is not sufficiently made clear in many accounts, e.g. Besselink 2007: 9–10 (compare Phelan 2014: 59–60).

[41] Davies 2012: 19. As far as this author is aware, none of scholarship asserting that national constitutional courts in the early decades of the Community would expect that Community law obligations would meet their own national standards for fundamental rights

To be sure, litigation over fundamental rights protections within the European Community, and now European Union, has only grown in scope and importance since the Court began to take on this role in *Internationale Handelsgesellschaft*, *Stauder*, and other cases. The Charter of Fundamental Rights of the European Union, first proclaimed by the European institutions in 2000, and the continuing debates over whether the European Union should itself become a member of the European Convention on Human Rights show that the law and politics of fundamental rights protections continue to be important aspects of the development of the European Union. The growing significance of fundamental rights questions over time within the European legal order should not distract, however, from a better understanding of the historical context of the Court's judgment in *Internationale Handelsgesellschaft*, which involved on the one hand the Court of Justice motivated primarily by the objective of protecting the supremacy of Community law, and on the other hand, national constitutional courts finding a way to apply their pre-existing flexible and accommodating postwar approach to possible conflicts between treaties and national fundamental rights to the peculiarities of European integration.

We introduced this discussion of *Internationale Handelsgesellschaft* in comparative context by observing that the question of conflicts between treaty obligations and national fundamental rights protections is rarely prominent in mainstream discussions of enforcement and escape in international trade politics. We will conclude by noting that this observation should counsel us towards not overestimating the practical importance of the national fundamental rights challenge facing the early Community legal order. There is of course a natural interest, particularly for national constitutional lawyers, in these tensions between the Court of Justice and the constitutional courts of leading European states. There are nonetheless strong temptations to exaggerate the importance of this topic, even to allow it to dominate our whole understanding of the development of the direct effect and supremacy doctrines of Community law. A clear grasp of the ways in which the postwar Italian and German constitutional courts addressed similar problems in other treaty contexts will help us avoid such an overemphasis. Just as *Internationale Handelsgesellschaft*

protections, or would find it difficult to accept that European obligations could lead their citizens to lose any of their constitutional protections, has based such assertions on an analysis of how such national constitutional courts ordinarily addressed potential conflicts between treaty obligations and national constitutional rights in the postwar era.

should be understood in the context of *Solange*, so *Solange* in turn should be understood in the context of the *Saar Agreement* judgment.

Writing in *L'Europe des juges*, judge Lecourt explained that he was only discussing "the rights of the person" at the halfway point of the book because "these rights were overwhelmingly understood by the Treaties as a function of the unity of the market. . . . The fate of persons was to be sure not ignored, but their rights derived first and foremost from the suppression of borders between the States. . ."[42] Seen in comparative context, and in line with Lecourt's description, the individual rights provided for by the direct effect doctrine have had a much greater impact, at once practical and revolutionary, through their distinctive approach to organizing enforcement and escape in the *market* between the member states, in conjunction with judgments such as *Pork Products* and *Dairy Products*, than through their connection with the development of a role for the Court of Justice in the protection of fundamental rights, in judgments such as *Internationale Handelsgesellschaft*. Our understanding of the relative importance of the landmark early judgments of the Court of Justice should bear that constantly in mind.

[42] Lecourt 1976a: 155. Lecourt's emphasis of the "rights of the person" is characteristic of left-leaning Catholic thought in mid-twentieth-century France.

10

States and Individuals in the Great Judgments of the European Court of Justice, 1961–1979

The European legal order was created by the Treaty of Rome and its Court of Justice. Because the Treaty was silent on many vital issues, the early judgments of the Court itself decisively shaped the way that Community law developed. It is therefore natural, and correct, that the essential doctrines of the European legal order are learnt through the study of the "great judgments" of the Court of Justice in the 1960s and 1970s. This was an era of fundamental judicial decisions without which the Common Market could not have been realized, and during which the Court itself grew from childhood to capable maturity.[1] Such were the achievements of the Court during this period that in 1976 retiring judge Robert Lecourt could declare, on the final page of *L'Europe des juges*, that "judicial Europe" had by then already been "made".[2]

In conventional accounts of the early development of European law, the *Van Gend en Loos–Costa* v. *ENEL* sequence in 1963–1964 is taken to mark the momentous birth of a new legal order. The special distinction of European law was to be found in the role of the private individual, empowered by the doctrine of direct effect to vindicate rights derived from the Treaties before their own national courts. This new role for national courts was confirmed and strengthened by the Court's declaration of the supremacy of Community law over conflicting national law, particularly subsequently enacted national law. These profound developments were derived by the Court of Justice partly from the text of the Treaty, above all from the preliminary reference procedure in Article 177 and the direct applicability of Regulations in Article 189, and partly from the Court's understanding of the underlying logic and spirit of the Treaty of Rome, as the Court explained in *Van Gend en Loos* and *Costa* v. *ENEL*. So the litigating private individual, above all, became both the Community legal order's "new actor" and the main beneficiary of doctrines set

[1] Lecourt 1987: 25, 31.

[2] *L'Europe judiciaire est faite*: Lecourt 1976a: 309.

out in the Court's landmark early judgments. It is in that sense that *Van Gend en Loos* founded a new European "citizenship", albeit primarily a "market citizenship", and placed "the individual" at the centre of the European legal order.[3] It is no wonder that much analysis of the "interests" underlying the creation and development of the Community legal order stresses the "bottom-up'" benefits of this new system for these litigating individuals and the newly empowered national courts.[4]

This conventional account, however, fails to sufficiently engage with the essential distinctions between the European legal order and the enforcement and escape systems commonly employed in other trade treaty systems. In fact, one of the characteristic features of European law scholarship is its persistent neglect of any detailed attempt to integrate the doctrinal novelties of the Court of Justice with the interests of the European states in the organization of a reliable intra-European market between themselves. It is far from unusual to read lengthy and learned monographs on the role of national courts in Community law, or collections of distinguished essays on the doctrine of direct effect, which contain either a single-paragraph treatment of "to-be-sure-the-provision-of-direct-effect-in-one-state-benefits-other-states"[5] or even no discussion at all of how these new individual rights and roles for national courts were connected to important international collective action problems and inter-state relationships.[6] In domestic law, it is of course widely

[3] Robert 1963, Everson 1995, Weiler 2014: 103.

[4] Most influentially, Weiler 1991.

[5] Claes's well-known monograph, *The National Courts' Mandate in the European Constitution*, provides a convenient illustration. This highly commendable and very extensive discussion of the role of national courts in European law appears to contain just a single-sentence discussion of how this relates to inter-state politics or provides benefits from one member state to another: "Probably the Member States do recognise the advantages of the doctrine of ordinary supremacy within the first pillar: it forces not only themselves, but more importantly the other Member States to comply with Community law and obliges their courts to enforce Community law against an unwilling State" (Claes 2006: 567). Even this modest and rather indirect comment by Claes demonstrates more engagement with this aspect of the direct effect and supremacy doctrines than many scholarly discussions of the enforcement role of individuals and national courts in the European legal order.

[6] To take one prominent example, the stimulating collection of essays on *Van Gend en Loos* from the Court of Justice's fiftieth-anniversary commemoration event does not contain a single direct discussion of how the direct-effect doctrine connects to inter-state relationships within the European legal order, or any comparison of the direct-effect doctrine within the European legal order with the enforcement mechanisms of other international economic treaties (Tizzano et al. 2013). The only mention of how direct effect might be involved in international relationships or in removing retaliation as a treaty enforcement

recognized that while public law questions before the courts are commonly presented as issues between the state and the rights of the individual, in reality they are often issues between different groups of citizens.[7] Similarly, while European law questions before the courts are commonly presented as issues between the European treaty system, the rights of the individual, and the litigating individual's own state, many of them are in reality issues that structure the relationship between the various European states.[8] Although it came to make use of individual rights as an enforcement mechanism, the Treaty of Rome was not a human rights treaty, of the sort where states often have little material interest in how carefully their treaty partners fulfil their obligations.[9] Rather the Treaty of Rome established a Common Market where state policy-makers and influential business interests had a very concrete economic interest in how effectively policy-makers in other states were carrying out their commitments.

If then there is a central intellectual flaw in many leading approaches to understanding the founding of the European legal order, it is in

mechanism relates to a discussion of whether WTO dispute settlement outcomes might in the future be granted direct effect in the European legal order (Jacqué 2013: 131–132, Ruiz Fabri 2013: 193–195). As so often, commentators have a clearer understanding of the impact of direct effect when looking at its possible extensions to new horizons, than when examining the role it has played where it is now already well-established. Note however the association by Louis 2013: 208 of *Dairy Products* with *Van Gend en Loos and Costa* v. *ENEL*, emphasizing the similarity of wording between *Dairy Products* and *Van Gend en Loos*.

7 Lord Sumption, "The Limits of Law", 27th Sultan Azan Shah Lecture, Kuala Lumpur, 20 November 2013.

8 Why the inter-state aspects of the direct-effect doctrine have been so neglected in European law scholarship must be a matter of speculation. Perhaps an almost exclusive emphasis on the role of litigating individuals and national courts appears best to suit the education of lawyers who need to understand opportunities for national litigation of European law and its relationship with national constitutional law more pressingly than they need to understand the distinctive trade-related treaty system that these litigation opportunities contribute to supporting. After all, national lawyers "make use" of *Van Gend en Loos* more directly than, for example, *Dairy Products*. That imperative – for the new national lawyer to learn to look "up" at the Court of Justice – might indeed contribute to an excessively "worm's eye" view of the achievements of European legal order. Even lawyers in training would benefit from a fuller and more complete understanding of the purposes and effects of *Van Gend en Loos*, however.

9 A paper on "Diagonal Enforcement in International Trade Politics" by this author provides a theoretical discussion of the way that individual rights and national court enforcement of treaty obligations affect inter-state relationships within the context of the scholarly literature on "vertical" and "horizontal" approaches to international law, and on debates about the differences between human rights and trade treaty systems (Phelan 2016a).

understanding the new doctrines – above all, direct effect – contained in the great judgments of the Court of Justice in the 1960s and 1970s only by contrast with the compliance procedures explicitly set out in Articles 169, 170, and 171 of the Treaty of Rome. That aspect of the story is, of course, a vital one. However, one of the most illuminating ways to understand any new institutional system is by comparison with other real-world institutions covering similar issue-areas where the novelties in question are lacking. Thus, the doctrines set out in the great judgments of the Court of Justice in the 1960s and 1970s should also be understood in the context of another contrast – a contrast with the enforcement and escape mechanisms commonly in use in other trade-related treaty systems, including the postwar GATT, forerunner of today's WTO.[10] That second story is just as important and sheds considerable new light on the achievements of Court of Justice in its most creative years. Any answer to such questions as "why are national courts involved with Community law at all?" must discuss the concrete alternative state behaviours likely to flourish in the absence of such national court involvement.[11] This is what comparative analysis helps us to identify.

Detailed comparisons with the enforcement and escape mechanisms common to other trade-related treaty systems regularly identify the European legal order's distinctive features as its rejection of inter-state retaliation mechanisms and its prohibition on the unilateral availability of safeguard mechanisms to policy-makers in the member states.[12] The availability of such mechanisms is certainly widespread in many other

[10] Scholarship sometimes shows a tendency to contrast direct effect with the Article 169 and 170 procedures while describing the latter straightforwardly as "traditional-public-international-law-type provisions" or as embodying a "classic international-law approach" (e.g. Lenaerts 1992: 98, Fennelly 2010: 42). Such descriptions rarely provide concrete examples of other treaty systems embodying such apparently "traditional" or "classic" approaches. The traditional or classic approach to enforcement in a trade-related treaty system such as the Treaty of Rome would be more convincingly described as involving state-to-state-complaints as well as the possibility of enforcing declaratory dispute settlement outcomes through inter-state reciprocity or countermeasures, a description that can be illustrated by many examples including the postwar GATT and today's WTO. Lecourt's 1963 reference to reciprocity as the "classic method" of enforcing treaty obligations is more convincing here (Lecourt and Chevallier 1963: 275–276).

[11] Temple Lang 1997: 4.

[12] On self-help, e.g. Simma 1985, Weiler 1991, Dero 2006, Gradoni 2008, Phelan 2012. On safeguards, e.g. Gori 1967, Roitinger 2004: 207, Teh et al. 2007: 26, Voon 2010: 647, Pelc 2016: 186. See also Phelan 2015a for discussion of differences between the European legal order and enforcement and escape in the Andean Community.

trade-related treaty systems.[13] Indeed, it is almost impossible to imagine that such mechanisms could have been comprehensively relieved of their essential roles in, say, the postwar GATT regime or even the WTO of today. Yet, the Community legal order has persistently rejected both since the early 1960s.

Prompted by this comparative perspective, we can derive a second, less conventional approach to understanding the great judgments of the Court of Justice between 1961 and 1979. On this alternative account, it is the *Pork Products–Dairy Products* sequence in 1961–1964 that signals the profound novelties of the European legal order, which lie in its persistent and effective rejection of the unilateral adoption of safeguards by the participating states, even when facing exceptional difficulties, and in equally in its persistent and effective rejection of retaliatory self-help as an enforcement mechanism – or "no escape" and 'no self-help', for short. These novelties were derived partly from the text of the Treaty, above all the structure of the general safeguards clause in Article 226, and partly from the Court of Justice's understanding of the underlying logic and spirit of the Treaty of Rome, as the Court explained in *Dairy Products*.

[13] European law's emphasis on the suppression of self-help retaliation and unilateral safeguards has recently re-emerged as the United Kingdom prepares to leave the European Union and searches for a new relationship outside the direct jurisdiction of the Court of Justice. Indeed, the imminence of the UK's departure from the EU has come, rather belatedly, to focus attention on concrete alternatives to the European legal order. The British government's August 2017 paper on "Enforcement and Dispute Resolution" after "Brexit" therefore candidly states that "In international agreements, final remedies are principally retaliatory in nature and implemented unilaterally by the parties. This includes the ability to take safeguard measures to mitigate any negative effects from the other party's noncompliance as well as the option to suspend all or part of the agreement", and supports this claim with illustrations of suspension and safeguard mechanisms in the EU–Canada Comprehensive Economic and Trade Agreement (CETA), the European Economic Area (EEA) Agreement, and the WTO among others. The ability of the EU's legal system to do without such mechanisms is "exceptional", notes the document. Thus, the state behaviours that were firmly and remarkably suppressed by Community law in the early years of the Court of Justice are being unearthed from obscurity as the Court of Justice's role within the UK legal order appears to be coming to an end (Department for Exiting the European Union 2017: 11 – this document attributes the EU's legal system's ability to avoid retaliatory mechanisms to the Court of Justice's power to fine: "The ability of the European Commission and the CJEU within the EU legal system to impose sanctions, such as fines for non-compliance with EU rules, is exceptional." However, as we have explained, the Court of Justice had rejected self-help retaliation and safeguard mechanisms thirty years before the Court was first granted or first employed its power to fine the member states, and it is instead the pervasive granting of direct effect to European law within the national legal systems that has primarily acted as a substitute for self-help and unilateral safeguards within the European legal order.).

This understanding of the early years of the European legal order has many advantages. It places an appreciation of state-to-state behaviours at the heart of its understanding of the development of the European legal order. It concentrates our attention on features of the European legal system that are genuinely astonishing in the long history of international law as well as in contemporary trade politics. It recognizes distinctions of the European legal order that have been highlighted by scholars and members of the Court alike.[14] It is arguably a better understanding of the essential novelties and principles of European law than the conventional *Van Gend en Loos–Costa* v. *ENEL* version because it focuses on well-defined impacts of the Court's judgments for European states and their societies as a whole, rather than the role of litigating individuals and courts in producing those outcomes.

Let us elaborate on this last point. Imagine for a moment a world, much like our own, in which several continents are constantly disturbed by the latent possibility, and intermittent reality, that states in their region make use of war – self-help in the form of armed force – as an instrument to settle their disputes, as states have often done over many centuries. In one continent, however, a remarkable treaty system seems to manage the same issues – reallocation of territories, adjustments to domestic governance in response to demands from neighbouring states, redistribution of international prestige – among its constituent states while effectively banning any threat or use of war between its participating states. Indeed, the possibility of war appears to have been so thoroughly suppressed that many people are not aware of this achievement, even though war and threat of war remain pervasive in other parts of the world. Upon further examination, it turns out that this treaty system grants direct rights to private individuals to make complaints before national courts which, in cooperation with a treaty-based tribunal and building on layers of agreements between the participating states, enforce the necessary changes in national policy.

Now in such a world, we can confidently say that commentators who, perhaps distracted by the novelties of this "legal individualism" or by lawyerly self-absorption, primarily highlighted the behaviours of, and

[14] Simma 1985, Weiler 1991, Dero 2006, Gradoni 2008. As Advocate General Léger declared in 1996, "Nothing is more alien to Community law than the idea of a measure of retaliation or *reciprocity* proper to classical public international law", Case C-5/94 *The Queen* v. *Ministry of Agriculture ex parte Hedley Lomas* [1996] ECR I-2553, emphasis in the original. Similarly, e.g. Kovar 1981: 109.

benefits to, litigating private individuals and judges in national courts within this treaty system, would be recognized as having missed the bigger picture. The real alternative to such a treaty system would be war and threat of war. Its beneficiaries would therefore include everyone (including of course non-litigants) whose interests might be injured by states' resort to armed self-help as a means of settling their disputes.

As it is in fact widely understood to be selfish and myopic private individuals and narrow interest groups that are the actors underlying states' incentives to take on the risks and material destruction of war, such a system could accurately be described as systematically subordinating the preferences of many private individuals and narrow lobby groups in the interest of an important national public good, the avoidance of war, by the state and its population as a whole.[15] This would be true even if the mechanism activating the dispute resolution mechanism appears to represent the triumphant role of individual empowerment. Such an outcome would of course represent a profound foreign policy achievement for any state or group of states.

Now let us return to our own world, one in which trade on and across several continents is constantly disturbed by the latent possibility, and intermittent reality, that states in their region make use of trade retaliation – self-help in the form of economic countermeasures – as an instrument to settle their trade disputes, as states have often done over many centuries. In one continent, however, a remarkable treaty system seems to manage the same issues – the enforcement of, and escape from, demanding trade treaty obligations – among its constituent states while effectively banning any threat or use of inter-state retaliation as a mechanism to address disputes, as well as prohibiting unilateral use of safeguard mechanisms. Indeed, the possibility of inter-state retaliation or unilateral use of safeguards appears to have been so thoroughly suppressed that many people within this group of states are unaware of it, even though retaliation or safeguards remain in pervasive use in other parts of the world, and within the global trading system. Upon further examination, it turns out that this treaty system grants direct rights to private individuals to make complaints before national courts which, in cooperation with a treaty-based tribunal and building on layers

[15] E.g. Angell 1911, Olson 1965, Doyle 1986, Kant 2003 [1795]. It is policy-makers in undemocratic states, with relatively narrow support bases in their domestic societies, who are particularly likely to behave in ways that promote the possibility of war with other states. This is not in the general interest of these societies.

of agreements between the participating states, enforce the necessary changes in national policy.

In our own world, however, there is no shortage of commentators who primarily highlight the behaviours of, and benefits to, litigating private individuals and judges in national courts within from this treaty system. Such approaches, however, similarly miss the bigger picture. The real alternative to such a treaty system is enforcement through inter-state reciprocity and retaliation mechanisms, and the ready use of unilateral safeguard mechanisms. Its beneficiaries therefore include everyone (including of course non-litigants) whose interests might be injured by states' resort to retaliatory self-help or unilateral safeguards.

As it is in fact widely understood to be selfish and myopic private individuals and narrow interest groups that are the actors underlying states' incentives to take on the risks and economic loss arising from trade retaliation and "temporary" safeguards,[16] such a system could accurately be described as systematically subordinating the preferences of many private individuals and narrow lobby groups in the interest of an important national public good, the avoidance of retaliatory trade disputes, and the cluttering of market opportunities by unilateral safeguards, in vitally important trading relationships, by the state and its population as a whole. This observation holds true even if the mechanism activating the dispute resolution mechanism appears to represent the triumphant role of individual empowerment. The European legal order is thus revealed as a remarkable trade policy achievement providing very concrete and specific benefits to policy-makers and business in the European member states. This is the Common Market whose principles the Court of Justice founded and developed over the 1960s and 1970s.

If a straightforward emphasis on the *Pork Products–Dairy Products* sequence as identifying the distinguishing features of the European legal order is arguably an improvement over the conventional emphasis on *Van Gend en Loos* and *Costa* v. *ENEL* alone, it nonetheless contains a severe limitation of its own. State use of both unilateral safeguard mechanisms and self-help enforcement behaviours are often accepted largely on the basis that there are no viable substitute mechanisms to manage

[16] Olson 1965, Downs and Rocke 1995, Downs et al. 1996, Rosendorff and Milner 2001. It is thus relatively small but well-organized interest groups such as US steelworkers that are willing to press their national policy-makers to violate treaty obligations in ways that provoke trade retaliation by the United States' WTO trading partners (Devereaux et al. 2006). This is not in the general interest of American society or business.

the underlying political and legal problems that these behaviours rather crudely and disruptively address. Dependable prohibitions thus appear impossible. The real distinction of Community law is therefore that its prohibitions of unilateral safeguard mechanisms and of self-help retaliatory behaviours by its member states have over time become remarkably *effective*. An appreciation of the novelty of the European legal order requires both an understanding of the new prohibitions on state behaviours contained in *Pork Products* and *Dairy Products* and an understanding of how these prohibitions were made effective. That brings us back to the direct effect and supremacy doctrines because the new prohibitions depended for their effectiveness on the new enforcement roles for private individuals and national courts that the Court of Justice was simultaneously in the process of constructing.

The connections between the Community's embrace of direct effect and its rejection of inter-state retaliation and unilateral safeguard mechanisms are numerous and compelling. It would obviously be difficult to sustain an effective prohibition on unilateral adoption of safeguard measures if the only available enforcement mechanism were an *ex post* declaratory judgment by a treaty-based tribunal. It would similarly be difficult to sustain an effective trade-related treaty system ruling out any possible use of reciprocity and retaliation mechanisms between its participating states if the only available enforcement mechanism were an *ex post* declaratory judgment by a treaty-based tribunal. In both cases, enforcement of treaty obligations by private individuals before national courts addresses the real weaknesses of the compliance and safeguards systems explicitly provided for by the Treaty of Rome.

These powerful logical connections are supported by the historical evidence drawn from the texts of the Court's landmark early judgments and from then contemporary scholarly debates. Wenner's commentary on the 1961 *Pork Products* judgment suggested that the Treaty's prohibition on unilateral safeguard mechanisms could be made effective by the Court's adoption of the doctrine of direct effect.[17] Paolo Gori, influential legal *attaché* to judge Trabucchi, later justified the Community legal order's rejection of unilateral safeguards, as first set out in *Pork Products*, by referring to the special role granted to individuals by the Community's "new legal order", and to the supremacy of European law.[18] The Court

[17] Wenner 1962.
[18] Gori 1967.

justified its supremacy doctrine in the 1964 *Costa* judgment by a straightforward reference to the Treaty's prohibitions on unilateral safeguard mechanisms, and the commentary on *Costa* published by the then recently retired ECJ judge Catalano considered that the division of competences between the Community and member states, illustrated by Community control of these derogation mechanisms, almost the only justification in *Costa* worth mentioning.[19] The dispute at issue in *Costa* was also one where the supremacy doctrine served to suppress a scenario, explicitly raised by the Italian Constitutional Court, that might incur the international responsibility of the Italian state, with all the possibilities that self-help retaliation and countermeasures might follow one step behind.[20] Judge Lecourt explained in 1963 than the ineffectiveness of an Article 171 finding by the Court might lead to a fall-back on classical reciprocity methods of treaty enforcement, but suggested instead a greater role for private individuals in enforcing Directives in national courts. Lecourt explained again in 1965 that the doctrines of direct effect and supremacy were required because, as the *Dairy Products* judgment made clear, the member states had renounced the possibility of employing self-help mechanisms to enforce their legal rights.[21] Lecourt's elaboration of the "*logique communautaire*" of the supremacy of European law in *L'Europe des juges* connected the supremacy doctrine both with the suppression of unilateral safeguards and with the end of self-help by the member states.[22] Finally, this approach to understanding the logic and purpose of direct effect offers a new and compelling explanation, more focused on the international collection action problems being addressed by Community law, for the Court's expansion of the scope of direct effect and the role of "lower" national courts in later decisions such as *Van Duyn* and *Simmenthal.*

Admittedly, the contemporary writings that connect the direct effect and supremacy doctrines to Community law's rejection of ordinary forms of self-help and safeguards in the 1960s and 1970s constitute a thin strand of legal scholarship. Contributions to this literature by judge Lecourt and *attaché* Gori, however, show that this approach was

[19] Catalano 1964. Arguably the reference to "institutions endowed with sovereign rights" in the Court's *Van Gend en Loos* judgment should also be understood to refer to the right of the European Commission to authorize safeguards and derogations.

[20] [1964] CMLR 425, 430–436.

[21] Lecourt 1965.

[22] Lecourt 1976a: 285.

embedded in the thinking of individuals at the very heart of the Court of Justice's internal deliberations. These influential lawyers appear clear-sighted when we observe that the role of direct effect as a substitute for retaliatory enforcement and as a control on unilateral use of safeguard mechanisms is recognized throughout the large scholarship that discusses the possibility of direct effect for GATT or WTO obligations within the European legal order.

Those at the centre of the Court's decision-making therefore appear to have had a good understanding of how Community law's new role for individuals was related to the elimination of unilateral safeguards and reciprocity measures in the newly developing Common Market. The Court was providing new solutions to international collective action problems that a familiarity with enforcement and escape issues in international trade politics brings immediately to light. It is only later scholarship that has tended to forget this. Indeed, the inclusion of an explicit discussion of the challenge of suppressing unilateral resort to safeguards can serve as a good indicator of whether a historical account of the early years of the European legal order is sufficiently embedded in the trade-related problems that the Court of Justice was facing at the time that it developed the direct-effect doctrine.

In a third and final account, therefore, it is the Court of Justice's *Pork Products–Van Gend en Loos–Costa* v. *ENEL–Dairy Products* sequence in 1961–1964 that marks the momentous birth of a new legal order. In these extraordinary years, the Court both prohibited common forms of state behaviour in trade politics and simultaneously created new enforcement roles for private individuals and national courts. These profound novelties were derived by the Court of Justice partly from the text of the Treaty, above all from the preliminary reference procedure in Article 177, the direct applicability of Regulations in Article 189, and the general safeguards clause in Article 226, and partly from the Court's understanding of the underlying logic and spirit of the Treaty of Rome, as the Court explained in *Van Gend en Loos*, *Costa* v. *ENEL*, and *Dairy Products*.[23]

This third understanding of the founding of the European legal order has the advantage of encompassing both the judgments that created these remarkable new relationships between the European states and

[23] This formulation correctly recognizes the general safeguards clause in Article 226 of the Treaty of Rome as equally essential to the development of the European legal order as the preliminary reference procedure in Article 177 and the direct applicability of Regulations in Article 189.

the judgments that newly empowered private individuals and national courts. It combines "state-to-state" and "bottom-up" perspectives on the novelties of the European legal order, and reveals how each is connected to the other. It shows how the interest of litigants in vindicating their European law rights before national courts was compatible with the interests of state policy-makers, and of firms not directly involved in litigation, in efficient and binding mechanisms of mutual control and in the development of a reliable Common Market. It is the best way to understand the landmark judgments of the early Court of Justice, bringing new expectations about state behaviours and new forms of individual rights together in the founding of a new legal order.

This approach differs profoundly from diverse strands of previous scholarship. Compared to so many accounts that introduce the achievements of *Van Gend en Loos* in strict quarantine from the detailed necessities of international trade politics, here the direct-effect doctrine is correctly recognized a means of enforcing *a treaty*, that is to say an instrument to change *state behaviours* and to structure relationships – in this case, particularly trade relationships –*between states.* Leading scholarship on the *Dairy Products* judgment has, to its credit, never overlooked that aspect of the Treaty of Rome. Compared to the impressive accounts by Simma and Gradoni, however, here *Dairy Products* is understood as intimately connected with the Community's approach to safeguards, and thus to *Pork Products*, and placed firmly in the midst of the larger number of the Court's landmark judgments in these crucial decades. After all, retaliatory self-help is a type of "exception based on reciprocity",[24] no ban on self-help would have been effective without an reliable prohibition on unilateral escape mechanisms, unilateral safeguard mechanisms often allow for reciprocal measures to be adopted by trading partners,[25] the controlled use of Community-authorized safeguards was discussed as an alternative to self-help arguments in both the *Dairy Products* and *Sheep Meat* disputes, and the Court's *International Fruit* judgment demonstrates how unilateral safeguards and retaliatory enforcement mechanisms, both together, can be contrasted with the logic of direct effect.

On the other hand, the importance of the *Dairy Products* judgment is here further extended, because the principle set out by the Court in November 1964 can be understood as the master principle of the entire

[24] Kovar 1981: 109.

[25] Gori 1967: 78, also 36, 80.

European legal order, from which the doctrine of direct effect itself can in turn be straightforwardly derived. After all, opposition to the use of inter-state retaliation is a common source of inspiration for the introduction of direct effect for treaty obligations, as debates over the possibility of direct effect for GATT obligations make clear. And indeed in 1963 – European law's *annus mirabilis* – we can see judge Lecourt doing just that, deriving the relevance of European law enforcement by individuals and national courts exactly from an aversion to falling back on more common methods of enforcing treaty obligations through retaliation and inter-state reciprocity.[26]

This new approach to the development of the European legal order does not in any way neglect the "European individual" or the "Community citizenship" that the Court of Justice founded through its the doctrine of direct effect. The empowerment of individuals to enforce their European law rights before national courts was undeniably a crucial decision. It claims only that characterizations of this citizenship as merely an "economic" or "market" citizenship are too limited. The citizenship founded in *Van Gend en Loos* was an "international collective action problem citizenship" – a "*Pork* and *Dairy* citizenship", closely linked to the Court's pioneering decisions on safeguards and self-help by the member states. The role of the individual in the European legal order has therefore from the beginning been at once less economic and more political – specifically, more international-political – than has yet been widely understood.

In short, therefore, whether one's primary interest is in European law's creation of individual rights to be protected by national courts or in European law's break with inter-state retaliation, it is essential in either case to recognize that European law's creation of individual rights to be protected by national courts was directly related to European law's break with inter-state retaliation.

To be sure, the obligations of the Treaty of Rome were never solely related to the expansion of trade between the participating states, and the scope of European obligations has only increased since the 1960s. The direct effect and supremacy doctrines established by the Court of Justice

[26] Lecourt and Chevallier 1963. Lecourt and Chevallier derived the enforcement of European obligations by private individuals before national courts from the principle that would be set out in the 1964 *Dairy Products* judgment *even before that judgment was decided by the Court*, perhaps unsurprisingly in light of Lecourt's long-standing interest in the suppression of self-help in legal disputes.

in its early years do of course facilitate the enforcement of a wide variety of European obligations, including non-trade obligations involving issues such as the free movement of persons, equal pay for men and women, environmental regulation, cross-border access to healthcare, and so on. That a large and growing number of non-trade issues have come to benefit from these enforcement mechanisms does not however displace the centrality of trade politics either from the Treaty of Rome or from the European legal order as the Court of Justice developed it from the Treaty's sparse provisions. "Although pursuing a more general Community objective, the purpose of the Treaties was in effect essentially, although not solely, economic," as judge Lecourt explained in *L'Europe des juges*.[27] It is therefore no surprise that, of all the available treaty systems, it was the GATT multilateral trade regime that *attaché* Gori employed as his foil when developing his study of the European legal order in comparative context.[28] Given the essentially economic purpose of the Treaty of Rome, the Court was facing many of the same challenges that confronted the GATT but sought to obtain a very different set of outcomes.

This understanding of the early judgments of the European Court of Justice may perhaps disappoint some readers. After all, it turns out that a central function of the new "European individual" was, and indeed is, to substitute for the use of inter-state countermeasures and prevent the unilateral adoption of safeguard mechanisms by the European states. Further reflection may however suggest a more positive assessment. The account advanced here places rather more achievements to the Court of Justice's credit than more conventional versions, and emphasizes that the beneficiaries of these decisions included a wider portion of European society than either the litigating individuals or national judges empowered by direct effect. More fundamentally, ambitious improvements in any institutional system are effectively built by directly addressing, rather than ignoring, the humdrum and mundane challenges facing participants in more primitive arrangements. Understanding how such ambitious improvements have been achieved in the past therefore requires a similar engagement with the concrete practical problems facing their less effective predecessors and contemporaries. Certainly, in the case of the European legal order the pedestrian problems of trade treaty systems were at the heart of the great judgments of the European

27 Lecourt 1976a: 155.

28 Gori 1967.

Court of Justice in the 1960s and 1970s. And, where politics and economics allow,[29] similar mechanisms stand available for policy-makers and lawyers who wish to restrict or eliminate the use of unilateral safeguard systems and retaliatory enforcement mechanisms in other trade treaty systems too, as Tumlir and others have advocated.

So far this book has tended to avoid describing the development of European law over the 1960s and 1970s as part of a process of "constitutionalizing" the Treaties. It is of course common to portray the growth of European law, and particularly the famous early decisions of the Court of Justice, as establishing a "constitution" for Europe.[30] The Court of Justice itself in 1986 described the Treaty of Rome as the "basic constitutional charter" of the EEC, and in 1991 again referred to the Treaty as the "constitutional charter of a Community based on rule of law", deriving this description explicitly from *Van Gend en Loos* and the direct effect and supremacy doctrines.[31]

There are certainly strong affinities between the European legal order and widely held understandings of constitutions and constitutionalism. These include, above all, the claim of European law to direct effect and supremacy in the national legal orders, and the widespread practical effect given to those claims by many courts in the European member states, which parallel the claims and influences of federal constitutions

[29] Phelan 2015b, Phelan 2018.

[30] Scholarship discussing European law in constitutional terms is extensive. Prominent contributions include Stein 1965, Stein 1981, MacCormick 1999, Weiler 1999, Douglas-Scott 2002, Walker 2003, Lenaerts and Van Nuffel 2005, de Búrca and Scott 2006, Lindseth 2016, Schütze 2016.

[31] Case 294/83 *Parti écologiste "Les Verts"* v. *European Parliament* [1986] ECR 1339: "It must first be emphasized in this regard that the European Economic Community is a community based on the rule of law, inasmuch as neither its member states nor its institutions can avoid a review of the question whether the measures adopted by them are in conformity with the basic constitutional charter, the Treaty." Opinion 1/91 *Re the Draft Agreement on a European Economic Area* [1991] ECR I-6079: "In contrast, the EEC Treaty, albeit concluded in the form of an international agreement, none the less constitutes the constitutional charter of a Community based on the rule of law. As the Court of Justice has consistently held, the Community treaties established a new legal order for the benefit of which the States have limited their sovereign rights, in ever wider fields, and the subjects of which comprise not only Member States but also their nationals (see, in particular, the judgment in Case 26/62 *Van Gend en Loos* [1963] ECR 1). The essential characteristics of the Community legal order which has thus been established are in particular its primacy over the law of the Member States and the direct effect of a whole series of provisions which are applicable to their nationals and to the Member States themselves."

within the court systems of their participating state or provincial jurisdictions. On the other hand, the European legal order as founded in *Van Gend en Loos* also demonstrates profound differences from widely held understandings of constitutions and constitutionalism.[32] After all, many constitutions are designed to structure mass participation in democratic self-government or to protect minority rights and civil liberties, neither of which was a direct concern of *Van Gend en Loos*. Furthermore, the widespread effect given to the direct effect and supremacy doctrines by many member state courts coexists with a profound and continuing rejection by those same courts of any claim that European law itself determines the basis of European law's application in the national legal orders.[33] National courts insist instead that European law obligations only receive national legal effect because national statutory and constitutional provisions continue to so provide and require. Such a proviso is profoundly at odds with the "constitutionalist" vision of this relationship, because it holds out the possibility of national courts refusing to apply directly effective European law obligations on grounds that these exceed the competences granted by the member states to the European institutions, or would conflict with national constitutional fundamental rights, national constitutional values, or a unilaterally enacted national statute or constitutional amendment deliberately designed to selectively oust the domestic application of European obligations.[34]

Discussion of the European legal order as a constitution therefore tends to drift into "is-it-a-real-constitution-or-not?" debates, which are not always particularly illuminating. Only a heavily qualified applicability of a wider constitutional model can possibly be compelling. Simple characterizations of the European legal order as a transnational constitution, or the Court of Justice as having created a "constitution by judicial fiat" in its *Van Gend en Loos* and *Costa* v. *ENEL* judgments, may be acceptable perhaps as intellectual provocations, but they are not convincing overall assessments.[35]

Compared to many discussions of the 'constitutional development' of the European legal order, this book's approach to the Court of Justice's

[32] Here we are particularly influenced by Isiksel 2016.

[33] E.g. Hogan and Whelan 1995, Rossa Phelan 1997. National courts therefore reject the Court of Justice's foundational claim in *Van Gend en Loos* that European law is applied "independently of the legislation of the member states" (Phelan 2010: 256).

[34] Phelan 2008, Phelan 2010.

[35] Cf. Stein 1965.

early landmark judgments is more compelling because it is more concrete. It cannot be denied that regulating the use of self-help retaliation and the unilateral activation of safeguards were profound challenges facing the early Treaty of Rome, just as they would be for any demanding international trade treaty. Indeed, these problems appear to have been central preoccupations of some of the Court's most influential lawyers.[36] The Court of Justice went on to comprehensively prohibit such behaviours within the Common Market in its *Pork Products* and *Dairy Products* judgments. The mechanism for making these ambitious prohibitions effective was, above all, the doctrine of direct effect. *Van Gend en Loos* was thus primarily concerned with specific problems of *inter-state trade politics*. In this respect the European legal order itself is widely accepted as providing the model against which the progress of other trade treaty systems can be measured.[37]

This is not to deny the value of continuing debate about the constitutional status of the European legal order, but rather to suggest that this discussion must be carefully advanced. Understanding the direct-effect doctrine as a remarkable instrument of inter-state trade politics without engaging with the constitutional debate is more than defensible: after all, the transformation of trade relationships within the European legal order is genuinely astonishing when compared to many other trade treaty systems. Understanding the direct-effect doctrine *both* as a very specific instrument of inter-state trade politics *and* as the potential basis for a constitutional understanding of the Treaty of Rome builds on these profound practical effects by bringing out the grandeur of the Court of Justice's ambitions and the wider role that *Van Gend en Loos* would come to play in promoting European unity. Understanding the direct-effect doctrine as the potential basis for a constitutional understanding of the Treaty of Rome *without* recognizing its specific contributions to inter-state trade politics cannot be recommended, however. Here theoretical discussion is liable to be insufficiently grounded in the particular problems that the Court was addressing at the time of *Van Gend en Loos*, and the "constitutional varnish" will likely obscure, rather than enhance, the plain timber of European trade integration to which it is applied.

For the avoidance of any misunderstanding, we should emphasize that the legal principles set out by the Court in the 1960s and 1970s were

[36] E.g. Lecourt 1931, Lecourt and Chevallier 1963, Lecourt 1965, Gori 1967, Lecourt 1968a, Lecourt 1991.
[37] E.g. Tumlir 1983a.

neither instantly effective nor did their eventual acceptance by governments, courts, and private actors derive from the Court's judgments alone. It took of course a long while for many national courts and lawyers to actively accept the new roles that the direct effect of European law had granted them, and indeed all the principles established in the Court's early judgments only became reasonably practically (if still imperfectly) effective over many years.

Furthermore, the ability of the European legal order to achieve a considerable degree of acceptance among its member states over time was assisted by a wide range of more political and economic factors. Growing and intense economic interdependence among the European states created demand for an unusually effective system for enforcing international trade obligations.[38] The rise of intra-industry trade – the exchange of similar goods between trading states – entailed a demanding trade relationship with relatively limited adjustments costs on firms and workers.[39] The postwar growth of the welfare state ensured that those facing economic dislocations were better compensated and protected than at any point in previous European history, and provided governments a wider range of financial instruments to manage the challenges facing affected firms and industries, in place of inefficient trade barriers.[40] New forms of parliamentary and administrative governance in the post-1945 European states stabilized national policy-making and helped states to reliably fulfil their international commitments.[41] The postwar European states therefore had both unusually strong incentives to obtain effective control over their trading partners' policy-making and unusually strong abilities to manage the adjustment costs of trade integration. The uniformly democratic basis of politics in the integrating European states provided the possibility of using national court systems to enforce treaty obligations. These features of inter-state trade

[38] Mongelli et al. 2005. The member states therefore had incentives to accept a much more demanding and effective treaty system would have been the case at lower levels of interdependence.

[39] Milward et al. 1992: 124.

[40] E.g. Cameron 1978, Ruggie 1982, Nord 2010. For the argument that the use of GATT-style safeguards is derivative of the political difficulty of raising taxes to act as an alternative insurance system for adversely affected industries (with the implication therefore that welfare states should need less GATT-style safeguards in their trading relationships), see Fischer and Prusa 2003.

[41] Above all, Lindseth 2010; see also Lindseth 2002, Lindseth 2016.

and domestic politics distinguished postwar western Europe from other trading regions, and from the global trade regime.

All this has been told in fuller detail elsewhere.[42] Even within this favourable environment, however, the "Lecourt years" of the Court of Justice (as judge Pescatore later described them) had a major role to play, by constructing a new legal order whose essential principles set out to reject the approaches to enforcement and escape found in more common forms of trade treaty.[43] All legal institutions are necessitated by facts, as Lecourt had emphasized in his early scholarship, and in the 1960s and 1970s the political-economy facts of an integrating Europe were matched by new and ambitious legal institutions.[44]

We will finish by briefly returning to Lecourt himself. Today's European legal order is the result of many and diverse influences, which include the contributions of the Court of Justice as well as those of the legal services of the European Commission, national judges, litigants both strategic and opportunistic, policy-makers in national governments, legal scholars and teachers, and, in the background, the growing interdependence of the postwar European states. However, no single individual can claim a more profound influence on European law than judge Lecourt.

Despite the destruction of his private papers and the inaccessibility of the most sensitive parts of the Court's own archives, it is clear that Lecourt brought many talents to the Court. His extensive involvement in journalism and party- political organizing was valuable background for a Court that needed to publicize its ground-breaking doctrines in the media and legal networks.[45] He also held a long-standing commitment to ambitious forms of international law and organization. In his 1937 article on "politics as an obligation", for example, Lecourt called not only for the

[42] By this author in Phelan 2015b, Phelan 2018. (For an earlier, more theoretical, discussion of how a trade regime might operate without retaliatory enforcement mechanisms, see Phelan 2011a.) The list of important economic and political influences could be further elaborated of course, including the relative equality in size between the larger member states, inhibiting the imposition of a unilateral solution to trade politics problems by a dominant power, and the role of the Common Agricultural Policy in making agricultural liberalization politically acceptable through common agreements to ensure high incomes for producers.

[43] Pescatore 2005: 595.

[44] Lecourt 1931: 11.

[45] Lecourt was, for example, the driving force behind the monthly periodical *Route des Jeunes*, which was affiliated with the French prewar Christian Democratic party, Parti Démocrate Populaire (Lecourt 1935).

reform of capitalism and a minimum wage, but also for the "submission" of "all peoples" to "a supranational authority, which is to say a limitation of sovereignty for each state".[46] His prominent participation in the Catholic and Gaullist Resistance movements in occupied France demonstrated his willingness to take risks for his commitments.

Lecourt had many years of experience in France's constitutional debates and, as parliamentary party leader for the *Mouvement Républicain Populaire*, familiarity in managing strong-willed individuals working towards a collective goal. No newcomer to the challenges of European unity, Lecourt was active in the transnational discussions of postwar Europe with his French, German, Italian, and other counterparts among Europe's newly influential Christian Democratic parties.[47] As for Lecourt's views on the law, his early scholarship on French property disputes repeatedly admired the way in which the courts themselves had developed the law in response to economic and social needs, even though such a role was rejected by French legal tradition.[48] Thus in personal experience and attitude, and perhaps also in religion at a time when Catholics were showing a new openness to rights and international law,[49] Lecourt had much to contribute to a Court of Justice that, with a coherence of purpose over many years, limited the sovereign rights of the European states and created a new legal order from the terse provisions of the Treaty of Rome.

Above all, the profound rejection of self-help in the resolution of disputes, demonstrated in Lecourt's early legal scholarship, appears to have been the beginning of a strong and continuing interest in alternatives to self-help methods of enforcing international obligations. As he explained in 1931, in his view international organizations were called upon to "prohibit nations, just as it has long been forbidden to individuals, from taking the law into their own hands".[50] Lecourt was thus well prepared to recognize the extraordinary potential of the direct-effect

46 Lecourt 1937: 34, within the context of a call to reinvigorate the League of Nations.

47 Pappini 1996.

48 Lecourt 1931: 236, 282.

49 Moyn 2015, Duranti 2017. Continuing research into Lecourt's life and contributions to European law is supported by the Jean Monnet Chair on EU Politics and Law at Trinity College Dublin.

50 Lecourt 1931: 284–285 on international law. The rejection of self-help activities in French property disputes is the central theme of Lecourt's dissertation as a whole. As for Lecourt's continuing interest in this aspect of international law, see his final book chapter on European law, published 15 years after his retirement from the Court of Justice (Lecourt 1991). There is therefore a certain consistency in Lecourt's intellectual interests over the sixty years from 1931 to 1991 (Phelan 2017).

doctrine to act as a substitute for the reciprocity principles of classical international law.[51] The prohibition of inter-state retaliation is an essential part of what has made the European legal order "something new", and its roots can be found much more clearly in Lecourt's intellectual commitments than in the text of the Treaty itself.[52] Today's European legal order, from which Europe has benefited so much, may, in this important sense, be Robert Lecourt's particular accomplishment.

[51] Lecourt and Chevallier 1963.
[52] Weiler 1991: 2422.

BIBLIOGRAPHY

Angell, Norman (1911). *The Great Illusion: A Study of the Relation of Military Power in Nations to Their Economic and Social Advantage*. London, Heinemann.

Arnull, Anthony (2006). *The European Union and Its Court of Justice*. Oxford, Oxford University Press.

Axelrod, Robert M. (1984). *The Evolution of Cooperation*. New York, Basic Books.

Azzalini, Marco and Claudia Sandei (eds) (2008). *La formazione del diritto europeo: Giornata di studio per Alberto Trabucchi nel centenario della nascita*. Padua, CEDAM.

Bailleux, Julie (2013). "Michel Gaudet, a Law Entrepreneur: The Role of the Legal Service of the European Executives in the Invention of EC Law and the Birth of the Common Market Law Review". *Common Market Law Review* 50: 359–368.

Barile, Giuseppe (1987). *Costituzione e Rinvio Mobile a Diritto Straniero, Diritto Canonico, Diritto Comunitario, Diritto Internazionale*. Padova, CEDAM.

Barton, John, Judith Goldstein, Timothy Josling and Richard Steinberg (2006). *The Evolution of the Trade Regime: Politics, Law, and Economics of the GATT and the WTO*. Princeton, NJ, Princeton University Press.

Bellanger, François (1968). "Contribution a L'Etude de la Nature Juridique des "Accords de Luxembourg" du 29 January 1966". *Nederlands Tijdschrift voor Internationaal Recht* 15: 179–196.

Bernier, Alexandre (2018). "La France et le droit communautaire 1958–1981: Histoire d'une réception et d'une coproduction". PhD thesis, University of Copenhagen.

Berri, Mario (1966). "Annotation on *San Michele* Decision of the Italian Constitutional Court". *Common Market Law Review* 4: 238–242.

Besselink, Leonard F. M. (2007). *A Composite European Constitution*. Groningen, Europa Law Publishing.

Boerger, Anne and Morten Rasmussen (2017). "The Making of European Law: Exploring the Life and Work of Michel Gaudet". *American Journal of Legal History* 57: 51–82.

Boulouis, Jean and R. M. Chevallier (1978). *Grands Arrêts de la Cour de Justice des Communautés européennes*, vol. 1. Paris, Dalloz.

Bown, Chad P. (2009). *Self-Enforcing Trade: Developing Countries and WTO Dispute Settlement*. Washington, DC, Brookings.

Brewster, Rachel (2011). "The Remedy Gap: Institutional Design, Retaliation, and Trade Law Enforcement". *George Washington Law Review* 80(1): 102–158.

Bribosia, Hervé (1997). "Report on Belgium", in A-M. Slaughter, Alec Stone Sweet and J. H. H. Weiler (eds) *The European Courts and National Courts: Doctrine and Jurisprudence*. Oxford, Hart: 3–39.

Byberg, Rebekka (2017). "The History of the Integration Through Law Project: Creating the Academic Expression of a Constitutional Legal Vision for Europe". *German Law Journal* 18(6): 1531–1556.

Cameron, David (1978). "The Expansion of the Public Economy". *American Political Science Review* 72: 1243–1261.

Cameron, Maxwell A. and Brian W. Tomlin (2000). *The Making of NAFTA: How the Deal was Done*. Ithaca, NY,"Cornell University Press.

Cannizzaro, Enzo (1991). *Trattati Internazionali e Guidizio di Costituzionalità*. Milano, Guiffrè.

Carreau, Dominique (1978). "Droit Communautaire et Droits Nationaux: Concurrence ou Primauté: La Contribution de l'arrêt Simmenthal". *Revue trimestrielle de droit européen*: 381–418.

Cassuto, Thomas (ed.) (2015). *L'Europe du droit face aux entreprises planétaires: Exposés, débats et perspectives*. Bruxelles, Bruylant.

Catalano, Nicola (1964). "Portée des Traités Instituant les Communautés Européennes et Limites des Pouvoirs Souverains des États Membres". *Le Droit et Les Affaires* 49 (Document LXXXVI).

Chalmers, Damian, Gareth Davies and Giorgio Monti (2014). *European Union Law: Text and Materials*. Cambridge, Cambridge University Press.

Chase, Claude, Alan Yanovich, Jo-Ann Crawford and Pamela Ugaz (2013). *Mapping of Dispute Settlement Mechanisms in Regional Trade Agreements – Innovative or Variations on a Theme?* WTO Working Paper ERSD-2013-07.

Claes, Monica (2006). *The National Courts' Mandate in the European Constitution*. Oxford, Hart.

Cottier, Thomas (2002). "A Theory of Direct Effect in Global Law", in Armin von Bogdandy, Petros Mavroidis and Yves Mény (eds) *European Integration and International Co-ordination: Studies in Transnational Economic Law in Honour of Claus-Dieter Ehlermann*. The Hague, Kluwer Law International: 99–123.

Craig, Paul (1992). "Once upon a Time in the West: Direct Effect and the Federalization of EEC Law". *Oxford Journal of Legal Studies* 12(4): 453–479.

(2009). "The Legal Effect of Directives: Policy, Rules, and Exceptions". *European Law Review* 34(3): 349–377.

Craig, Paul and Gráinne de Búrca (eds) (2011). *The Evolution of EU Law*. Oxford, Oxford University Press.

Craig, Paul and Gráinne de Búrca (2015). *EU Law: Text, Cases and Materials*. Oxford, Oxford University Press.

Cremona, Marise (2013). "The Judgment – Framing the Argument", in Antonio Tizzano, Juliane Kokott and Sacha Prechal (eds) *50th Anniversary of the Judgement in Van Gend en Loos 1963–2013*. Luxembourg, Court of Justice of the European Union: 23–27.

Da Cruz Vilaça, José Luís (2014). "Are there Substantive Limits to the Amendment of the Treaties?", in José Luís Da Cruz Vilaça (ed.) *EU Law and Integration: Twenty Years of Judicial Application of EU law*. Oxford, Hart: 13–43.

Dani, Marco (2010). "Remedying European Legal Pluralism: The FIAMM and Fedon Litigation and the Judicial Protection of International Trade Bystanders". *European Journal of International Law* 21(2): 303–340.

Dashwood, Alan, Michael Dougan, Barry Rodger, Eleanor Spaventa and Derrick Wyatt (2011). *Wyatt and Dashwood's European Union Law*. Oxford, Hart.

Däubler, Wolfgang (1968). "Die Klage der EWG-Kommission gegen einen Mitgliedstaat". *NJW*(8): 325–331.

Davies, Bill (2012). *Resisting the European Court of Justice: West Germany's Confrontation with European Law, 1949–1979*. Cambridge, Cambridge University Press.

Davis, Christina (2012). *Why Adjudicate? Enforcing Trade Rules in the WTO*. Princeton, NJ, Princeton University Press.

de Búrca, Gráinne and Joanne Scott (eds) (2006). *Law and New Governance in the EU and the US*. Oxford, Hart.

De Witte, Bruno (1986). "Retour à Costa – La primauté du droit communautaire à la lumière du droit international", in Werner Maihofer (ed.) *Selected Working Papers of the European University Institute*. Fiesole, European University Institute: 257–289.

(1999). "Direct Effect, Supremacy, and the Nature of the Legal Order", in Paul Craig and Gráinne de Búrca (eds) *The Evolution of EU Law*. Oxford, Oxford University Press: 177–213.

(2011a). "Direct Effect, Primacy, and the Nature of the Legal Order", in Paul Craig and Gráinne de Búrca (eds) *The Evolution of EU Law*. Oxford, Oxford University Press: 323–362.

(2011b). "The European Union as an International Legal Experiment", in Gráinne de Búrca and Joseph H. H. Weiler (eds) *The Worlds of European Constitutionalism*. Cambridge, Cambridge University Press: 19–46.

(2013). "The Impact of *Van Gend en Loos* on Judicial Protection at European and National Level: Three Types of Preliminary Questions", in Antonio Tizzano, Juliane Kokott and Sacha Prechal (eds) *50th Anniversary of the Judgement in Van Gend en Loos 1963–2013*. Luxembourg, Court of Justice of the European Union: 93–101.

Dehousse, Renaud (1998). *The European Court of Justice: The Politics of Judicial Integration*. Basingstoke, Macmillan.

Delvolve, Jean-Louis (1968). "Le Pouvoir Judiciaire et le Traité de Rome ou la diplomatie des juges". *Juris-Classeur Périodique* I, 2184.

Department for Exiting the European Union (2017). *Enforcement and Dispute Resolution: A Future Partnership Paper*. London, HM Government.

Dero, Delphine (2006). *La Réciprocité et le Droit des Communautés et de L'Union Européenne*. Bruxelles, Bruylant.

Devereaux, Charan, Robert Z. Lawrence and Michael D. Watkins (2006). *Case Studies in US Trade Negotiation*, Vol. 2: *Resolving Disputes*. Washington, DC, Institute for International Economics.

Donner, Andreas (1968). *The Role of the Lawyer in the European Communities*. Edinburgh, Edinburgh University Press.

Dougan, Michael (2007). "When Worlds Collide! Competing Visions of the Relationship Between Direct Effect and Supremacy". *Common Market Law Review* 44: 931–963.

Douglas-Scott, Sionaidh (2002). *Constitutional law of the European Union*. Harlow, Longman.

Downs, George W. and David M. Rocke (1995). *Optimal Imperfection? Domestic Uncertainty and Institutions in International Relations*. Princeton, NJ, Princeton University Press.

Downs, George W., David M. Rocke and Peter N. Barsoom (1996). "Is the Good News about Compliance Good News about Cooperation?" *International Organization* (3): 379–406.

Doyle, Michael W. (1986). "Liberalism in World Politics". *American Political Science Review* 80(4): 1151–1169.

Duranti, Marco (2017). *The Conservative Human Rights Revolution: European Identity, Transnational Politics, and the Origins of the European Convention*. Oxford, Oxford University Press.

Easson, A. J. (1979). "The 'Direct Effect' of EEC Directives". *International and Comparative Law Quarterly* 28(3): 319–353.

ECLR Editorial Comments (2014). "For History's Sake: On *Costa* v. *ENEL*, André Donner and the Eternal Secret of the Court of Justice's Deliberations". *European Constitutional Law Review* 10(2): 191–198.

Edward, David (2001). "Lord Mackenzie-Stuart of Dean LLB, LLD", in *Yearbook of the Royal Society of Edinburgh*. Edinburgh, RSE Scotland Foundation: 180–182.

Eeckhout, Piet (2002). "Judicial Enforcement of WTO Law in the European Union – Some Further Reflections". *Journal of International Economic Law* 5(1): 91–110.

(2011). *EU External Relations Law*. Oxford, Oxford University Press.

Eisemann, Pierre Michel (ed.) (1996). *The Integration of International and European Community Law into the National Legal Order: A Study of the Practice in Europe*. The Hague, Boston, Kluwer Law International.

Elagab, Omer Yousif (1988). *The Legality of Non-Forcible Counter-Measures in International Law*. Oxford, Clarendon Press.

Everson, Michelle (1995). "The Legacy of the Market Citizen", in J. Shaw and G. More (eds) *New Legal Dynamics of the European Union*. Oxford, Clarendon Press: 73–89.

Fennelly, Nial (2010). "The European Court of Justice and the Doctrine of Supremacy: *Van Gend en Loos*; *Costa* v *ENEL*; *Simmenthal*", in Miguel Poiares Maduro and Loic Azoulai (eds) *The Past and Future of EU Law: The Classics of EU Law Revisited on the 50th Anniversary of the Rome Treaty*. Oxford, Hart: 39–46.

Fischer, Ronald D. and Thomas J. Prusa (2003). "WTO Exceptions as Insurance". *Review of International Economics* 11(5): 745–757.

Foster, Nigel (2016). *EU Law Directions*. Oxford, Oxford University Press.

Fritz, Vera (2018). *Juges et avocats généraux de la Cour de Justice de l'Union européenne (1952–1972): une approche biographique de l'histoire d'une révolution juridique*. Frankfurt, Klostermann.

Froese, Marc D. (2014). "Regional Trade Agreements and the Paradox of Dispute Settlement". *Manchester Journal of International Economic Law* 11(3): 367–396.

Frowein, Jochen A. and Michael J. Hahn (1991). "The Participation of Parliament in the Treaty Process in the Federal Republic of Germany". *Chicago-Kent Law Review* 67: 361–389.

Frowein, Jochen A. and Karin Oellers-Frahm (1996). "Allemagne Germany", in Pierre Michel Eisemann (ed.) *The Integration of International and European Community Law into the National Legal Order: A Study of the Practice in Europe*. The Hague, Boston, Kluwer Law International: 69–114.

Gaudet, Michel (1965). "Exposé de M. Michel Gaudet devant la Commission juridique en sa réunion du 18 février 1965". *Revue trimestrielle de droit européen*.

Gianelli, Alessandra (2004). "Aspects of the Relationship between the Law of Treaties and the State Responsibility". *Studi di diritto internazionale in onore di Gaetano Arangio-Ruiz. Naples, Editoriale Scientifica* 2: 757–805.

Gori, Paolo (1967). *Les Clauses de Sauvegarde des Traités CECA et CEE*. Heule, Belgium, Editions UGA.

(2013). "Souvenirs d'un survivant", in Antonio Tizzano, Juliane Kokott and Sacha Prechal (eds) *50th Anniversary of the Judgment in Van Gend en Loos, 1963–2013*. Luxembourg, European Union: 29–35.

Gradoni, Lorenzo (2008). *"Regime failure" nel diritto internazionale*. Padova, CEDAM.

Gradoni, Lorenzo and Attila Tanzi (2008). "*Diritto comunitario: una* lex specialis *molto speciale*", in Lucia Serena Rossi and Giacomo Di Federico (eds) *L'incidenza del Diritto dell'Unione Europea sullo Studio delle Discipline Giuridiche*. Rome, Editoriale Scientifica: 37–70.

Grayson, George W. (1995). *The North American Free Trade Agreement: Regional Community and the New World Order*. Lanham, MD, University Press of America.

Griller, Stefan (2000). "Judicial Enforceability of WTO Law in the European Union: Annotation to Case C-149/96 *Portugal* v. *Council*". *Journal of International Economic Law* 3: 441–472.

Gubin, Éliane (2008). *Éliane Vogel-Polsky: A Woman of Conviction*. Brussels, Institute for the Equality of Women and Men.

Hall, D. F. (1979). "'Plus ça change…'". *The Law Society's Gazette* 76(39): 1089.

Hartley, Trevor C. (2000). "International Law and the Law of the European Union – A Reassessment". *British Yearbook of International Law*: 1–35.

(2014). *The Foundations of European Union Law: An Introduction to the Constitutional and Admnistrative Law of the European Union*. Oxford, Oxford University Press.

Hilf, Meinhard (1996–1997). "The Role of National Courts in International Trade Relations". *Michigan Journal of International Law* 18: 321–356.

Hockin, Thomas A. (2003). *The American Nightmare: Politics and the Fragile World Trade Organization*. Lanham, MD, Lexington.

Hogan, Gerard and Anthony Whelan (1995). *Ireland and the European Union: Constitutional and Statutory Texts and Commentary*. London, Sweet & Maxwell.

Hübner, Denise Carolin (2016). "The 'National Decisions' database (Dec.Nat): Introducing a database on national courts' interactions with European Law". *European Union Politics* 17(2): 324–339.

Hufbauer, Gary Clyde, Jeffrey J. Schott and Yee Wong (2003). *NAFTA Dispute Settlement Systems*. Institute for International Economics Working Paper.

Ipsen, Hans Peter (1964–1965). "The Relationship Between the Law of the European Communities and National Law". *Common Market Law Review* 2: 379–402.

(1965). "Das Verhältnis des Rechts der europäischen Gemeinschaften zum nationalen Recht", in *Aktuelle Fragen des europäischen Gemeinschaftsrechts*. Stuttgart, Ferdinand Enke: 1–27.

Isiksel, Turkuler (2016). *Europe's Functional Constitution: A Theory of Constitutionalism Beyond the State*. Oxford, Oxford University Press.

Jacqué, J.-P. (2013). "Third Working Session – The Future Prospects – Introduction", in Antonio Tizzano, Juliane Kokott and Sacha Prechal (eds) *50th Anniversary of the Judgement in Van Gend en Loos, 1963–2013*. Luxembourg, Court of Justice of the European Union: 129–134.

Jensen, Theresa (2011). "The Role of Dispute Settlement Mechanisms in the Constitutionalization of Regional Trade Agreements". Master of Law thesis, University of Toronto.

Kaczorowska, Alina (2013). *European Union Law*. Abingdon, Routledge.

Kant, Immanuel (2003 [1795]). *To Perpetual Peace: A Philosophical Sketch*. Indianapolis, Hackett.

Kapteyn, Paul Joan George (1964–1965). "EUROPA-RUBRIEK". *Ars Aequi*: 238–244.

Kapteyn, Paul Joan George and Pieter VerLoren Van Themaat (1973). *Introduction to the Law of the European Communities: After the Accession of the New Member States*. London, Deventer, Sweet & Maxwell, Kluwer.

(1989). *Introduction to the Law of the European Communities: After the Coming into Force of the Single European Act*. Deventer, Kluwer Law.

(1998). *Introduction to the Law of the European Communities: From Maastricht to Amsterdam*. London, Kluwer Law International.

Kapteyn, Paul Joan George, A. M. McDonnell, K. J. M. Mortelmans, Christian W. A. Timmermans and L. A. Geelhoed (2008). *The Law of the European Union and the European Communites: With Reference to Changes To Be Made by the Lisbon Treaty*. Alphen aan den Rijn, Wolters Kluwer.

Kim, SooYeon (2010). *Power and the Governance of Global Trade: From the GATT to the WTO* Ithaca, NY, Cornell University Press.

Kischel, Uwe (2000). *The State as a Non-Unitary Actor: The Role of the Judicial Branch in International Negotiations*. Working Paper 23, Mannheimer Zentrum für Europäische Sozialforschung.

Kovar, Robert (1981). "Affaire 232/78". *Journal de Droit International*: 108–110.

Kuilwijk, Kees J. (1996). *The European Court of Justice and the GATT Dilemma*. Beuningen, Nexed.

Le Beguec, Gilles (1989). "L'entrée au Palais Bourbon : les filières privilegiées d'accès à la fonction parlementaire (1919–1939)". Doctoral thesis, Lille, Université de Paris X, Nanterre.

Lecourt, Robert (1931). *Nature juridique de l'action en réintégrande: étude de la jurisprudence française* Paris, A.-D.

(1935). "Les J. D. P. presentent … La Route des Jeunes". *Route des Jeunes* 1(May).

(1937). "La Politique est un devoir social". *L'Homme Réel. Revue Mensuelle du Syndicalisme et de l'humanisme* 4(48): 28–34.

(1963). "Role de la Cour de Justice Dans Le Développement de L'Europe". *Revue de Marché Commun* (July–August): 273–275.

(1964a). "Le rôle du droit dans l'unification européenne". *Gazette du Palais* 1: 49–54.

(1964b). "Le rôle du droit dans l'unification européenne". *Bulletin des juristes européens* 17–18: 5–23.

(1965). "La Dynamique Judiciaire dans l'Édification de l'Europe". *France-Forum* 64(April–May): 20–22.

(1966). "Diagnostic judiciaire de l'europe". *Le Monde* (25 July).

(1967). "L'Heure des Juges dans Le Marché commun". *Le Monde* (17 April).

(1968a). "Allocution prononcée par le président de la Cour, M. Robert Lecourt". *Dixième anniversaire 1958–1968*. Luxembourg: 15–24.

(1968b). "Barometre judiciaire de l'Europe". *Le Monde* (15 January).

(1970). *Le juge devant le Marché commun*. Genève, Graduate Institute of International Studies

(1973a). "Allocution Prononcée par Monsieur le President Robert LECOURT lors de l'audience solennelle du 9 Octobre 1973: Acceuil de Monsieur Reischl", in *Audiences Solennelles 1973*. Luxembourg, Cour de Justice des Communautes Europeennes.

(1973b). "[Speech at 'Grand Night']". *Graya* 77: 171–173.

(1974–1975). "Speech delivered by Mr R. Lecourt to commemorate the 25th anniversary of the Robert Schuman Declaration", in *Formal Hearings of the Court of Justice of the European Communities 1974–1975*. Luxembourg, Court of Justice of the European Communities: 25–27.

(1976a). *L'Europe des juges*. Bruxelles, Bruylant.

(1976b). "Speech delivered by Mr R Lecourt, President, at the formal hearing on 7 October 1976 on the occasion of his departure", in *Formal Hearings of the Court of Justice of the European Communities*. Luxembourg, Court of Justice of the European Communities: 49–53.

(1976c). "Speech delivered by Mr R. Lecourt, President, at the formal hearing on 7 October 1976 on the occasion of the departure of Mr A. Trabucchi, Advocate-General", in *Formal Hearings of the Court of Justice of the European Communities*. Luxembourg, Court of Justice of the European Communities: 27–30.

(1979). "Interférences entre la Convention européenne des droits de l'homme et le Droit de la Communauté au regard du controle judiciaire communautaire et national". Actes du Colloque sur la Convention européenne des Droits de l'homme par rapport à d'autres instruments internationaux pour la protection des droits de l'homme, Athens.

(1981). "La Cour de Justice des Communautes europeennes vue de l'interieur", in *Europäische Gerichtsbarkeit und nationale Verfassungsgerichtsbarkeit: Festschrift zum 70. Geburtstag von Hans Kutscher*. Baden-Baden, Nomos: 261–272.

(1984). "Le Role Unificateur du Juge dans La Communauté", in *Études de Droit des Communautés Européennes: Mélanges offerts à Pierre-Henri Teitgen*. Paris, Pedone: 223–237.

(1987). "Quelques souvenirs d'un passé anterieur", in *XXXV ANNI: 1952–1987*. Luxembourg, CURIA.

(1991). "Quel eut été le droit des Communautés sans les arrêts de 1963 et 1964?", in *Mélanges Jean Boulouis: l'Europe et le droit*. Dalloz: 349–361.

Lecourt, Robert and R. M. Chevallier (1963). "Chances et malchances de l'harmonisation des législations européennes". *Recueil Dalloz*: 273–283.

Lenaerts, Koen (1992). "Some Thoughts about the Interaction between Judges and Politicians". *University of Chcago Legal Forum* 1992(1): 93–133.

Lenaerts, Koen and Piet Van Nuffel (2005). *Constitutional Law of the European Union*. London, Thomson, Sweet & Maxwell.

Lindseth, Peter L. (2002). "The Contradictions of Supranationalism: European Integration and the Constitutional Settlement of Administrative Governance". PhD thesis, Columbia University.

(2010). *Power and Legitimacy: Reconciling Europe and the Nation-State*. Oxford, Oxford University Press.

(2016). "The Perils of 'As If' European Constitutionalism". *European Law Journal* 22(5): 696–718.

Lipset, Seymour Martin (1993). "Pacific Divide: American Exceptionalism –Japanese Uniqueness". *International Journal of Public Opinion Research* 5(2): 121–166.

Louis, Jean-Victor (1966). "Troisième Colloque de Droit Européen, Paris, 25–27 novembre 1965". *Cahiers du Droit Europenne*: 90–96.

(2013). "Concluding Remarks", in Antonio Tizzano, Juliane Kokott and Sacha Prechal (eds) *50th Anniversary of the Judgement in Van Gend en Loos, 1963–2013*. Luxembourg, Office des publications de l'Union européenne: 205–225.

MacCormick, Neil (1999). *Questioning Sovereignty? Law, State and Nation in the European Commonwealth*. Oxford, Oxford University Press.

Maduro, Miguel Poiares and Loic Azoulai (2010). *The Past and Future of EU Law: The Classics of EU Law Revisited on the 50th Anniversary of the Rome Treaty*. Oxford, Hart.

Maher, Imelda (1994). "National Courts as European Community Courts". *Legal Studies* 14: 226–243.

Malenovský, Jiří (2013). "La contribution ambivalente de la Cour de justice de l'Union européenne à la saga centenaire de la domestication du droit international public", in V. Kronenberger, M. T. D'Alessio and V. Placco (eds) *De Rome à Lisbonne: les juridictions de l'Union Europeenne à la croisée des chemins. Mélanges en l'honneur de Paolo Mengozzi*. Brussels, Bruylant: 25–59.

Mayer, Frederick (1998). *Interpreting NAFTA: The Science and Art of Political Analysis*. New York, Columbia University Press.

Mendez, Mario (2013). *The Legal Effects of EU Agreements*. Oxford, Oxford University Press.

Michelet, Élisabeth (1973). *La règle du non-cumul du possèssoire et du pétitoire*. Paris, Librairie générale de droit et de jurisprudence.

Milward, Alan S., George Brennan and Federico Romero (1992). *The European Rescue of the Nation-State.* London, Routledge.

Mongelli, Francesco Paolo, Ettore Dorrucci and Itai Agur (2005). *What Does European Institutional Integration Tell Us about Trade Integration?* ECB Occasional Paper Series 40, Frankfurt.

Moyn, Samuel (2015). *Christian Human Rights.* Philadelphia, University of Pennsylvania Press.

Nicola, Fernanda and Bill Davies (eds) (2017). *EU Law Stories: Contextual and Critical Histories of European Jurisprudence.* Cambridge, Cambridge University Press.

Nord, Philip (2010). *France's New Deal: From the Thirties to the Postwar Era.* Princeton, NJ, Princeton University Press.

Olson, Mancur (1965). *The Logic of Collective Action: Public Goods and the Theory of Groups.* Cambridge, MA, Harvard University Press; Oxford University Press.

Oppenheimer, Andrew (ed.) (1994). *The Relationship between European Community Law and National Law: The cases, Volume 1.* Cambridge, New York, Cambridge University Press.

Pappini, Roberto (1996). *The Christian Democrat International.* Lanham, MD, Rowman & Littlefield.

Pelc, Krzysztof (2016). *Making and Bending International Rules: The Design of Exceptions and Escape Clauses in Trade Law.* Cambridge, Cambridge Cambridge University Press.

Pescatore, Pierre (1968). "Les Droits de l'Homme et L'Intégration Européenne". *Cahiers de Droit Européen*: 629–673.

(1981). "Aspects judiciaires de l' 'acquis communautaire'". *Revue trimestrielle de droit européen* 17(4): 617–651.

(2005). "Robert Lecourt (1908–2004). Eloge funèbre prononcé par Pierre Pescatore ancien Juge de la Cour, à l'audience solennelle du 7 mars 2005". *Revue trimestrielle de droit européen* (3): 589–596.

Petersmann, Ernst-Ulrich (1983). "Application of GATT by the Court of Justice of the European Communities". *Common Market Law Review* 20: 397ff.

(1985). "International and European Foreign Trade Law: GATT Dispute Settlement Proceedings Against the EEC". *Common Market Law Review* 22: 441ff.

(1995). "Proposals for a New Constitution for the European Union: Building-Blocks for a Constitutional Theory and Constitutional Law of the EU". *Common Market Law Review* 32: 1123–1175.

Phelan, William (2008). "Can Ireland Legislate Contrary to European Community Law?" *European Law Review* 33(4): 530–549.

(2010). "Political Self-Control and European Constitution: The Assumption of National Political Loyalty to European Obligations as the Solution to the

Lex Posterior problem in the National Legal Orders". *European Law Journal* 16(3): 253–272.

(2011a). "Open International Markets without Exclusion: Encompassing Domestic Political Institutions, International Organization, and Self-Contained Regimes". *International Theory* 3(2): 286–306.

(2011b). "Why do the EU Member States Accept the Supremacy of European Law? Explaining Supremacy as an Alternative to Bilateral Reciprocity". *Journal of European Public Policy* 18(5): 766–777.

(2012). "What is *Sui Generis* about the European Union? Costly International Cooperation in a Self-Contained Regime". *International Studies Review* 14: 367–385.

(2013). "The European Union's Next Nobel Peace Prize". *E-International Relations*, from www.e-ir.info/2013/08/05/the-european-unions-next-nobel-peace-prize/.

(2014). "The Limited Practical Relevance of National Constitutional Rights as a Constraint on the National Application of European Law in the Early Decades of European Integration". *Irish Journal of European Law* 17(1): 43–61.

(2015a). "Enforcement and Escape in the Andean Community: Why the Andean Community of Nations is not a Replica of the European Union". *Journal of Common Market Studies* 53(4): 840–856.

(2015b). *In Place of Inter-State Retaliation: The European Union's Rejection of WTO-style Trade Sanctions and Trade Remedies*. Oxford, Oxford University Press.

(2015c). "The Troika: The Interlocking Roles of Commission *v.* Luxembourg and Belgium, Van Gend en Loos and Costa *v.* ENEL in the Creation of the European Legal Order". *European Law Journal* 21(1): 116–135.

(2016a). *Diagonal Enforcement in International Trade Politics*. EUI Working Paper SPS 2016/1. Fiesole, EUI.

(2016b). "Safety Valves and Complete Exits in European Treaty Politics". *German Law Journal* 17 (Brexit Supplement): 93–94.

(2016c). "Supremacy, Direct Effect, and *Dairy Products* in the Early History of European Law". *International Journal of Constitutional Law* 14(1): 6–25.

(2017). "The Revolutionary Doctrines of European Law and the Legal Philosophy of Robert Lecourt". *European Journal of International Law* 28(3): 935–957.

(2018). "European Legal Integration: Towards a More Liberal Intergovernmentalist Approach". *Journal of Common Market Studies* 56(7): 1562–1577.

Plender, Richard (1976). "An Incipient Form of European Citizenship", in Francis Jacobs (ed.) *European Law and the Individual*. Amsterdam, North Holland.

Plötner, Jens (1997). "Report on France", in Anne-Marie Slaughter, Alec Stone Sweet and J. H. H. Weiler (eds) *The European Courts and National Courts: Doctrine and Jurisprudence*. Oxford, Hart: 43–75.

Prechal, Sacha (2005). *Directives in EC Law*. Oxford, Oxford University Press.

Rasmussen, Hjalte (1983). "The Court of Justice", in *Thirty Years of Community Law*. Luxembourg, European Community Information Service.

(1986). *On Law and Policy in the European Court of Justice: A Comparative Study in Judicial Policymaking*. Dordrecht, M. Nijhoff.

(2009). Legal Opinion about The European Court of Justice's Competence Transgressions, Poor Reasonings and the Complete Non-transparency of *Willensbildung. Unpublished Paper.*

Rasmussen, Morten (2008). "The Origins of a Legal Revolution – The Early History of the European Court of Justice". *Journal of European Integration History* 14(2): 77–98.

(2010). "Constructing and Deconstructing 'Constitutional' European Law: Some Reflections on how to Study the History of European Law", in Henning Koch, Karsten Hagel-Sørensen, Ulrich R. Haltern and J. H. H. Weiler (eds) *Europe: The New Legal Realism: Essays in Honour of Hjalte Rasmussen*. Copenhagen, Djøf Publishing: 639–660.

(2012). "Establishing a Constitutional Practice of European Law: The History of the Legal Service of the European Executive 1952–65". *Contemporary European History* 21(3): 375–397.

(2014). "Revolutionizing European Law: A History of the Van Gend en Loos judgment". *International Journal of Constitutional Law* 12(1): 136–163.

(2017). "How to Enforce European Law? A New History of the Battle over the Direct Effect of Directives, 1958–1987". *European Law Journal* 23: 290–308.

Reuter, Paul (1968). "La Cour de justice des Communautés européennes et le droit international", in *Recueil d'études de droit international en hommage à Paul Guggenheim*. Geneva, Éditions de la Faculté de Droit de l'Université de Genève/Institut Universitaire de Hautes Études Internationales: 665–686.

(1969). "Le Droit International comme Source de Droit Communautaire", in W. J. Ganshof van der Meersch (ed.) *Droit des Communautés européennes*. Bruxelles, Larcier: 437–440.

Robert, Jean (1963)."Sur une Égalité de Droits devant La Communauté Économique Européenne Des Ressortissants Des États Membres Avec Ces États Eux-Mêmes". *Recueil Sirey* (Mai): 29–33.

Roitinger, Alexander (2004). "The Institutional Design of Trade Policy Flexibility in the World Trading Order: Analysis and New Direction for Reform". PhD thesis, St Gallen.

Rosendorff, B. Peter and Helen V. Milner (2001). "The Optimal Design of International Trade Institutions: Uncertainty and Escape". *International Organization* 55(4): 829–857.

Rossa Phelan, Diarmuid (1997). *Revolt or Revolution: The Constitutional Boundaries of the European Community*. Dublin, Round Hall Sweet & Maxwell.

Rudden, Bernard and Diarmuid Rossa Phelan (1997). *Basic Community Cases*. Oxford, Oxford University Press.

Ruggie, John (1982). "International Regimes, Transactions, and Change: Embedded Liberalism in the Postwar Economic Order". *International Organization* 36(2): 379–425.

Ruiz Fabri, Helene (2013). "Conjuguer justice et prudence: commentaire sur le développement de l'effet direct du droit international en droit de l'Union", in Antonio Tizzano, Juliane Kokott and Sacha Prechal (eds) *50th Anniversary of the Judgement in Van Gend en Loos 1963–2013*. Luxembourg, Court of Justice of the European Union: 189–196.

(2014). "Is There a Case – Legally and Politically – for Direct Effect of WTO Obligations?" *European Journal of International Law* 25: 151–173.

Rupp, Hans G. (1977). "Judicial Review of International Agreements: Federal Republic of Germany". *American Journal of Comparative Law* 25(2): 286–302.

Savatier, René (1960). "Le Marché commun au regard du droit internationale privé", in Colloque des facultés de droit (ed.) *Les Problèmes juridiques et économiques du Marché commun*. Lille, Librairies techniques: 55–71.

Schermers, Henry G. (1975). "Community Law and International Law". *Common Market Law Review* 12: 77–90.

(1977). "*L'Europe des Juges* by Robert Lecourt". *Common Market Law Review* 14: 261–262.

Schütze, Robert (2016). *European Constitutional Law*. Cambridge, Cambridge University Press.

Scott, Joanne (1995). "GATT and Community Law: Rethinking the 'Regulatory Gap'", in J. Shaw and G. More (eds) *New Legal Dynamics of the European Union*. Oxford, Clarendon Press: 147–164.

Secretaría General (2006). *Comunidad Andina: Avances y Perspectivas*. Lima: Documento informativo SG/di 800.

Simma, Bruno (1985). "Self-Contained Regimes". *Netherlands Yearbook of International Law* 16: 111–136.

(1994). "Counter-Measures and Dispute Settlement: A Plea for a Different Balance". *European Journal of International Law* 5: 102–105.

Simma, Bruno and Dirk Pulkowski (2006). "Of Planets and the Universe: Self-Contained Regimes in International Law". *The European Journal of International Law* 17(3): 483–529.

(2010). "*Leges Speciales* and Self-Contained Regimes", in James Crawford, Alain Pellet and Simon Olleson (eds) *The Law of International Responsibility*. Oxford, Oxford University Press: 138–163.

Simmonds, K. R. (1975). "*Van Duyn* v. *The Home Office*: The Direct Effectiveness of Directives". *International and Comparative Law Quarterly* 24(3): 419–437.

Simon, Denys (2000). "The Sanction of Member States' Serious Violations of Community Law", in D. O'Keeffe (ed.) *Liber Amicorum in Honour of Lord Slynn of Hadley*. The Hague, Kluwer 1: 275–286.

Slobodian, Quinn (2018). *Globalists: The End of Empire and the Birth of Neoliberalism*. Cambridge, MA, Harvard University Press.

Somek, Alexander (2017). "Is Legality a Principle of EU Law?", in Stefan Vogenauer and Stephen Weatherill (eds) *General Principles of EU Law: European and Comparative Perspectives*. Oxford, Hart: 53–75.

Stein, Eric (1965). "Toward Supremacy of Treaty – Constitution by Judicial Fiat in the European Economic Community". *Rivista di Diritto Internazionale* 48: 3–28.

(1981). "Lawyers, Judges and the Making of a Transnational Constitution". *American Journal of International Law* 75(1): 1–27.

Tancredi, Antonello (2004). "EC Practice in the WTO: How Wide is the 'Scope for Manoeuvre'?" *European Journal of International Law* 15(5): 933–961.

Teh, Robert, Thomas J. Prusa and Michele Budetta (2007). *Trade Remedy Provisions in Regional Trade Agreements*. WTO Staff Working Paper ERSD-2007–03.

Temple Lang, John (1997). "The Duties of National Courts under Community Constitutional Law". *European Law Review* 22: 3–18.

Thies, Anne (2013). *International Trade Disputes and EU Liability*. Cambridge, Cambridge University Press.

Thompson, Dennis (1962). "The Bosch Case". *International and Comparative Law Quarterly* 11(3): 721–741.

Tizzano, Antonio, Juliane Kokott and Sacha Prechal (2013). *50th Anniversàry of the Judgement in Van Gend en Loos, 1963–2013*. Luxembourg, Court of Justice of the European Union.

Torrelli, Maurice (1968). "La Cour Constitutionnelle Fédérale Allemande et le Droit Communautaire: Note de Jurisprudence". *Revue de Marché Commun*: 719–723.

Trebilcock, M., R. Howse and A. Eliason (2013). *The Regulation of International Trade*. London and New York, Routledge.

Tumlir, Jan (1983a). "International Economic Order and Democratic Constitutionalism". *ORDO* 34: 71–83.

(1983b). "Need for an Open Multilateral Trading System". *The World Economy*: 393–408.

Van Leeuwen, Karin (2012). "On Democratic Concerns and Legal Traditions: The Dutch 1953 and 1956 Constitutional Reforms 'Towards' Europe". *Contemporary European History* 21(3): 357–374.

Vauchez, Antoine (2010). "The Transnational Politics of Judicialization, *Van Gend en Loos* and the Making of EU Polity". *European Law Journal* 16(1): 1–28.

(2015). *Brokering Europe: Euro-Lawyers and the Making of a Transnational Polity*. Cambridge, Cambridge University Press.

Vinuesa, Raúl Emilio (2005). "Enforcement of Mercosur Arbitration Awards within the Domestic Legal Orders of Member States". *Texas International Law Journal* 40: 425–442.

Voon, Tania (2010). "Eliminating Trade Remedies from the WTO: Lessons from Regional Trade Agreements". *International and Comparative Law Quarterly* 59: 625–667.

Waelbroeck, Michel (1967). "The Application of EEC Law by National Courts". *Stanford Law Review* 19(6): 1248–1276.

(1969). *Traités internation »aux et juridictions interns dans les pays du Marché commun*. Bruxelles, CIDC.

(1974). "Effect of GATT within the Legal Order of the EEC". *Journal of World Trade Law* 8: 614–623.

Walker, Neil (ed.) (2003). *Sovereignty in Transition*. Oxford and Portland, OR, Hart Publishing.

Weatherill, Stephen (2014). *Cases and Materials on EU Law*. Oxford, Oxford University Press.

Weiler, J. H. H. (1986). "Eurocracy and Distrust: Some Questions concerning the Role of the European Court of Justice in the Protection of Fundamental Human Rights within the Legal Order of the European Communities". *Washington Law Review* 61: 1103–1142.

(1991). "The Transformation of Europe". *Yale Law Journal* 100: 2403–2483.

(1996). *The Jurisprudence of Human Rights in the European Union: Integration and Disintegration, Values and Processes*. Jean Monnet Chair Working Papers 2/96. Cambridge, MA.

(1999). *The Constitution of Europe: "Do the New Clothes have an Emperor?" and Other Essays on European Integration*. New York, Cambridge University Press.

(2003). "Rewriting *Van Gend en Loos*: Towards a Normative Theory of ECJ Hermeneutics" in Ola Wiklund (ed.) *Judicial Discretion in European Perspective*. The Hague, Kluwer Law International: 150–164.

(2014). "Van Gend en Loos: The Individual as Subject and Object and the Dilemma of European Legitimacy". *International Journal of Constitutional Law* 12(1): 94–103.

Wenner, Wolfgang (1962). "Zur Auslegung des EWG-Vertrages". *Aussenwirtschaftsdienst des Betreibs-Beraters* (4): 110–112.

Woods, Lorna and Philippa Watson (2014). *Steiner & Woods EU Law*. Oxford, Oxford University Press.

Wyatt, Derrick (1975). "Directly Applicable Provisions of EEC Law". *New Law Journal*: 458–460; 575–578; 669–672; 793, 794.

Zeitler, Franz-Christoph (1973). *Verfassungsgericht und völkerrechtlicher Vertrag*. Berlin, Dunkler & Humblot.

Zoller, Elisabeth (1984). *Peacetime Unilateral Remedies: An Analysis of Countermeasures*. Dobbs Ferry, NY, Transnational Publishers.

INDEX